I0816106

A History of the Gateway City in 40 Rare Maps

ANDREW W. HAHN

Copyright © 2024 by Reedy Press, LLC
Reedy Press
PO Box 5131
St. Louis, MO 63139, USA
reedypress.com

No part of this publication may be reproduced or transmitted in any form or by any means, electronic or mechanical, including photocopy, recording, or any information storage and retrieval system, without permission in writing from the publisher.

Permissions may be sought directly from Reedy Press at the above mailing address or via our website at reedypress.com.

Library of Congress Control Number: 2024939009

ISBN: 9781681065526

Cover and interior design by Eric Marquard

Front cover image courtesy of Campbell House Museum
Back cover image courtesy of St. Louis Public Library
All interior images are believed to be in the public domain unless otherwise noted.
Credits for map detail images can be found on their corresponding full map.

Printed in the United States of America
25 26 27 28 5 4 3

Dedication

To the many members of my St. Louis family, both past and present, who have made this city their home over the past 175 years; especially Valerie, Leo, and Alice Hahn, who inspire hope for the future of the Gateway City.

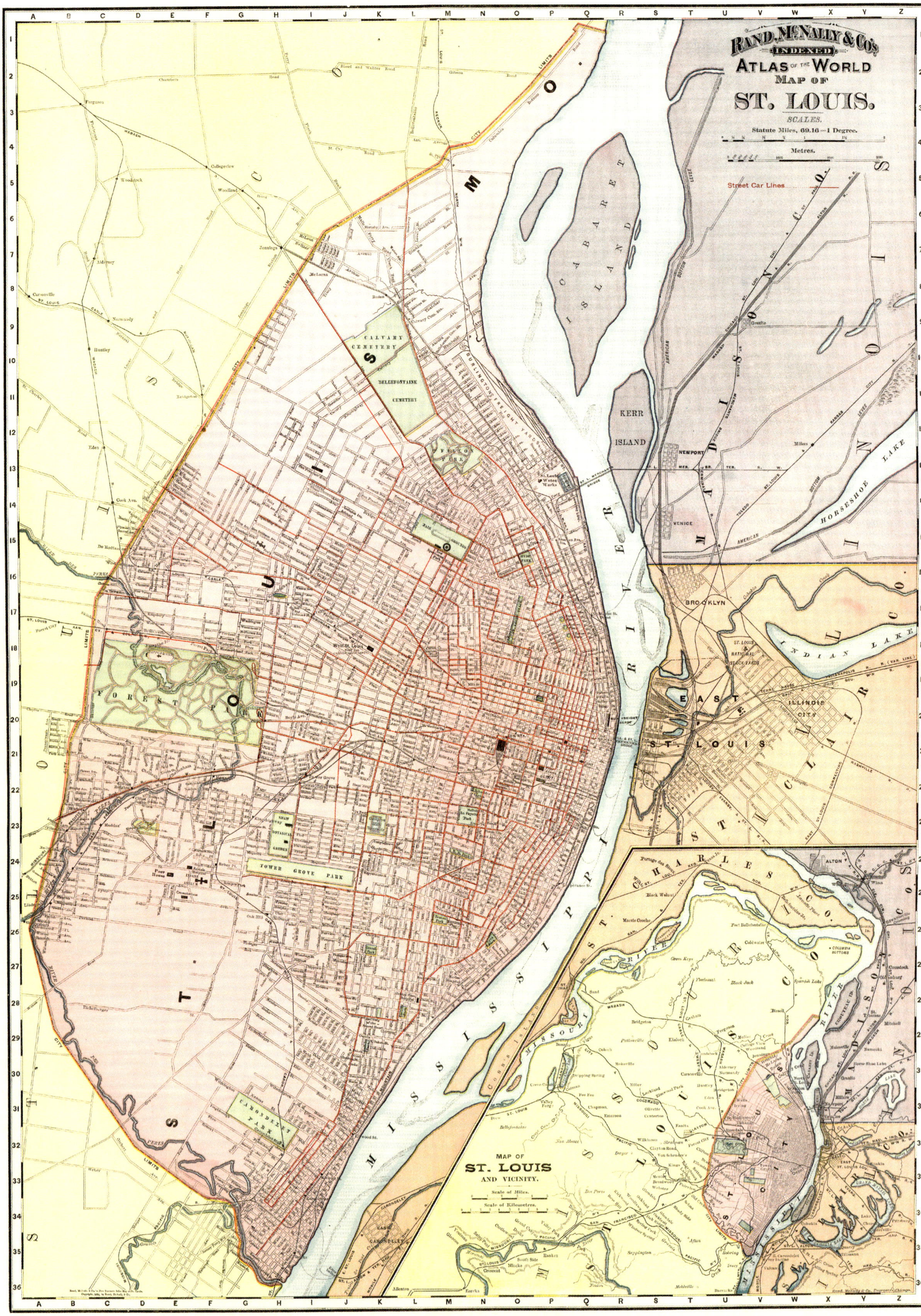
RAND, McNALLY & Co's
INDEXED
ATLAS OF THE WORLD
MAP OF
ST. LOUIS.
SCALES.
Statute Miles, 69.16=1 Degree.
Metres.
Street Car Lines
CALVARY CEMETERY
BELLEFONTAINE CEMETERY
FOREST PARK
TOWER GROVE PARK
CARONDELET PARK
MISSISSIPPI RIVER
CABARET ISLAND
KERR ISLAND
NEWPORT
VENICE
HORSESHOE LAKE
BROOKLYN
INDIAN LAKE
EAST ST. LOUIS
ILLINOIS CITY
ST. CLAIR CO.
MADISON CO.
ST. LOUIS CO.
EAST CARONDELET
ST. CHARLES CO.
MAP OF
ST. LOUIS
AND VICINITY.
Scale of Miles.
Scale of Kilometres.

Table of Contents

Map of St. Louis from the 1897 *Atlas of the World* by Rand, McNally & Company
COLLECTION OF THE AUTHOR

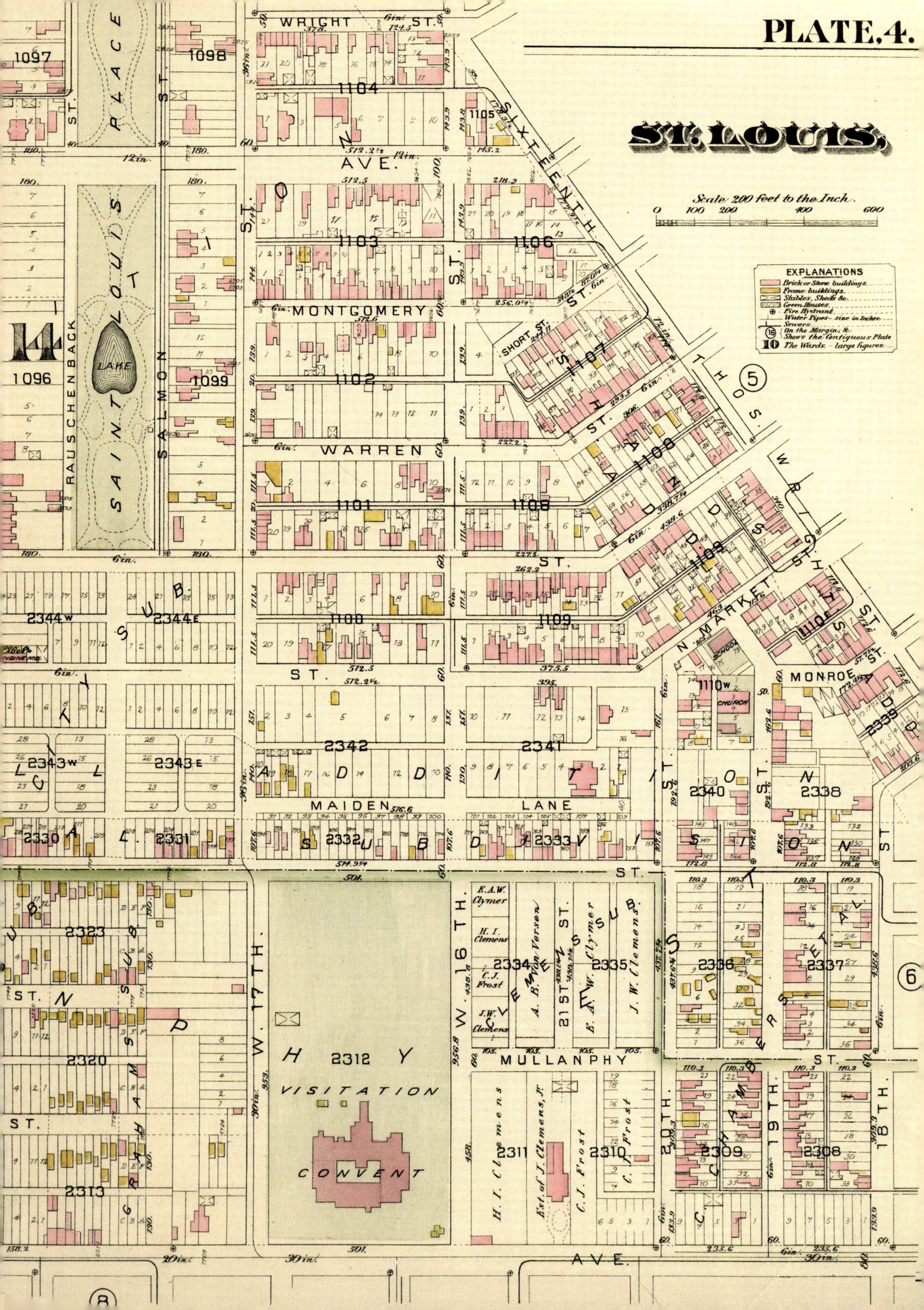
PLATE. 4.
ST. LOUIS,
Scale 200 feet to the Inch
0 100 200 400 600
EXPLANATIONS
Brick or Stone buildings
Frame buildings
Stables, Sheds &c.
Green Houses
Fire Hydrant
Water Pipes - size in Inches
Sewers
On the Margin, & Shows the Contiguous Plate
The Wards, - large figures.
WRIGHT ST.
SIXTEENTH
AVE.
MONTGOMERY
WARREN
ST.
MAIDEN LANE
MULLANPHY
AVE.
SHORT ST.
N. MARKET ST.
MONROE
RAUSCHENBACK
SALMON
SAINT LOUIS PLACE
LAKE
W. 17TH.
W. 16 TH.
21ST.
20TH.
19TH.
18TH.
SCHOOL
CHURCH
VISITATION CONVENT
E. A. W. Clymer
H. I. Clemens
C. J. Frost
J. W. Clemens
A. B. Van Versen
E. A. W. Clymer
J. W. Clemens
H. I. Clemens
Est. of J. Clemens, Jr.
C. J. Frost
C. J. Frost
14
5
6
8
1097
1098
1104
1105
1103
1106
1096
1099
1102
1107
1101
1108
1100
1109
1110w
2344w
2344E
2343w
2343E
2342
2341
2340
2338
2339
2330
2331
2332
2333
2323
2320
2313
2312
2334
2335
2336
2337
2311
2310
2309
2308

Acknowledgments

THIS BOOK melds two of my greatest interests—St. Louis history and maps. Growing up, a large *National Geographic* map of Europe on my bedroom wall helped me dream about future travels. As an adult, the 2001 edition of the Official Map of the City of St. Louis in my upstairs hallway has been the base for pinpointing the residences of my ancestors, most of whom came here in the mid-19th century. My job as the executive director of the Campbell House Museum has exposed me to a huge variety of St. Louis maps and introduced me to many people who share a passion for local history.

The seed of this book lies in the work of Emily Jaycox, librarian of the Missouri Historical Society. As the custodian of the premier collection of St. Louis maps, she has written and lectured extensively on this subject. I am very grateful for her generous support of my research and for her insightful thoughts in this book's foreword.

At the St. Louis Mercantile Library at the University of Missouri–St. Louis, both John Hoover and Charles Brown were very helpful in sharing the many special maps under their care. Dan Fuller with Bellefontaine Cemetery offered valuable comments about the cemetery's history along with the suggestion of the 1852 map included in this book. Francesca Griffero and Jenna Stout at the Richardson Memorial Library at the Saint Louis Art Museum supplied archival information about the early history of the Art Museum. Local artist Dan Zettwoch kindly allowed the reproduction of his skillfully drawn 21st-century St. Louis maps.

St. Louis is very fortunate to have a world-class public library. The library's special collections department is a treasure trove for the local historian. Librarians Adele Heagney, Amanda Bahr-Evola, and Kirwin Roach assisted me in understanding and accessing the rich map collection at the St. Louis Public Library.

Seasoned local authors Cameron Collins, John Guenther, and NiNi Harris all gave me advice on writing a book and on writing about St. Louis. Between them they have written more than 25 books on local topics, and I am fortunate for having their advice and friendship.

For more than 20 years, I have been entrusted with the care of the best-preserved 19th-century house in St. Louis—the Campbell House Museum. The Museum thrives because of its wonderful family of volunteers, who are the backbone of every aspect of the institution. From board members to docents, interns, shop attendants, and gardeners, this group has always given me the support and guidance that has fostered my love of St. Louis history.

While I am grateful for everyone at Campbell House both past and present, I would like to especially acknowledge: Eileen Carr, Jackie Chambers, Fritz Clifford, Suzanne Corbett, Scott Dolan, Louis Gerteis, Jane Gleason, Tom Gronski, Kathleen Horgan, Lynne Johnson, Tom and Lynne Keay, Patricia Lock-Buckley, Lisa McLaughlin, Dennis Rathert, Ginger Reinert, Tricia Schlafly, Celeste Sprung, and Jack Swanson.

And lastly, I am exceedingly thankful for Valerie Hahn and Tom Gronski, my best critics and first editors. They are both at the top of the game, Valerie the journalist and Tom the historian. *Mapping St. Louis* would not have been completed without their many insights.

— ANDREW W. HAHN

Plate 4 from the *Atlas of the City* of St. Louis, 1883.
COURTESY STATE HISTORICAL SOCIETY OF MISSOURI

Foreword

GAZING AT a historic map of a familiar place can feel like a form of time travel. Andy Hahn, a lifelong St. Louisan and longtime director of the Campbell House Museum, is well qualified to guide the readers of this book on a journey through past St. Louis with the aid of these fascinating maps.

Selected from notable collections, both local and national, the maps in this book span the entire history of St. Louis from the 1760s all the way up to the third decade of the 21st century. Some of these maps document conditions that were current at the time. Others, like the 1907 Civil Plan and the St. Louis Metro Fantasy of 2022, make bold proposals for the future.

Turning these pages you can watch the growth of St. Louis, which began as a small colonial village situated on a bluff near the confluence of two great rivers. Laid out and settled by French fur traders, the site would shortly find itself on an international border, governed by Spain for most of its first 40 years. After becoming absorbed into the United States in 1804 thanks to the Louisiana Purchase, St. Louis grew modestly until the era of the steamboat transformed the town into a bustling, explosively growing river port. As more people thronged to and settled there, St. Louis repeatedly annexed surrounding lands. These maps chronicle the city's increase in area, from the original village—located on today's Arch grounds—to its current footprint of over 61 square miles.

Evolving forms of transportation continued, and continue, to shape the St. Louis landscape, influencing the choices St. Louisans would make about where to live, work, and establish businesses. With the maps in this book, you can trace the ferry lines, run by a powerful lobby that resisted the construction of a railroad bridge over the Mississippi River—the majestic Eads Bridge ultimately spanning the river and connecting the eastern and western railroad networks; and the streetcar system that moved workers and shoppers before the automobile era.

Map of the City of St. Louis and Vicinity, drawn by J.H. Fisher, 1865.
COURTESY MISSOURI HISTORICAL SOCIETY, ST. LOUIS

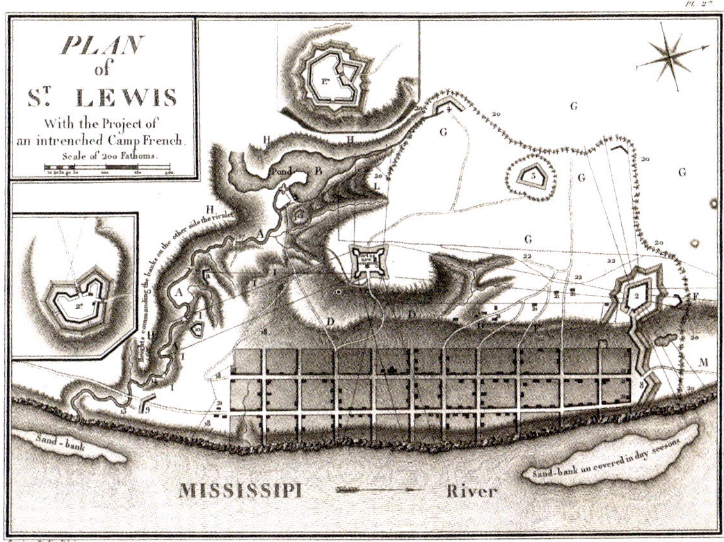

Plan of St. Lewis by Georges Collot, 1796.
COURTESY MISSOURI HISTORICAL SOCIETY, ST. LOUIS

A well-designed map can be a powerful tool to entice the traveler and can also help him or her navigate the city after arrival. As early as the 1820s, when Missouri had just achieved statehood, a map of St. Louis highlighted the institutions that had already been established in this frontier town: banks, churches, mills, ferries, and a jail. Later 19th century maps would add features such as hotels, schools, orphanages, engine houses, and the courthouse. By the 20th century, when St. Louis had established itself firmly as a regional cultural center, maps would give an increasingly prominent place to attractions such as parks, museums, and sports stadiums.

By 1900, St. Louis would rank as the fourth-largest US city by population. But it did not achieve this growth without challenges. Maps in this book document the Great Fire of 1849, the fortifications of this border city in the Civil War, and the Great Cyclone of 1896. St. Louis would survive these setbacks and triumphantly invite the world to visit the Louisiana Purchase Exposition, dramatically reshaping Forest Park to accommodate the grounds of the 1904 World's Fair.

After the Fair, St. Louis reconfigured Forest Park as a key public space, housing cultural attractions like the Saint Louis Art Museum, the Zoo, and the Jefferson Memorial (now the Missouri History Museum). Along with the Missouri Botanical Garden, those attractions have drawn visitors and offered enjoyment for generations of residents. Perhaps most dramatically, the riverfront was completely reshaped into a national park honoring St. Louis's role as Gateway to the West. But there was more to come: as Dan Zettwoch's map shows, a wealth of museums appealing to a wide variety of interests blanket the entire region.

St. Louis continued to be ranked in the top 10 US cities by population through 1960, but in the mid-20th century it increasingly faced aging infrastructure and significant demographic shifts. Meanwhile, residents occupying the oldest housing stock—generally those with fewest choices, including immigrants and people of color—were displaced and their neighborhoods razed as the City retrofitted its legacy streets and buildings to the age of the automobile, indoor plumbing, and other aspects of modern living that had become the norm. As part of efforts to expand the City's tax base, maps have been used to make a case for voting on bond issues or proposing a reunification of the City and County. The City's population continued to shrink each decade between 1950 and 2020; the 2021 map shows its new ward boundaries after the number of wards was reduced from 28 to 14, belatedly aligning the number of alderpersons with the shrinking St. Louis population.

Maps have many uses, including navigation, documentation, and persuasion. Beyond that, an artistically drawn map is just plain fun to look at. Throughout this book you will see examples of artists embellishing their maps with intricate borders, iconic landmarks, and moody landscapes. These creative touches bring the maps to life and can enhance our feeling of connection to the places they depict.

Like Andy, I have been fortunate to have been able to study maps of St. Louis for several decades as part of my work at the Library + Research Center. I hope you will enjoy these maps as much as we do.

— Emily Jaycox
Librarian, Missouri Historical Society

Preface

IN 1964, St. Louis celebrated its bicentennial with ceremonies, parades, and newly published books about the City. But the most lasting commemoration that year was the adoption of something simple: a new St. Louis flag. Since then, the flag has become a recognizable source of local pride.

Nearly unique among city or country flags, this symbol of St. Louis is also a map, albeit a basic one. Artist Theodore Sizer wrote that the core of his flag design was a depiction of the City's location at the confluence of North America's two greatest rivers—the blue and white wavy bands represent the Mississippi and Missouri. The gold disk emblazoned with the French fleur-de-lis pinpoints the location of St. Louis itself. As they are on the flag, the rivers are the dominant feature of the local geography and consequently the major element on any St. Louis map.

Mapping St. Louis charts the growth of the City from its founding in the 1760s to the present day. It does so by interweaving 40 maps along with short essays, detailed views, and captioned illustrations that provide stories and history that are only hinted at on each map. The featured maps are reproduced as large as each page will allow in order to afford the viewer as close a look as possible.

Maps of St. Louis are, more often than not, oriented to the west (west at the top of the page). This is contrary to the vast majority of maps, which are oriented to the north. This western orientation places the Mississippi River in a dominant position as it runs across the bottom of the map. This reinforces an attitude that has prevailed in the Gateway City since its founding: that its future and fortunes lie toward the West. It was a view west across the City that people first saw as they arrived on the riverfront, and it was to the west that lie the expanse and possibilities of the United States.

There are hundreds of maps that illustrate St. Louis's

Original artwork for the proposed flag design for the City of St. Louis by Theodore Sizer, 1963.
COURTESY MISSOURI HISTORICAL SOCIETY, ST. LOUIS

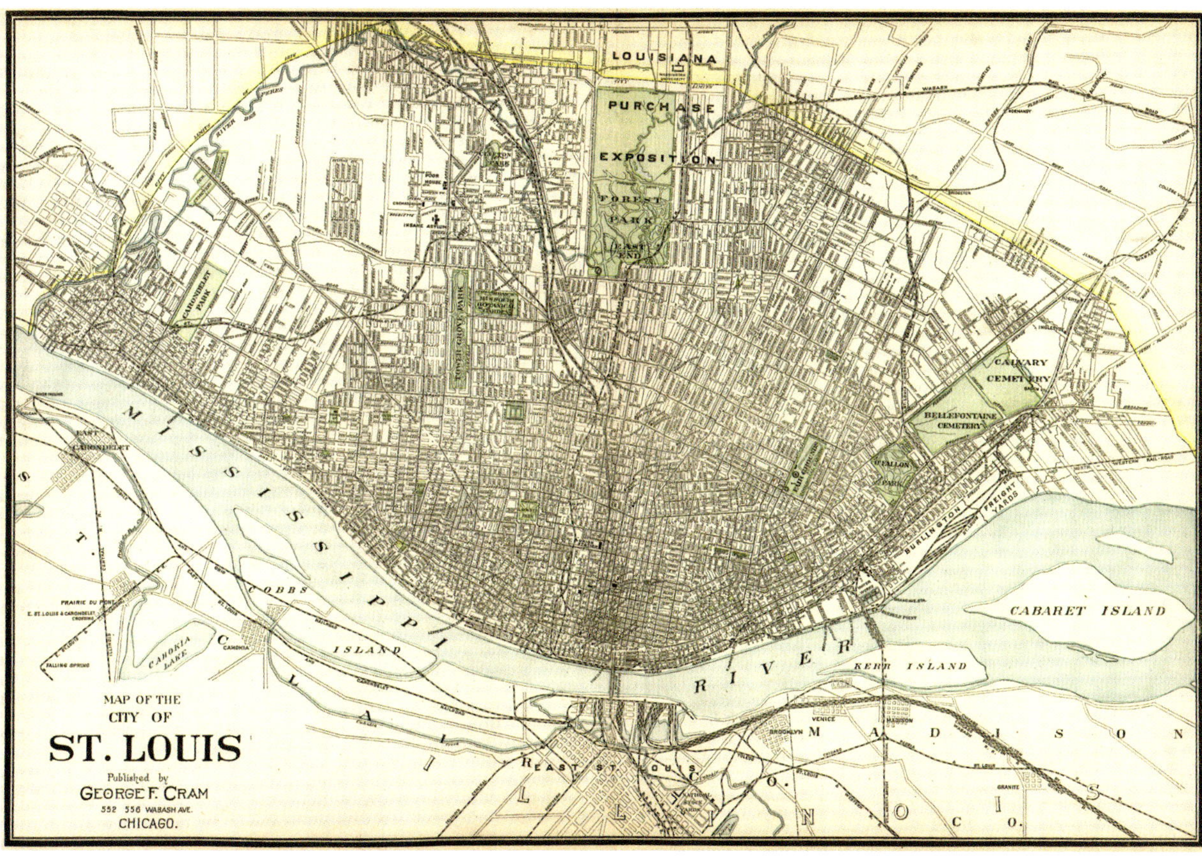

Map of the City of St. Louis, published by George F. Cram, 1907.
COLLECTION OF THE AUTHOR

geography and history. Ordered chronologically, the maps in this book can easily be grouped into themes that follow a historical progression: the founding of St. Louis and Colonial Era (1760–1810s); the Fur Trade Era and westward expansion (1820s–1850s); the Civil War and Reconstruction (1860s); the Gilded Age (1870s–1910s); Post–World War I, the Great Migration, and the Great Depression (1920s–1930s); Post–World War II and Urban Renewal (1940s–1970s); and finally 21st-Century St. Louis (2010s–2020s). These maps were created by a white-dominated culture. However, the story of Indigenous and Black St. Louisans has not been ignored. General themes like religion or sports are not discussed in this book, for lack of either space or a good map.

All of the 40 maps featured in this book focus on the City of St. Louis, though its connection with St. Louis County cannot be ignored. This focus was a deliberate decision that shaped the narrative. The many interesting maps of the greater St. Louis region and its municipalities are the subject for another book.

There are many different styles of maps featured—maps for exploration and navigation, pocket and atlas maps, development and planning maps, pictorial maps, and fantasy maps. Some maps in this book have rarely (or never) been reproduced in color. The 40 featured maps are cross-referenced throughout in order to highlight relationships among various maps. The first map, from 1767, for example, will be referred to in subsequent essays in italics as the *1767 map*.

The basic purpose of any map is as a tool for navigation—we think of maps as a means to show you where you are or where you want to go. But maps also provide an opportunity to reflect on where you have been. If a picture is worth a thousand words, then a map is worth 100,000. A map shows you many small pictures, some on the page and some in your mind, and a map places those pictures within both space and time. Some of the maps featured on these pages are large, some quite small, some beautifully ornate, and others simply utilitarian. All of them tell a diverse and fascinating story. In presenting these striking and interesting maps, it is the goal of this book to illustrate where St. Louis started, to show how it arrived at certain points in history, and to challenge the reader to consider where the City may be heading.

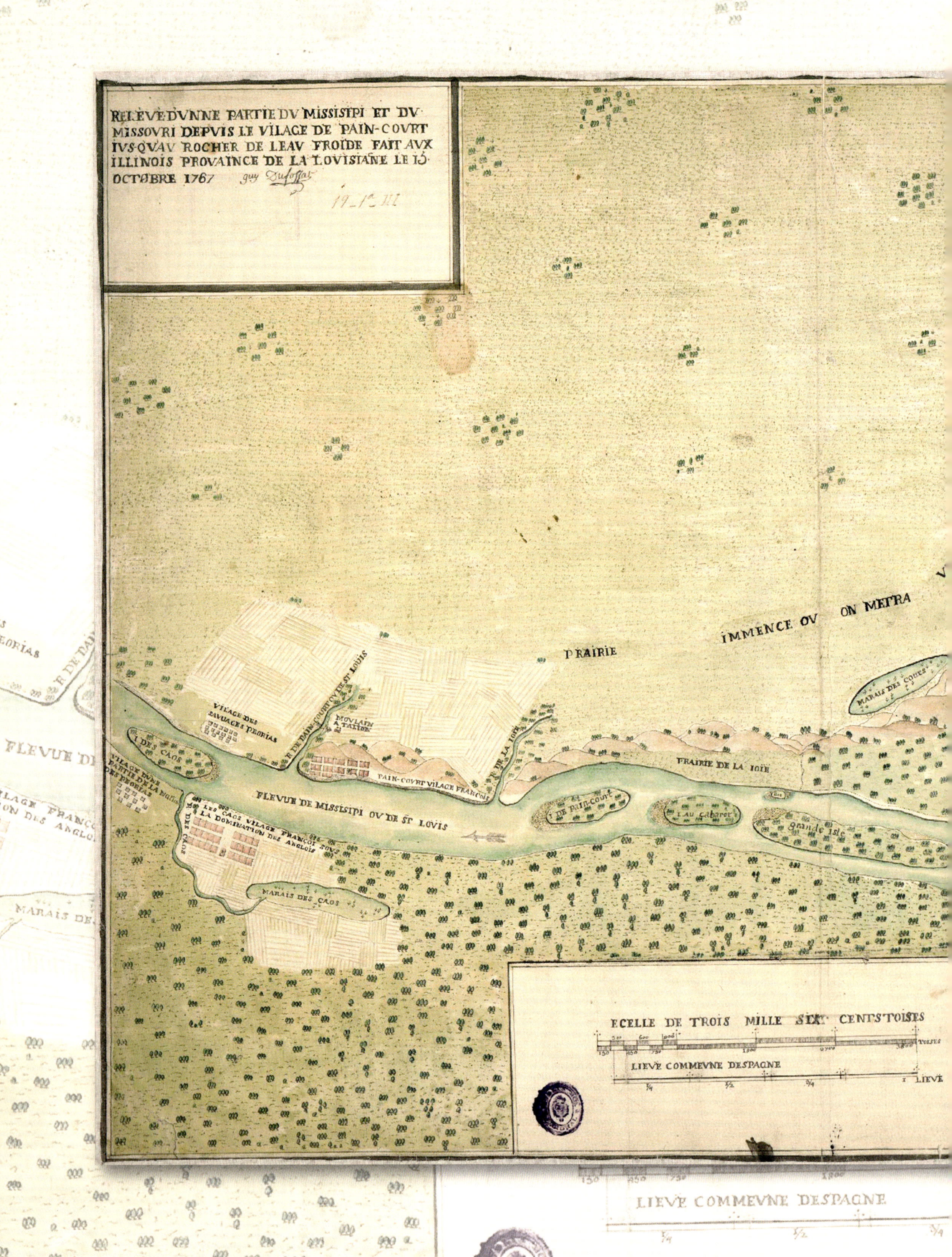
RELEVE DVNNE PARTIE DV MISSISIPI ET DV MISSOVRI DEPVIS LE VILAGE DE PAIN-COVRT IVS-QVAV ROCHER DE LEAV FROIDE FAIT AVX ILLINOIS PROVAINCE DE LA LOVISIANE LE 15 OCTOBRE 1767
PRAIRIE
IMMENCE OV
ON METRA
MARAIS DES COUES
VILAGE DES SAUVAGES PEORIAS
R DE PAIN-COURT OU DE ST LOUIS
MOULAIN A TABIDE
PAIN-COURT VILAGE FRANÇOIS
R DE LA JOIE
PRAIRIE DE LA JOIE
I DES CAOS
FLEVUE DE MISSISIPI OU DE ST LOUIS
I DE PAIN-COURT
I AU Cabaret
grande isle
LES CAOS VILAGE FRANÇOIS SOUS LA DOMINATION DES ANGLOIS
MARAIS DES CAOS
ECELLE DE TROIS MILLE SIX CENTS TOISES
LIEVE COMMEVNE DESPAGNE
LIEVE
FLEVUE DE
MARAIS DE
LIEVE COMMEVNE DESPAGNE

1767

The First Map of St. Louis

Survey of a Part of the Mississippi and the Missouri from the Village of Pain Court to Cold Water Rock Made in the Illinois Province of Louisiana on October 15, 1767

Guy Dufossat
(artist/cartographer)

Manuscript, black ink with green and sienna wash

19.69 x 26.77 inches

Biblioteca Nacional de España, Madrid

1767

ST. LOUIS was founded in February 1764 by Pierre Laclede and Auguste Chouteau on what was thought to be French territory. However, the new colony of St. Louis, located on the west bank of the Mississippi just below the confluence with the Missouri, was actually at that time a part of Spain. The land had been acquired from France in 1763 as a result of the Treaty of Paris, which ended the French and Indian War, the American theater of the global Seven Years' War. It took a year before that news traveled to Laclede and Chouteau all the way from Europe to the new village of St. Louis.

In the spring of 1767, a small convoy of soldiers under the command of the Spanish Captain Fancisco Ríu y Morales left New Orleans and headed up the Mississippi River to take stock of their new territory. The Treaty of Paris and the acquisition by Spain would have a lasting impact on the village of St. Louis, since it removed all French political influence from North America for the next 40 years. Regardless, the French language and culture would endure in St. Louis and other former French outposts.

Captain Morales's 1767 convoy included the French-speaking Guy Dufossat, a longtime officer in Louisiana who had served in the French army as far back as 1747. Dufossat was an engineer of some skill, and within one month of his arrival in St. Louis, in September 1767, he completed this map. This colorful and detailed depiction of the confluence of the Mississippi and Missouri rivers includes the first depiction of what historians have called the "geometric nucleus" of St. Louis. Quite simply, it was the first city street grid. This grid remained intact until the 1930s, when the Jefferson National Expansion Memorial project, today known as Gateway Arch National Park, destroyed it.

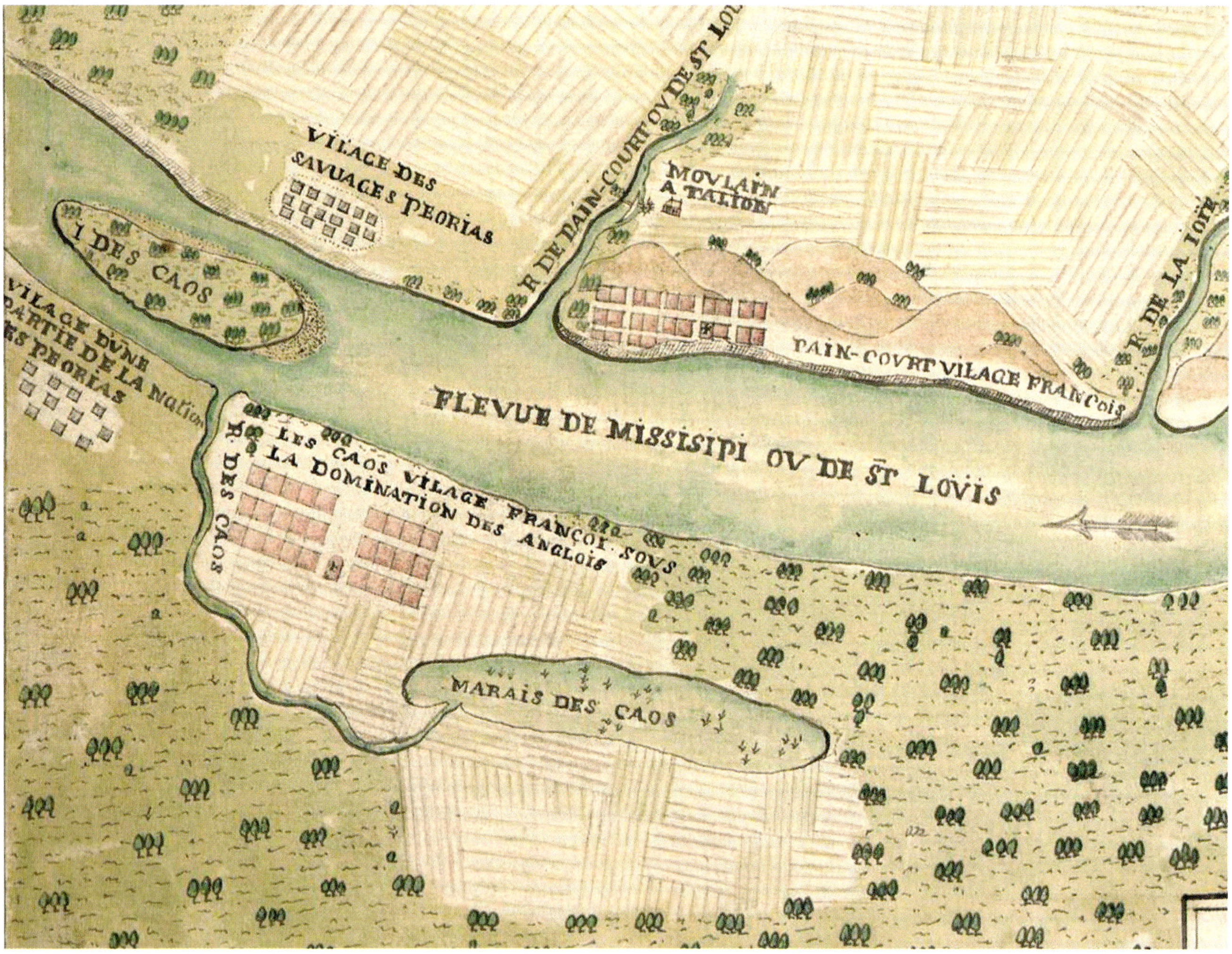

The audience for this map were the Spanish authorities, not the people of St. Louis or America. In fact, since shortly after its creation, this map has been part of the Spanish colonial archives now housed at the National Library of Spain in Madrid. Dufossat's map is one of the most beautiful maps of St. Louis, and it has rarely been reproduced, especially in color.

Dufossat's map shows a number of interesting features of early St. Louis. The most prominent feature near the new village of St. Louis (labeled *Pain-Court Village Francois* or French Village Short of Bread) was noted as the *Moulain a Talion* or Taillon's Mill.

JACQUES NOISÉ HOUSE

Built in the 1770s at the northwest corner of Main and Spruce Streets, this house was in a ruinous state when this photo was taken in 1850. The Noisé house is typical of the first buildings erected in St. Louis. It measured 22 feet × 30 feet and was built of vertical wood posts with an attached overhanging gallery on three sides. It is often called the McNair Mansion, as Missouri's first governor, Alexander McNair, owned the house for 13 years.
COURTESY MISSOURI HISTORICAL SOCIETY, ST. LOUIS

Just two months after this map was completed, the mill was sold by Joseph Taillon to Pierre Laclede, one of St. Louis's wealthiest early citizens. The bill of sale notes that the "mill belonged to Taillon because he had built it at his own expense within the royal domain, although without any official concession," meaning that it was not granted to him by the government. Taillon had occupied the land for a year and a day, had improved it, and thereby acquired title to it by "customary right."

Laclede paid Taillon 400 livres in silver or gold, which was rarely used in early St. Louis. Most transactions were made in animal skins and pelts. No dimensions were noted for the tract of real estate, which was simply defined as the land associated with the mill. Laclede took possession of the property in March 1768 and immediately began enlarging the mill. An ever increasing supply of flour was needed for the quickly growing village. This may be the root of St. Louis's early moniker *Pain Court* or "short of bread": if there was not enough capacity at the mill to grind wheat to flour, St. Louis would be short of bread.

The stone for the enlarged mill was brought downriver from the Cold Water Quarry, which is still the site of an active quarry today. After Laclede's death in 1778, Auguste Chouteau bought the mill and made improvements. Among them was the construction of a dam that created Chouteau's Pond, which would be a prominent feature on St. Louis maps until the 1850s.

Dufossat's map also shows the large numbers of Indigenous people living in organized settlements around the new village of St. Louis. Groups of Peoria Indians are shown living on both sides of the Mississippi, one directly south of St. Louis in what is now the Soulard neighborhood and a second group east of the river in what is now Sauget, Illinois. Although no Indigenous people lived directly on the site of St. Louis when it was founded, people had been living in the area for at least 1,000 years, as evidenced by the Mounds just north of the village that Dufossat drew on the map. Also shown across the Mississippi from St. Louis is the French village of Cahokia (*Caos*), which was then under British control.

Document F accompanying Report

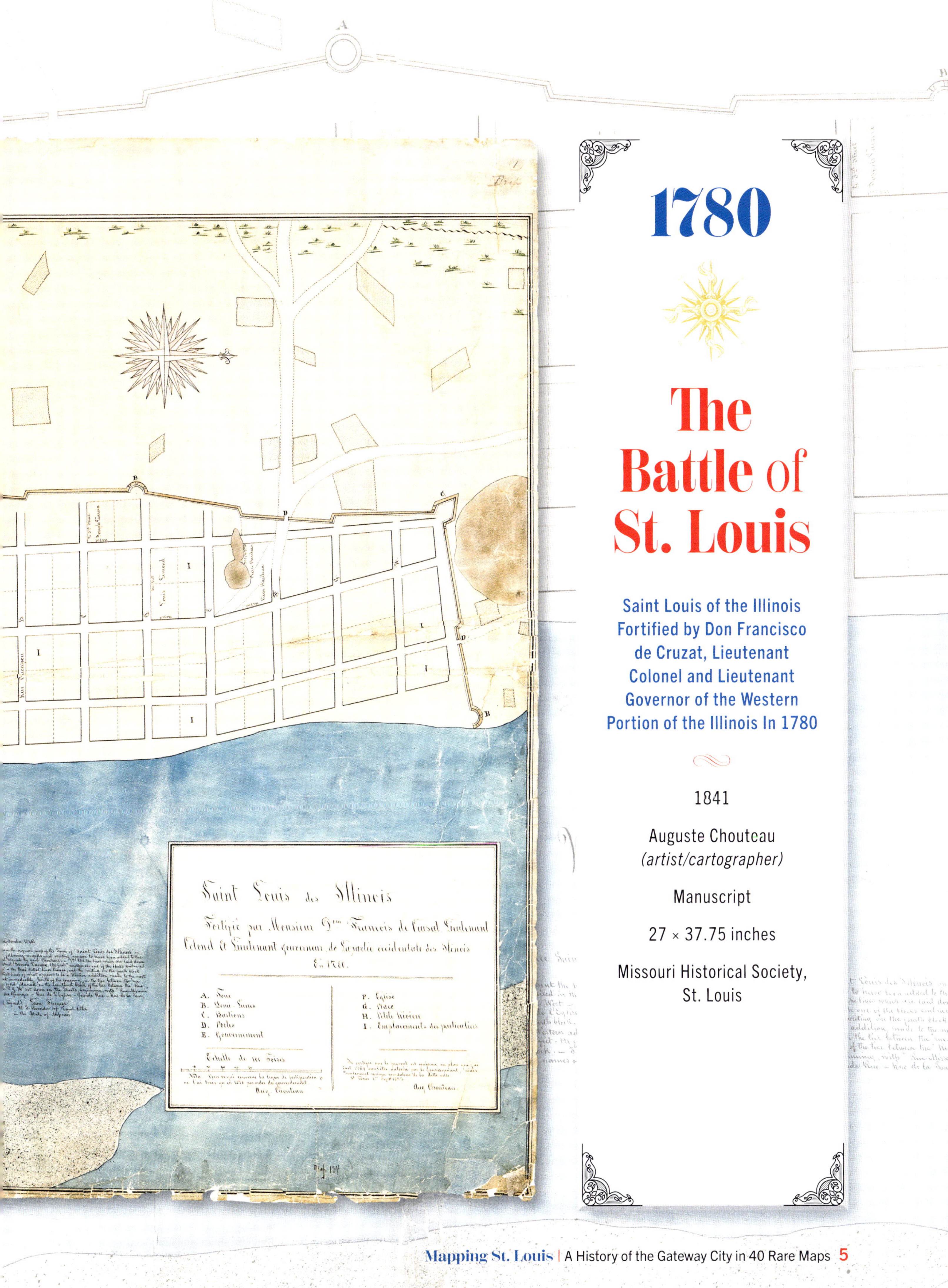

1780

The Battle of St. Louis

Saint Louis of the Illinois Fortified by Don Francisco de Cruzat, Lieutenant Colonel and Lieutenant Governor of the Western Portion of the Illinois In 1780

1841

Auguste Chouteau
(artist/cartographer)

Manuscript

27 × 37.75 inches

Missouri Historical Society, St. Louis

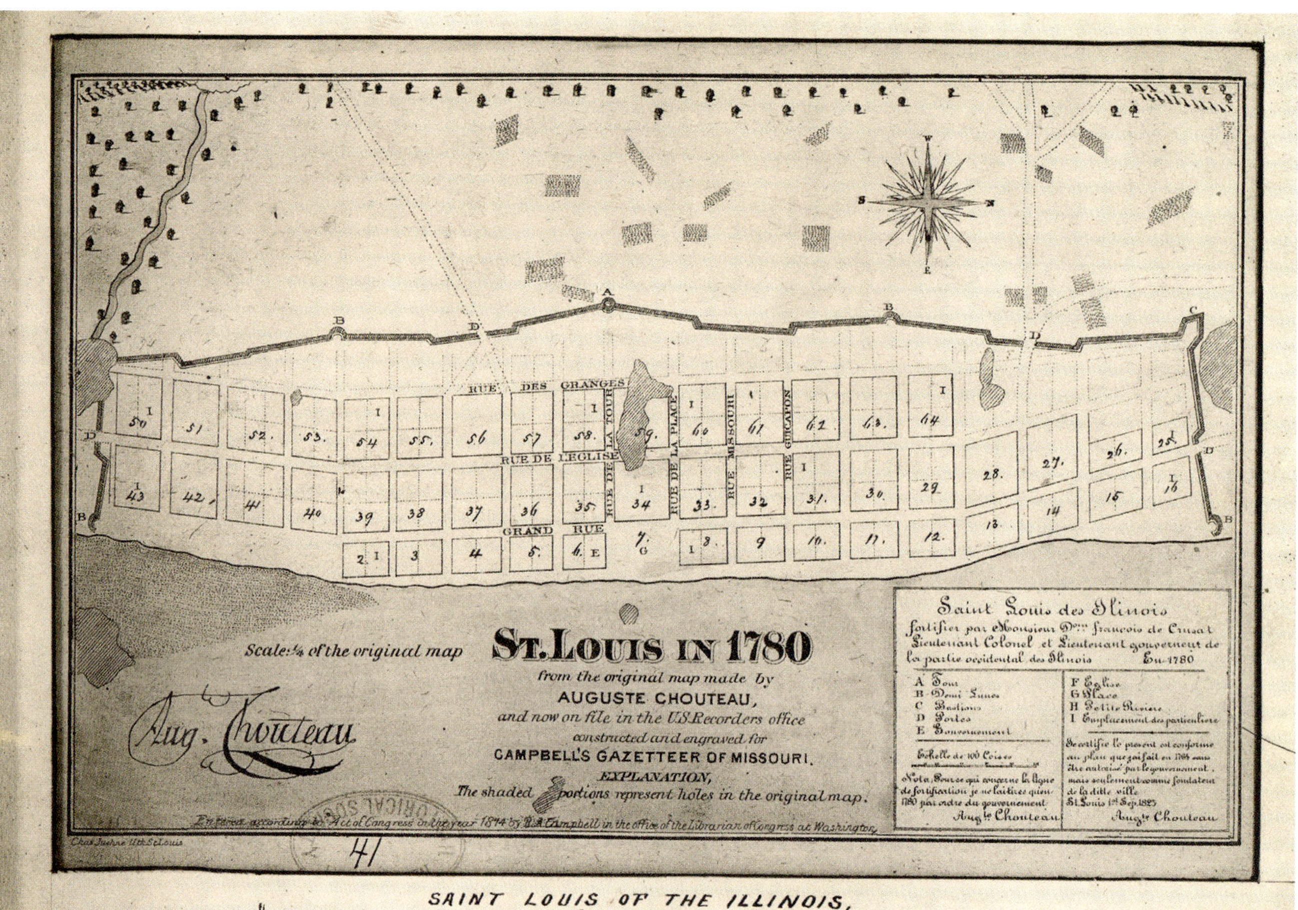

ON MAY 28, 1780, the Spanish colonial village of St. Louis was attacked in what would be the only battle of the American Revolution fought west of the Mississippi.

This hand-colored manuscript map was drawn in 1841, copying an older map depicting St. Louis as it was at the time of the battle. The map title begins with the phrase "Saint Louis of the Illinois." St. Louis was at the heart of French Illinois County, a large, ill-defined area encompassing the middle Mississippi Valley. The later term "Upper Louisiana" refers only to the land on the west side of the Mississippi. The map records the street grid of the village as three blocks deep from the river and 19 blocks long. It clearly shows the defenses that ring the town, including a large, round, stone tower, marked "A." Brown areas on the map represent holes in the original map that was copied.

In July 1779, Spain joined the American Revolutionary War against the British. Great Britain had ordered its generals in Canada to begin expeditions against Spanish settlements on the Mississippi River and to drive out American officer George Rogers Clark and his troops. Clark learned of this, and in March 1780 he warned the Spanish commandant at St. Louis, Don Fernando de Leyba, to prepare for an attack.

ANOTHER LOOK AT ST. LOUIS IN 1780

This map offers a more-detailed, though less-colorful, look at St. Louis at the time of the battle. It is also a copy of a now-lost original, which was prepared under the supervision of Auguste Chouteau, who had been present during the founding and initial survey of St. Louis in 1764. Chouteau had originally noted, in French, that "in regard to the line of fortification, I only traced it in 1780, by order of the government." This particular version of the 1780 map was printed in St. Louis in 1874 by R. A. Campbell, who produced a number of important maps of Missouri and St. Louis (see the *1882 map*). Campbell chose to include a facsimile of Chouteau's dramatic signature for effect.

COURTESY MISSOURI HISTORICAL SOCIETY, ST. LOUIS

Leyba began fortifying St. Louis. Through public subscription augmented by his own personal funds, he planned to construct a series of stone towers around the perimeter of the village. On April 17, construction of the first tower on the western boundary of the village began with a blessing by the Catholic priest Father Bernard. Amazingly, there is a record of this ceremony, which recorded Father Bernard as saying "bless this first stone of the fort on the hill behind the church, which is named Fort Don Carlos in the name of His Majesty, Carlos III."

Leyba also directed the villagers to dig a series of mile-long entrenchments consisting of ditches and earthen mounds that ran from either side of the tower along the edge of the village and down to the banks of the Mississippi. The tower was probably about 30 feet in diameter and between 30 and 40 feet tall. When the attack finally occurred, the tower was nearly complete, only missing its parapet wall. Five cannons were installed at the top of the tower before the attack commenced.

At around 1 p.m. on May 26, 1780, a band of more than 700 Indigenous people from the Sioux, Ojibwe, Menominee, and Ho-Chunk tribes led by Canadian fur traders and probably a few British army regulars commenced an attack from the north. Some villagers working in the fields were surprised by the attackers, and about 25 were killed and 70 captured. An alarm cannon shot was fired, marking the start of the defense of St. Louis by just 300 men.

According to Leyba, the Indians attacked "like madmen with an unbelievable boldness and fury, making terrible cries and a terrible firing." No doubt the attackers were surprised by the entrenchments and the heavy cannon fire from the tower. Leyba's preparations proved successful, and the attack was repelled after just a few hours. Leyba reported 21 defenders and just four attackers dead.

On the same day as the attack on St. Louis, George Rogers Clark and his men defeated another band of British and Indians just across the river at Cahokia. The attackers retreated up the river, and the Mississippi Valley was now safe from British control. St. Louis would remain part of Spain for 23 more years until the Louisiana Purchase in 1803.

Barely a month after the battle of St. Louis, Don Fernando de Leyba died and was buried in the church next to his wife. After his death, local tradition perpetuated the myth that Leyba was incompetent and even traitorous. Many resented his use of forced requisitions in constructing the fortifications. Curiously, this map notes that the fortifications at St. Louis were built under the direction of Don Francisco de Cruzat. Cruzat in fact succeeded Leyba as the commandant at St. Louis, and while he may have further developed the fortifications, they were conceived and begun by Leyba. Today, there is a local chapter of the Sons of the American Revolution named in Leyba's honor.

MARKING THE BATTLE
The site where the tower of Fort San Carlos stood is today at the corner of South Broadway and Walnut Streets. In 1946, the General Society of the Sons of the Revolution placed this bronze plaque on the corner to commemorate the battle. A local organization, the Commemoration Committee for the Battle of Fort San Carlos, annually honors the event by reading the names of the 21 defenders of St. Louis who lost their lives during the battle. The battle is also depicted in a somewhat fanciful mural painted in 1920 by artist Oscar Berninghaus in the Missouri State Capitol.
COURTESY OF THE AUTHOR

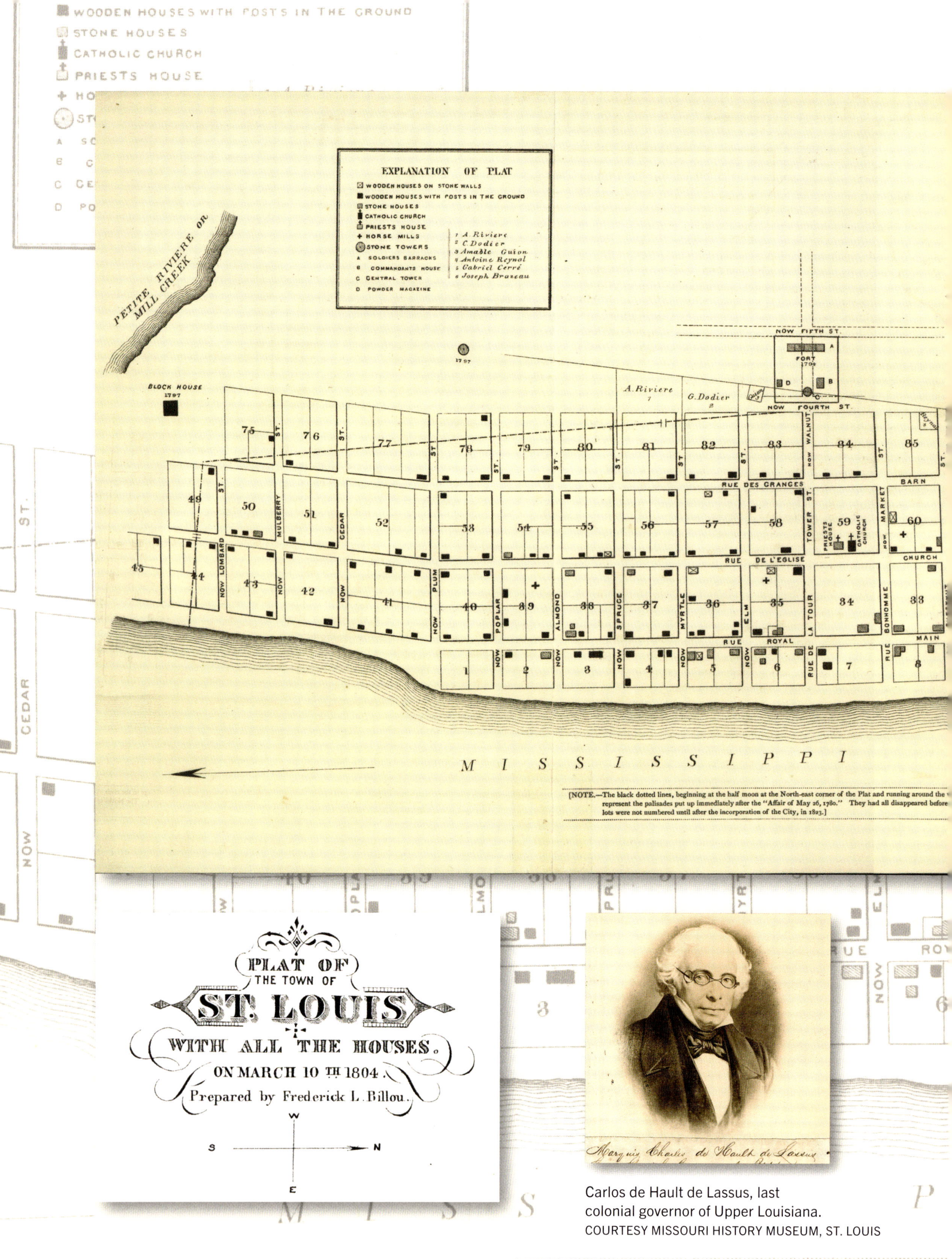

Carlos de Hault de Lassus, last colonial governor of Upper Louisiana.
COURTESY MISSOURI HISTORY MUSEUM, ST. LOUIS

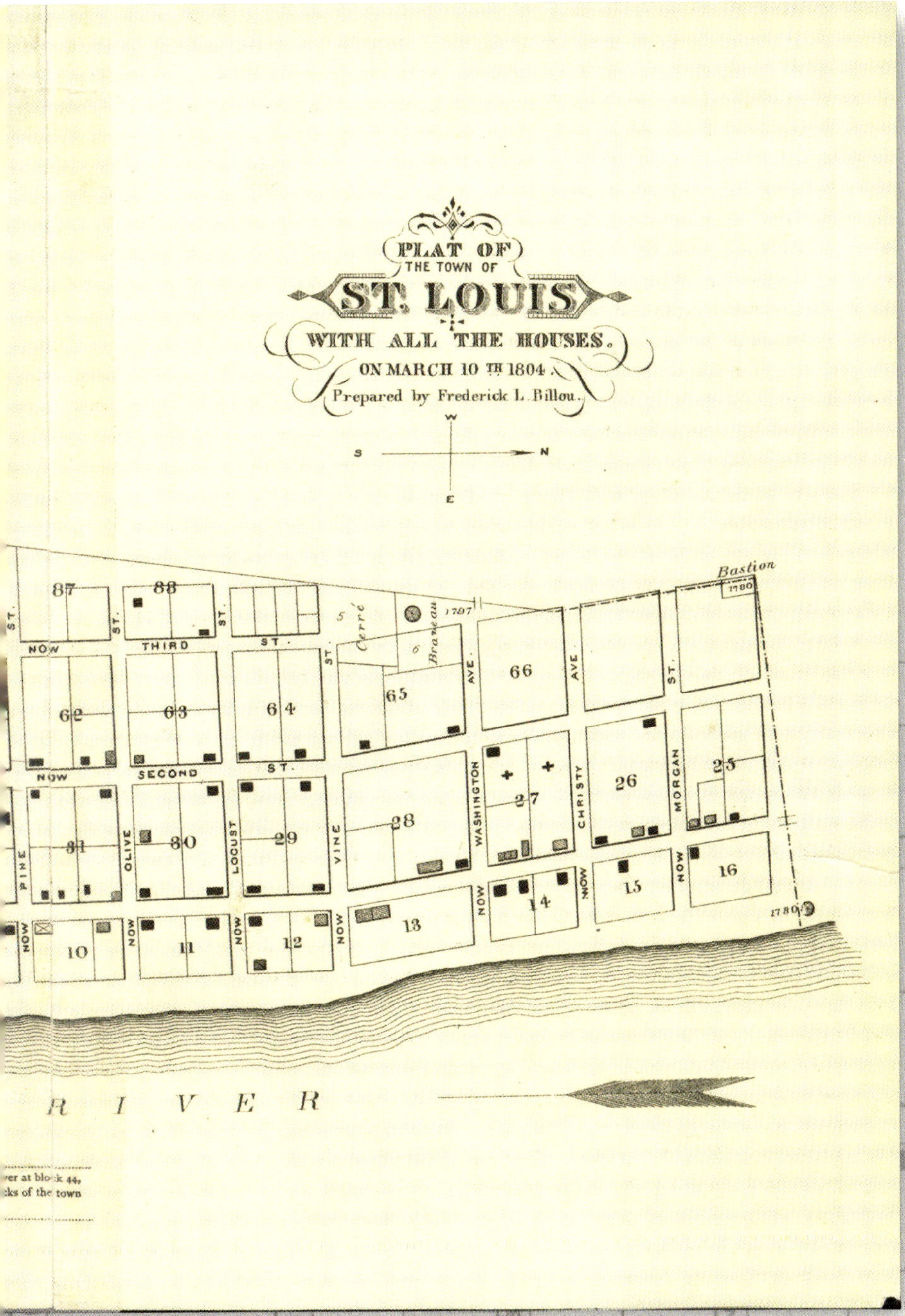

1804

St. Louis under Three Flags

Plat of the Town of St. Louis with all the Houses on March 10, 1804

1883

Frederic Billon
(artist/cartographer)

L.H. Everts and Co.
(publisher)

Lithograph

19.5 × 10.75 inches

Collection of the author

Signatures and seals on the official Louisiana Purchase document signed at St. Louis.
COURTESY MISSOURI HISTORY MUSEUM, ST. LOUIS

AS EVERY American school child knows, Thomas Jefferson transacted the largest land deal in American history in 1803, when he purchased the Louisiana Territory from France for $15 million. This territory extended from New Orleans to the Canadian Rockies. The purchase of some 530 million acres was a bold move with a complicated backstory.

In October 1800, the Louisiana Territory was transferred from Spain back to France as part of the Third Treaty of San Ildefonso. Napoleon desired France to regain its former colonies, and the Spanish were ready to be rid of Louisiana, as the territory was losing ten times as much money as it generated in taxes. Confusion was added to the complexity of this treaty because all its negotiations were secret and Spain continued to administer Louisiana, including St. Louis, to keep up appearances.

The prospect of French control of the Mississippi River and a revived French empire on America's doorstep alarmed Jefferson. The president sent negotiators to France with instructions to purchase New Orleans and as much of the Gulf Coast as they could for $2 million. In part because of the recent slave rebellion in Haiti, France offered to sell not just New Orleans but all of Louisiana for just four cents an acre. In a single stroke, the size of America doubled.

The official turnover of Louisiana to the United States took place in Paris on April 30, 1803. However, the process was complicated and slow, dragging on into the fall of 1803. Money eventually changed hands, and on December 20 there was a transfer ceremony in New Orleans.

Finally, by March 1804, word of the transfer reached St. Louis. The village was still administered by the

TRANSFER OF NORTHERN LOUISIANA, 1804
This depiction of the transfer of Louisiana to America shows the scene in front of the house of the last Spanish commandant, Carlos de Hault de Lassus. The French flag is lowered, and the American flag is raised for the first time over St. Louis. This postcard was created around 1904 and is No. 5 from the "St. Louis pageant series," which included other depictions of early St. Louis events, including Fr. Jacques Marquette's voyage past the future site of St. Louis in 1673.
COLLECTION OF THE AUTHOR

Spanish, and most of the local officials and soldiers did not know they had been technically working for the French. The last Spanish commandant of St. Louis, Carlos de Hault de Lassus, announced on March 8, 1804, that over the course of the following two days, St. Louis and Upper Louisiana would be transferred from Spain to France, and then finally to America.

On March 9, 1804, de Lassus and US Army representative Amos Stoddard signed a sheaf of papers. Then de Lassus spoke to the crowd, "By order of the King I am now about to surrender this post and its dependencies. The flag which has protected you during nearly 36 years will no longer be seen . . . From the bottom of my heart I wish you all prosperity." At his words, the flag of Spain was slowly lowered, and the flag of France rose in its place. The French flag was only supposed to fly for a total of six hours, but St. Louisans remembered their French roots—there was a cannon salute and a huge party. The Americans permitted the French flag to fly until noon the next day, when it was lowered and the stars and stripes took its place. St. Louis had been governed under three flags in just 24 hours.

This map was produced for the landmark two-volume book *History of Saint Louis City and County, from the Earliest Periods to the Present Day* by J. Thomas Scharf. These volumes contain dozens of illustrations of St. Louis and its most prominent citizens. This map is the most important one in the book and was prepared by amateur historian Frederic Billon.

When this map was published in 1883, there were few people who had lived in St. Louis for so long—Billon first arrived in 1818. His status as a member of the pioneering generation placed him in a good position to document the history of St. Louis, and he became the City's unofficial historian. He used "interviews with early inhabitants, research in territorial archives, scattered diaries, scrapbooks, journals, and other manuscript records to produce a detailed and useful chronology of early St. Louis." Late in life, he published two classic works of early local history, *Annals of St. Louis in Its Early Days under the French and Spanish Dominations, 1764–1804* and *Annals of St. Louis in Its Territorial Days from 1804 to 1821*. Today, Billon's *Annals* can still be consulted for information about early life in St. Louis.

THREE FLAGS DAY REENACTED

This photo was taken at the corner of First and Walnut Streets on March 9, 1935, the 131st anniversary of the transfer of Louisiana. The event reenacts the transfer of the Louisiana Purchase territory at St. Louis. From left to right are Gale F. Johnson as Charles Gratiot, Louis LaBeaume as Carlos de Hault de Lassus, Bernard Dickmann as Amos Stoddard, and two unidentified men as Indigenous peoples.
COURTESY MISSOURI HISTORICAL SOCIETY, ST. LOUIS

As noted in the upper left corner, the map shows the town "with all its houses" as they existed on the day of the transfer of Louisiana, March 10, 1804. This unusually precise map is the only one in the history of St. Louis purported to show the City as it existed on one specific day. The drawn detail includes a description of the construction type of each building—"wooden houses on stone walls, wooden houses with posts in the ground (poteaux-en-terre) and stone houses."

Street names are given in French and English, which represents the political change happening on that day. The black dotted lines at the bottom represent "the palisades put up immediately after the Affair of May 26, 1780." They had all disappeared before 1804.

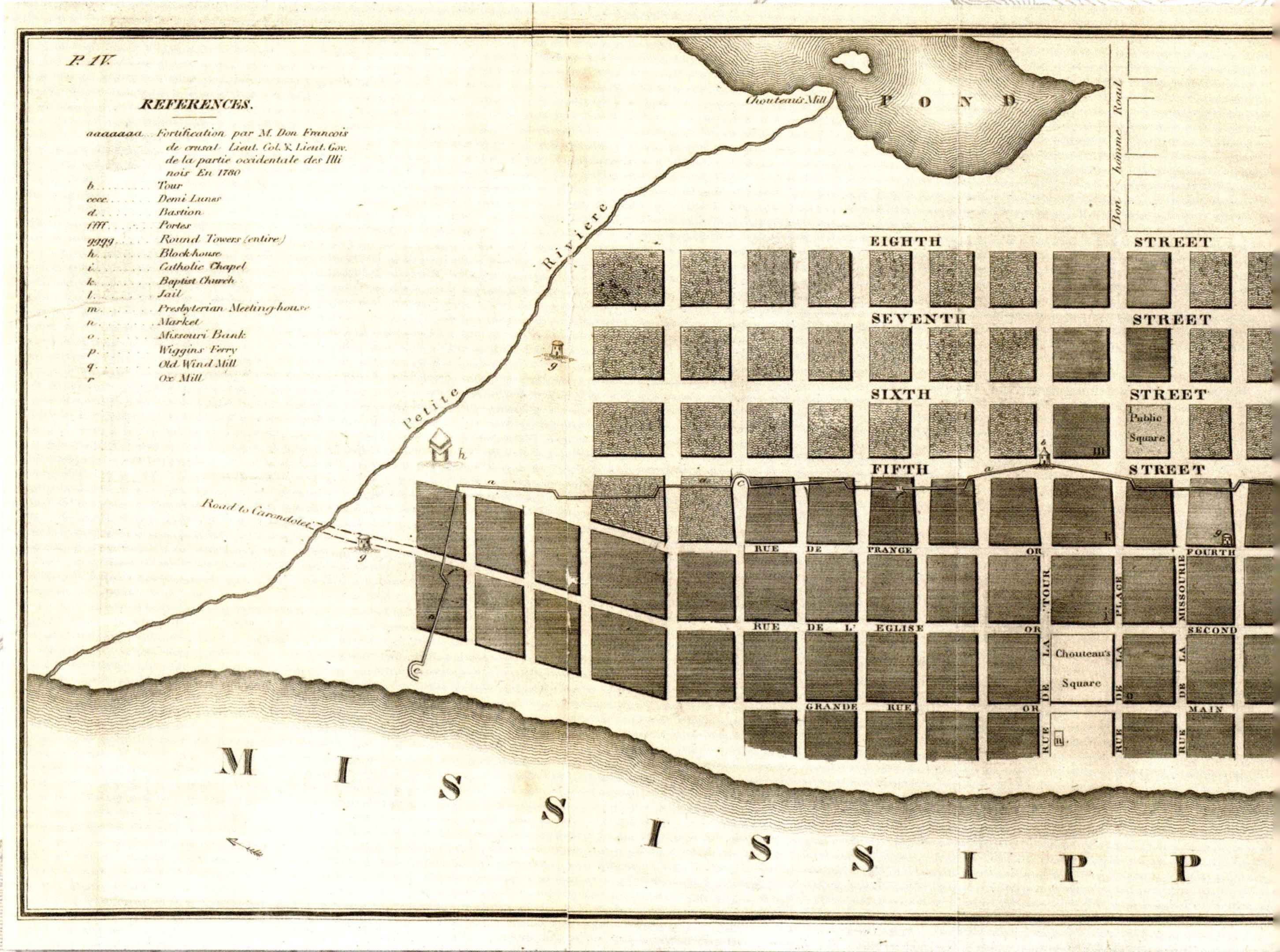

P. IV.
REFERENCES.
aaaaaaa. Fortification par M. Don Francois de crusat Lieut. Col. & Lieut. Gov. de la partie occidentale des Illinois En 1780
b. Tour
cccc. Demi Lunes
d. Bastion
ffff. Portes
gggg. Round Towers (entire)
h. Block-house
i. Catholic Chapel
k. Baptist Church
l. Jail
m. Presbyterian Meeting-house
n. Market
o. Missouri Bank
p. Wiggins Ferry
q. Old Wind Mill
r Ox Mill
Chouteau's Mill
POND
Bon homme Road
Petite Riviere
Road to Carondolet
EIGHTH STREET
SEVENTH STREET
SIXTH STREET
Public Square
FIFTH STREET
RUE DE PRANGE OR FOURTH
RUE DE L' EGLISE OR SECOND
GRANDE RUE OR MAIN
RUE DE LA TOUR
RUE DE LA PLACE
RUE DE LA MISSOURIE
Chouteau's Square
MISSISSIPPI

Plan
OF
St. LOUIS,
Including the late
ADDITIONS
Engraved for
BECK'S GAZETTEER 1822

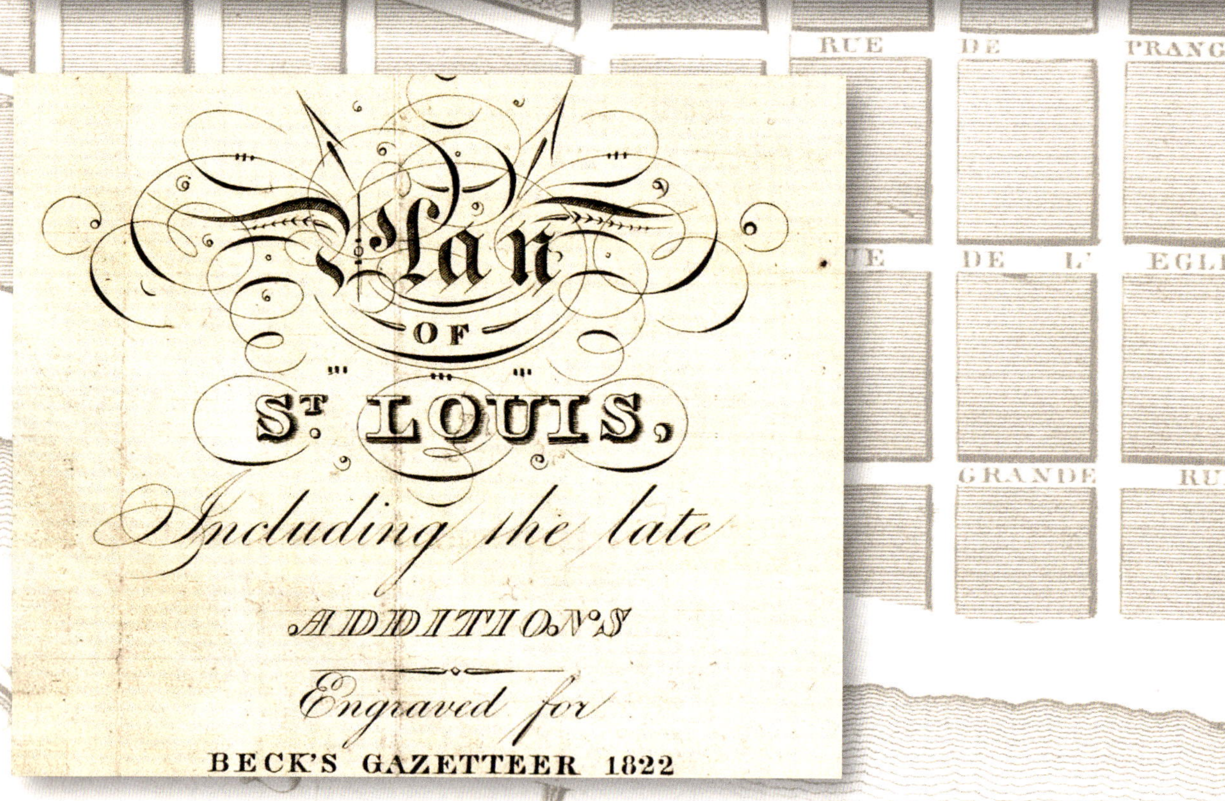

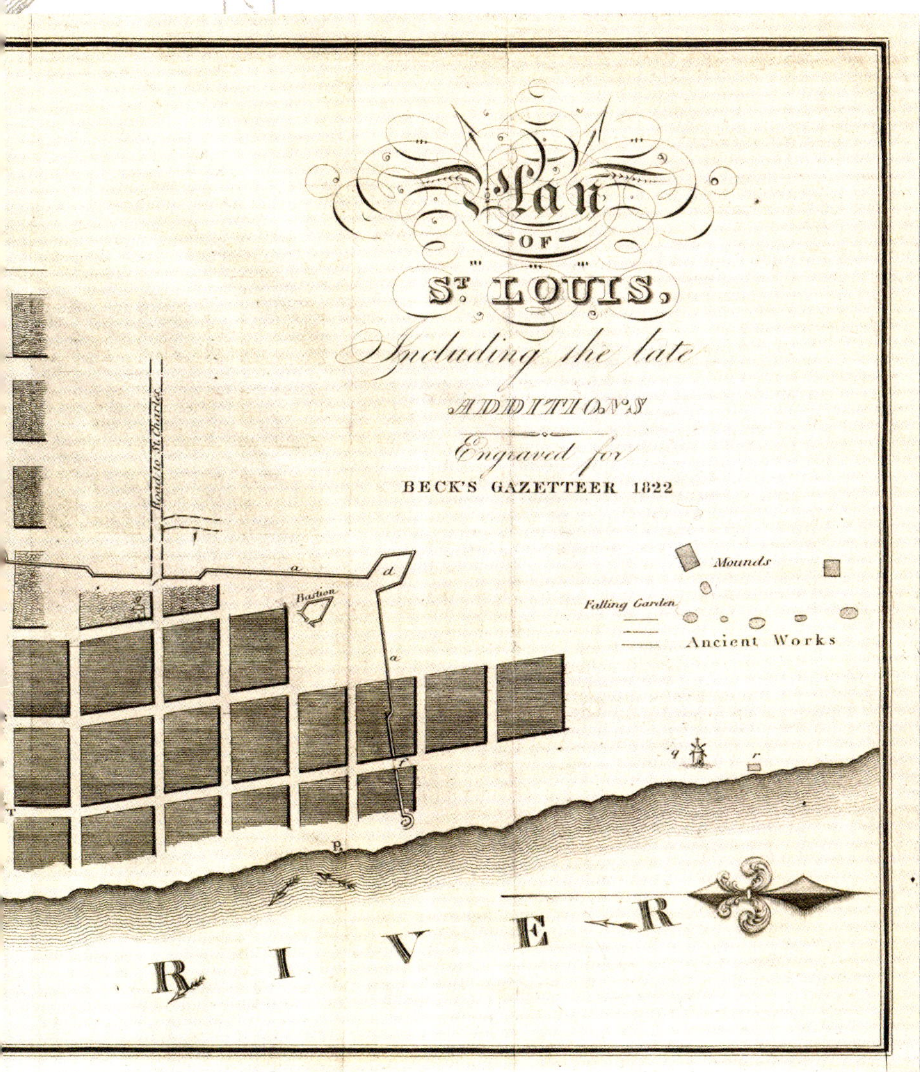

Major William Christy's house, 1818.
COLLECTION OF THE AUTHOR

1822

St. Louis, Missouri

Plan of St. Louis, Including the Late Additions

Lewis C. Beck
(artist/cartographer)

Charles and George Webster
(publisher)

Engraving

7.1 × 16.9 inches

David Rumsey Map Collection,
David Rumsey Map Center,
Stanford Libraries

ON AUGUST 10, 1821, 18 years after the Louisiana Purchase, St. Louis became part of Missouri, which had entered the Union as the 24th state. It was a time of rapid economic and physical growth for St. Louis. Illustrated here are "the late additions" to the City, or 33 new blocks laid out west of Fifth Street. This is the first map of St. Louis to show the expansion of streets and blocks outside of the original town site. It was noted by the map's artist that "soon after the American emigration commenced, four additional streets were laid out . . . and on account of the width of the streets, the coolness and airiness of the situation, it is preferred for places of residence." Importantly, this map also shows the routes out of St. Louis—"Road to Carondelet," "Road to St. Charles," and "Bon Homme Road," known today as Market Street.

Inexplicably left off most earlier maps of St. Louis, the oldest features shown on this map are the "mounds" and "ancient works" of Indigenous peoples. In 1822, at least 25 separate earthen mounds, including the so-called Big Mound that contained the remains of dozens of human burials, were spread across a small area just north of St. Louis. The mounds were constructed between 1000 and 1400 AD as part of a Indigenous American city that included an even larger group of mounds just across the river in Illinois. Called Cahokia by archeologists (we do not know what this civilization called itself), this ancient city had more than 20,000 inhabitants at its height. Cahokia is considered the largest and most complex

Old and new features of St. Louis are evident in this detail of the northern end of the City. The double line traces the fortifications built in 1780, including gates and bastions. Marked with a "P" along the edge of the river is the Wiggens Ferry landing. Samuel Wiggins started his ferry business at St. Louis just a few years before this map was made. The last Wiggins Ferry boat would cross the Mississippi in 1930. The *1897 map* details the history of the Wiggins Ferry Co.

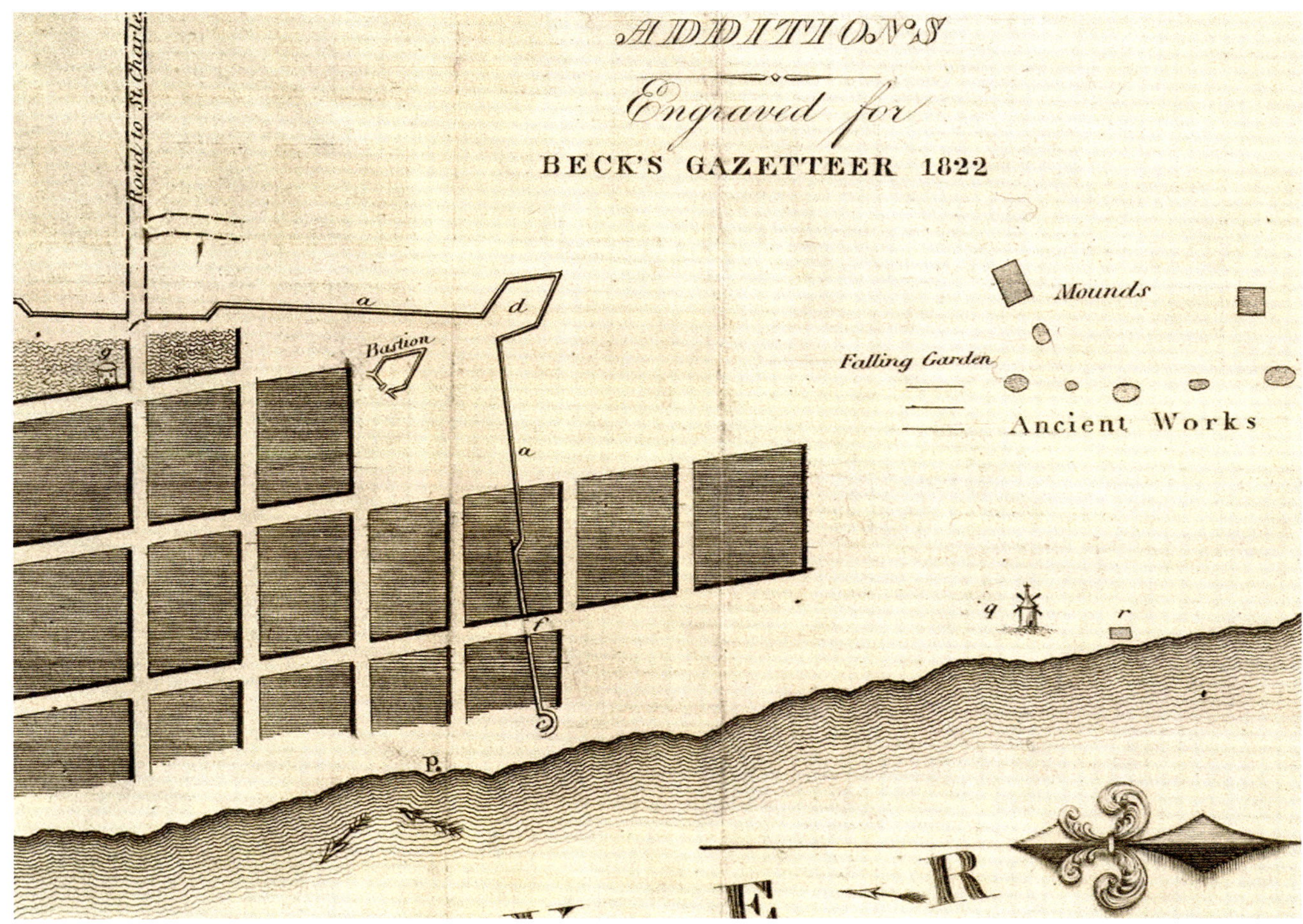

SECOND CATHOLIC CHURCH

In 1818, St. Louis's Catholics began the construction of a new church. Previously, there had been two wood churches on the same block. The new brick church was built under the direction of Bishop DuBourg, and it was the first to be designated a cathedral. Other features include the cemetery, priest's house, and a school, which would in a short time be called Saint Louis University. This brick church had been used for only 14 years when, just to its southwest, a much larger stone church was dedicated in 1834. That larger stone church is today referred to as the Old Cathedral. Both this drawing and that of the Missouri Hotel were prepared "under the direction of Frederic Billon" for his book *Annals of St. Louis in Its Territorial Days from 1804 to 1821*, published in 1888.
COLLECTION OF THE AUTHOR

archaeological site north of the great pre-Columbian cities in Mexico.

This map was engraved for the book *A Gazetteer of the States of Missouri and Illinois*, published in 1823. It is one of the earliest American books describing in any detail Illinois and Missouri, which became states in 1818 and 1821, respectively. In addition to this map of St. Louis, the book also included the first large-scale, intricate map of both states. The Missouri state map shows St. Louis as a large town, but Chicago, not yet sufficiently sized to justify a dot, is shown only by Ft. Dearborn and Chicago Creek on the Illinois map.

The book's author and the map's artist was Lewis C. Beck. Beck was born in upstate New York, where he earned a medical degree in 1818. In 1819, Beck moved to St. Louis, where he lived for the next three years while he prepared his book. During his time in Missouri, he developed a love for botany. Beck gathered an extensive collection of plants from the vicinity of St. Louis, and he later published a list of his plant collection in the leading science journals of the day. Among several new species he documented in St. Louis were the dwarf bluet (*Houstonia minima*) and a variety of sweet pea (*Lathyrus ochroleucus*).

In preparing this map, Beck copied the grid layout and old fortifications from a manuscript he "found in the possession of one of the old inhabitants of that place," adding "I have also added a plan of the ancient works in the vicinity, from actual survey, in which I was assisted by W.S. Hamilton, Esquire, of Illinois." Of the mounds, he noted "fragments of earthenware, arrow heads, and human bones are frequently found in their vicinity." The Big Mound of St. Louis was 30 feet high and more than 150 feet long. It was demolished in 1869, and the spot where it stood is marked with a plaque at the corner of Mound Street and North Broadway.

By the 1870s, St. Louis was popularly called Mound City. Locals viewed the mounds as curiosities, sketching and taking photos of them, building houses on them, and even constructing the City's first reservoir on top of one. While nearly all the mounds of St. Louis have been destroyed, at least one mound still stands. Sugar Loaf mound overlooks the Mississippi River, where Interstate 55 meets South Broadway. Today, it is owned by the Osage Nation.

NEW HOTEL FOR A NEW STATE

When it opened in 1820, the Missouri Hotel was one of the largest buildings in St. Louis. This large and impressive stone structure was on the southwest corner of Main and Oak (now Morgan) Streets. It was here on September 18, 1820, that the Missouri State legislature met for the first time. In 1873, the Missouri Hotel was razed to make way for the Raeder Place building, a landmark that still stands today on Laclede's Landing.
COLLECTION OF THE AUTHOR

Frac.al Township No 45 North Range No 7 East
St Louis Fields
See leaf 8th from this for subdivision
August Chouteau 1031 arpents equal 853 37/100 acres
Prairie De Noyer Fields
See the subdivision of them on leaf 7 from this
Charles Gratiott
Mississippi River
Arsenal Island
Saint Louis Common
Common field lands of Carondelet

Survey around Creve Coeur Lake
by Joseph C. Brown, circa 1825.
COURTESY MISSOURI HISTORICAL SOCIETY, ST. LOUIS

Survey of St. Louis in 1812 showing the common fields (top) and commons (bottom).
COURTESY MISSOURI HISTORICAL SOCIETY, ST. LOUIS

1829

St. Louis Commons & Common Fields

Township No. 45 North, Range No. 7 East

Joseph C. Brown
(artist/cartographer)

Manuscript, brown ink

18.5 × 12.5 inches

Missouri Historical Society, St. Louis

FROM THE CITY'S founding until the 1830s, the landscape of St. Louis had two distinct features: the commons and the common fields. The practice of setting aside land for common use by all its citizens goes back to the medieval era. By the 18th century, this practice had largely fallen out of use in Britain and France, but it had been vigorously maintained in Spain. The St. Louis commons were a large expanse of communal land that provided wood for burning and building, as well as space and grasslands for horses and livestock. These "public" spaces were crucial for the growth and stability of colonial settlements. St. Louis was not unique, as the nearby villages of Cahokia, Kaskaskia, and Prairie du Rocher also had designated common lands.

Anonymous surveyor, circa 1850.
COURTESY THE LIBRARY OF CONGRESS.

The commons were southwest of the village of St. Louis and were enclosed on all sides by a substantial wood fence. The strength of the fence was critical for the well-being of the village, as it corralled the livestock that were the livelihood of many villagers. According to rules established in 1782, the fence was collectively maintained by those families who used the commons, with specific families assigned to certain sections. The sections were marked with the name of the accountable family, and when the fence needed repair, that family would fix it at their own expense or pay a penalty. Every April, a group of 16 men would inspect the entire length of fence, looking for weak spots.

In 1775, the fence was described as being "made in various modes, some was made picket fashion, some worm fence, some with trees their full length and small stakes with riders on top." When St. Louis became part of the US in 1804, the commons encompassed nearly 4,000 acres (about 10 percent of the City of St. Louis). The eventual sale of this land to individuals would help fund the growth of the City. By the 1850s almost all of the commons would be gone. Today, all that remains of the St. Louis commons is Lafayette Park.

Completely separate from the commons were the common fields, or prairies, of St. Louis. The fields were laid out in long, narrow strips, sometimes called ribbon farms. These strips of land were measured in arpents and granted to specific villagers for their own use. An arpent is an old French measurement and can be used to denote either distance or area. One arpent is about 192 feet, or 0.85 acres, depending on the context. A typical arpent division for one common field was four arpents wide by 40 arpents deep (about 135 acres or 102 football fields), though this could vary. Common crops grown in St. Louis included Indian corn, rye, buckwheat, flax, oats, barley, beans, pumpkins, watermelons, muskmelons, and cotton.

There were five common fields around the colonial village—*Prairie de St. Louis* (today the neighborhoods of Downtown West, St. Louis Place, and Old North St. Louis); *La Grande Prairie* (today The Ville and Fairgrounds Park neighborhoods); *Prairie des Noyers* (today Shaw and Tower Grove South); *Prairie a Catalan* (today Dutchtown and Carondelet); and *Cul de Sac* (known today as Midtown).

Even though this map was produced in 1829, 25 years after the colonial period in St. Louis ended, the commons and common fields are still notated. The town of St. Louis is unlabeled, but it sits near the right-center of the map, between Arsenal Island and

THE GRAND PRAIRIE

The northernmost common fields were *La Grande Prairie*. This detailed survey, also completed by Joseph Brown in 1829, shows the division of these fields. The French families named are all early St. Louis residents, including Laclede, Chouteau, Taillon, Sarpy, and Kiercerau.
COURTESY MISSOURI HISTORICAL SOCIETY, ST. LOUIS

Chouteau's Pond. North of the pond are the "St. Louis Fields" or *Prairie de St. Louis*. Adjoining the pond to the west is a large plot of land owned by Auguste Chouteau, which measured "1031 arpents equal to 853 37/100 acres." At the very bottom of the map you can see "St. Louis Common," which had been greatly reduced in size since its maximum.

The map's cartographer was Joseph Cromwell Brown, a legendary surveyor and mapmaker in the Louisiana Territory and early Missouri. He laid down thousands of survey lines and monuments that literally shaped Missouri and surrounding states. Brown executed the first US surveys of St. Louis in the 1810s and 1820s and also served at various times as official county surveyor, St. Louis sheriff, and state senator.

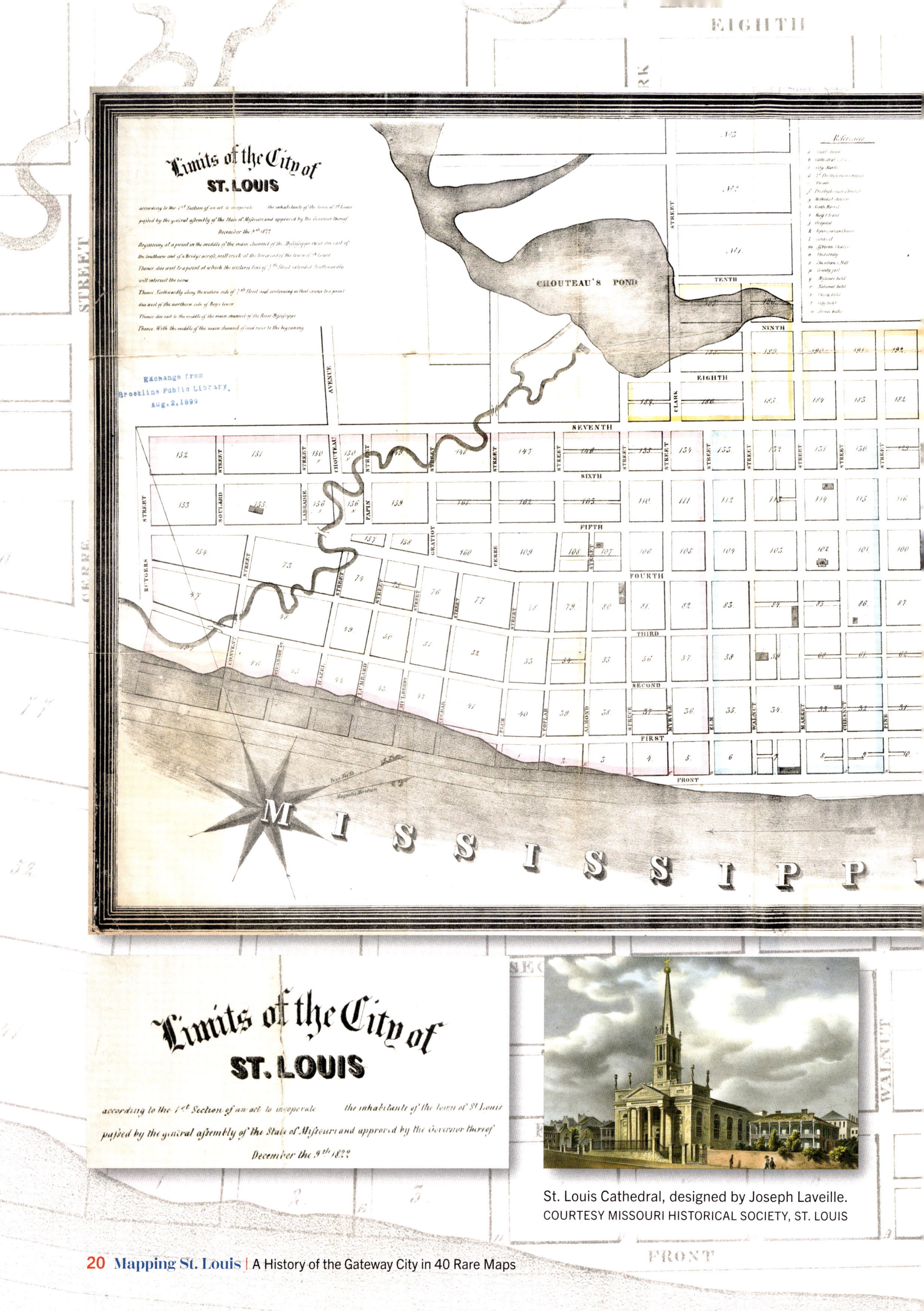

St. Louis Cathedral, designed by Joseph Laveille.
COURTESY MISSOURI HISTORICAL SOCIETY, ST. LOUIS

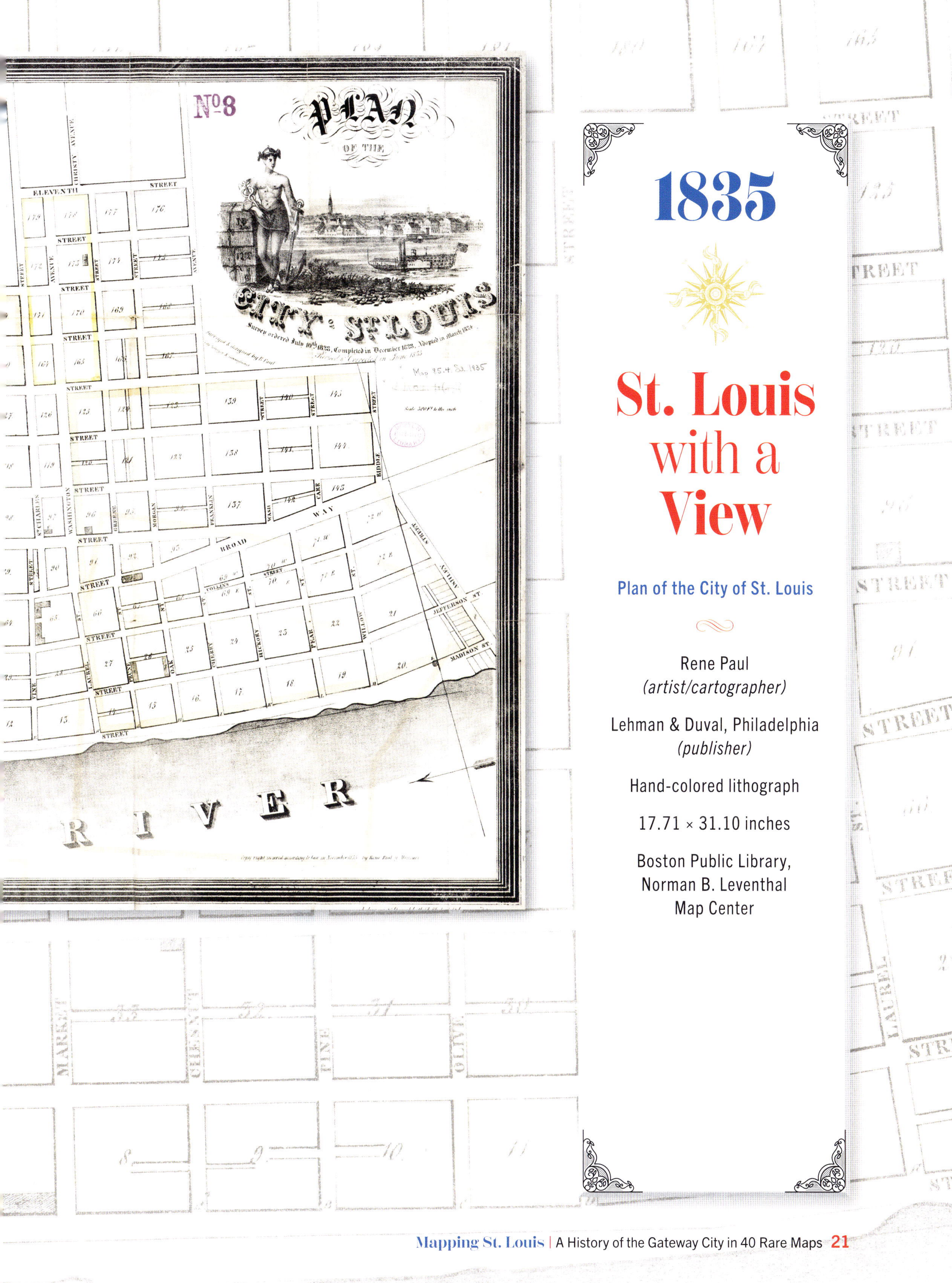

1835

St. Louis with a View

Plan of the City of St. Louis

Rene Paul
(artist/cartographer)

Lehman & Duval, Philadelphia
(publisher)

Hand-colored lithograph

17.71 × 31.10 inches

Boston Public Library,
Norman B. Leventhal
Map Center

1835

THIS MAP shows the dramatic growth of St. Louis in the years since the *1822 map* was published. The City now stretched as far west as 11th Street, nearly four times the depth of the original St. Louis plan.

The base of this map is a survey from December 1823, which was commissioned as part of the process to incorporate the town of St. Louis by the new Missouri state government. In June 1835, extensive "revisions and corrections" to the 1823 survey were completed by Rene Paul, resulting in the map shown here.

Two features on this map that appear here for the first time, and which will be seen on many future St. Louis maps, are a new system of street names and city block numbers.

In the mid-1820s, street commissioner Joseph Laveille established the naming system for the City's street grid, with ordinal numbers for north-south

The title block of this map includes a view of St. Louis—one of the earliest made of the City. The exaggeratedly tall spire is the Catholic Cathedral (the Old Cathedral), completed just a year before this map. Directly in front of the spire along the river is the Public Market, which doubled as the town hall. The large figure is Hermes, the Greek god of travelers, trade, and commercial success, all found in abundance in the quickly growing St. Louis of 1835.

ROY'S TOWER

A landmark along the river for more than 50 years, the round stone tower called Roy's Tower, or Roy's Mill, was built in 1797 by Antoine Roy. Used as a wind-powered grist mill until 1810, it also served for a time as the unofficial northern boundary of St. Louis. Marked with an "i" and a small dark circle, Roy's Tower is located on the far right side of the map along the river between Willow and Ashley Streets. It is one of 21 important places referenced with letters on this map. This photo of Roy's Tower was taken by Thomas Easterly before the tower was demolished in 1856.

COURTESY MISSOURI HISTORICAL SOCIETY, ST. LOUIS

streets and tree names for east–west streets. Gone are the French names *Rue de la Tour* and *Rue de L'Église*, now replaced with Walnut and Second Streets. Laveille was no doubt inspired by Philadelphia, which uses the same system for its downtown streets—tree streets run north–south and numbered streets run west from the Schuylkill River. Like many early city officials, Laveille earned his livelihood at another job. He was an architect, and he designed the early buildings at Jefferson Barracks as well as the Old Cathedral.

The blocks of the City were numbered as a result of the City's incorporation in 1823. Every official city block of St. Louis shown on this map is given a number, totaling 194 blocks on Paul's map. These city block numbers are still a critical reference, appearing in all the City's real estate records.

Another interesting feature of this map demonstrates the fluid power of the Mississippi. On the south end of the riverfront (the left side of the map), 14 blocks are printed as either partially or completely grayed out. The grayed-out blocks had been submerged by the movement of the river since they were first surveyed in 1823 and were part of Paul's revisions printed here.

This map's designer is a fascinating figure. Rene Paul was born in Haiti and educated as a military engineer in Paris. He had served as an officer in Napoleon's army and was wounded at the Battle of Trafalgar in 1805. He later immigrated to St. Louis, where he put his engineering background to good use by becoming a surveyor of the City. Paul married Eulalie Chouteau, whose father was none other than Auguste Chouteau, the prominent landowner who had helped found St. Louis in 1764. Paul's son Gabriel also had an illustrious military and engineering career. Graduating from West Point in 1834, Gabriel served with distinction in the Mexican–American War and was a brigadier general when he was wounded at the Battle of Gettysburg.

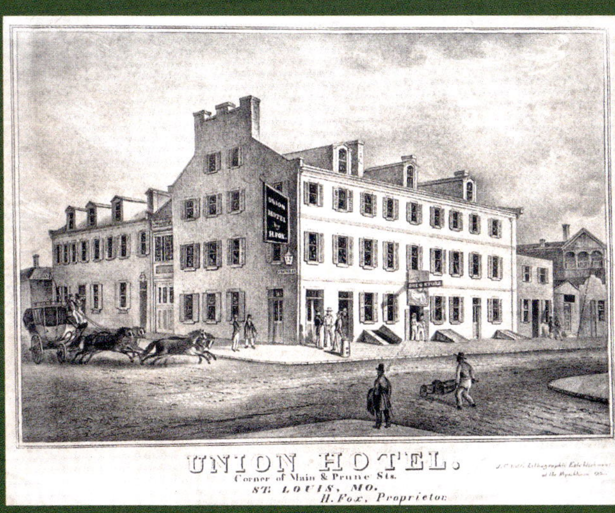

UNION HOTEL

By 1835, St. Louis boasted three hotels to serve visitors: the National Hotel, the Missouri Hotel, and the Union Hotel, all marked on this map. The Missouri and Union shared the same block just off the river. The Union was on the northwest corner of Main and Prune Streets, and it boasted "good food and first class servants." It was also frequently used as a polling place in the 1830s.

COLLECTION OF THE AUTHOR

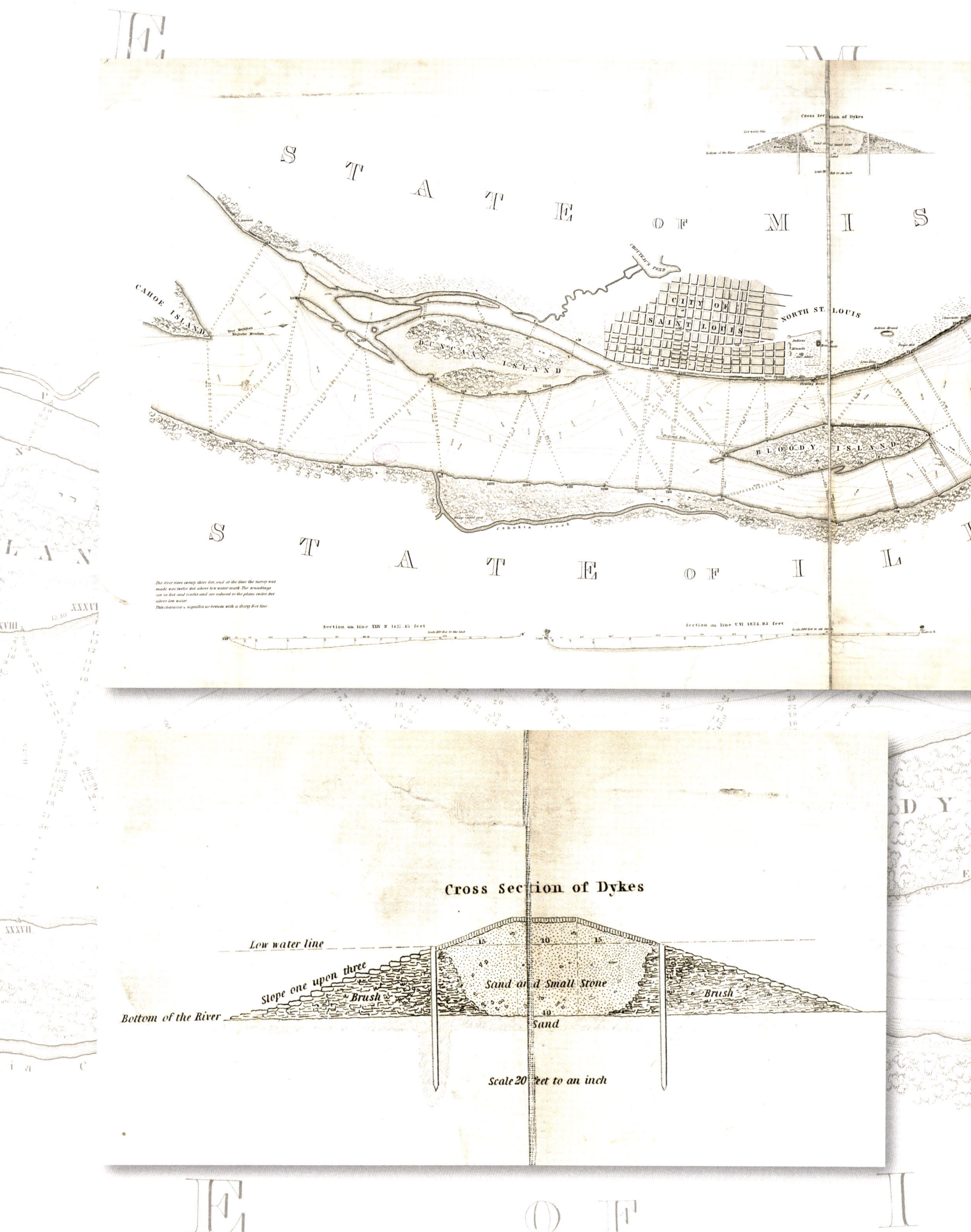
STATE OF MISS
STATE OF ILL
CITY OF SAINT LOUIS
NORTH ST. LOUIS
DUNCANS ISLAND
BLOODY ISLAND
CAHOE ISLAND
Cross Section of Dykes
Low water line
Slope one upon three
Brush
Sand and Small Stone
Bottom of the River
Sand
Scale 20 feet to an inch

Henry Kayser.
COURTESY MISSOURI HISTORICAL SOCIETY, ST. LOUIS

1837

The St. Louis Harbor

Map of the Harbor of St. Louis, Mississippi River, October 1837

Lt. Robert E. Lee
(surveyor)
& Lt. M.C. Meigs
(artist)

W.J. Stone, Washington DC
(printer)

Engraving

36.25 × 48.85 inches

Boston Public Library,
Norman B. Leventhal
Map Center

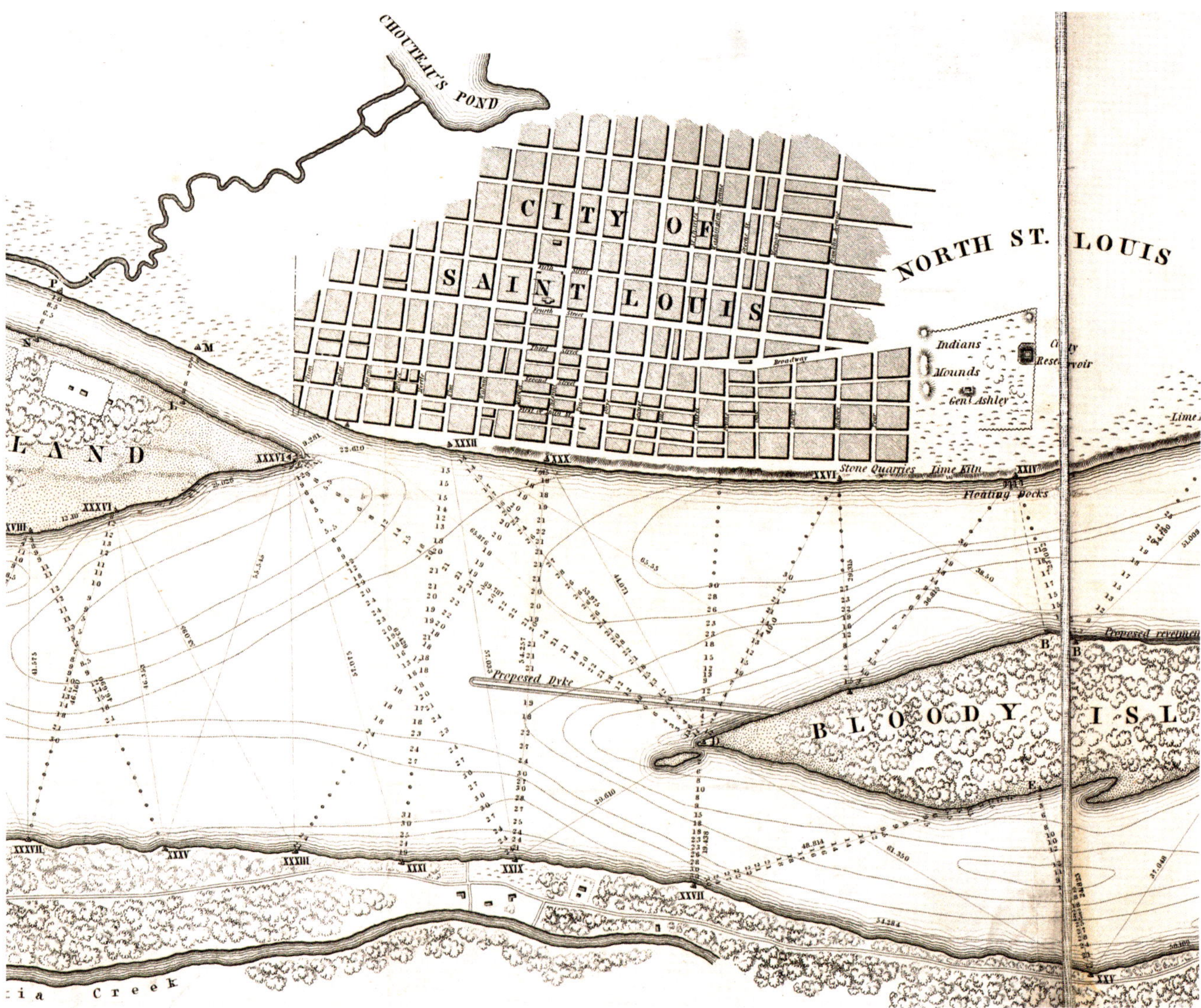

THE FIRST steamboat arrived in St. Louis in 1817. Just 20 years later, in 1837, St. Louis was at the heart of an ever-growing riverboat network. Steamboats quickly connected St. Louis to the major cities of the eastern United States via the Ohio River, to the Rockies and fur-trade posts via the Missouri River, and to New Orleans and the Gulf of Mexico (and also to points north) via the Mississippi. Previously, it had taken a keelboat about 95 days to travel from New Orleans to St. Louis. A steamboat journey averaged just 13 days.

In the early 1830s, St. Louis was designated by the US government as a port of entry for foreign goods. By the time this map was printed, more than 20,000 tons of cargo were being delivered via 1,400 steamboat landings each year. The *Missouri Republican* newspaper reported in 1835 that "every steamboat that arrives at our wharves is crowded with passengers. Some of the Louisville boats bring 300 at a time . . . many of these will stay with us."

There was, however, a problem that threatened the continued growth of this river traffic, and it is

Lee's survey of the St. Louis harbor shows the river as it flows past the City of St. Louis between Bloody Island on the left and Duncan's Island on the right. The numbers organized in diagonal lines across the river indicate the depth of the water. At the south entrance to the harbor or the top of Duncan's Island, the water was only five feet deep due to accumulating sand. In low water conditions it would be even shallower. One of Lee's proposed dikes can be seen in this detail extending out of the bottom of Bloody Island.

LT. ROBERT E. LEE

This portrait of Lee was painted in 1838 in the midst of his work on the St. Louis harbor. Lee was 31 at the time, and in July of that year he would be promoted to the rank of captain. He continued his work in St. Louis until the fall of 1840, when the project was completed.
COURTESY OF THE AUTHOR

documented in this map. The Mississippi was moving *away* from the St. Louis riverfront as sand bars were forming along the levee between Bloody and Duncan Islands. If not corrected, the flow of the river would direct all traffic to the Illinois, not the Missouri, side of the river. To remedy this, a young army lieutenant was assigned to inspect and improve the harbor. His name was Robert E. Lee.

After graduating from West Point in 1829, Lee earned a reputation as a first-class engineer. In 1837 he was assigned by US Army Chief Engineer Col. Charles Gratiot (a well-known St. Louisan) to try and solve the sand problem at the St. Louis harbor.

Lee reported that "a flat bar projects from the upper end of Duncan's Island to the foot of Bloody Island, opposite the town, which at low stage of the river, presents an obstacle to the approach of the City, and gives reason to apprehend that, at some future day, this passage may be closed." In other words, the riverfront at St. Louis was silting up, making it more difficult by the day for steamboats to land at the levee. Lee determined that the remedy was simple, at least on paper. He proposed to redirect the main channel of the river through a series of dikes so that it flowed right in front of the St. Louis levee. The fast current would wash away the loose sand bars and clear the harbor.

After three years of planning and work, the project was deemed a success. Eventually Duncan's Island completely washed away, and Bloody Island became part of the Illinois shore. Today, St. Louis remains a vital and active harbor as the second largest inland port in America, and we can largely credit the work of Robert E. Lee.

As part of Lee's survey and report, this detailed map of the St. Louis Harbor was created, denoting river widths and soundings along with proposed dikes to save the St. Louis Harbor. As noted in the lower right corner, the map was "surveyed by Lt. R.E. Lee, Corps of Engineers" and he was "assisted by Lt. M.C. Meigs, J.S. Morehead, and H. Kayser."

The H. Kayser listed as assisting with this map was Henry Kayser, who, unlike Lee, would continue to play an important role in the growth of St. Louis. Kayser resigned his army position to become St. Louis's first city engineer. He oversaw street, sewer, and water main and public buildings for almost 20 years.

STEAMER *METEOR*

In the 1830s steamboats like the *Meteor* moved both passengers and freight along American rivers. In this era, on any given day, there could be dozens of boats lined up at the St. Louis levee. This rare steamboat view was printed in St. Louis about 1841, bearing the boast, "the finest passenger steamer afloat, and the fastest steam vessel in the world."
COLLECTION OF THE AUTHOR

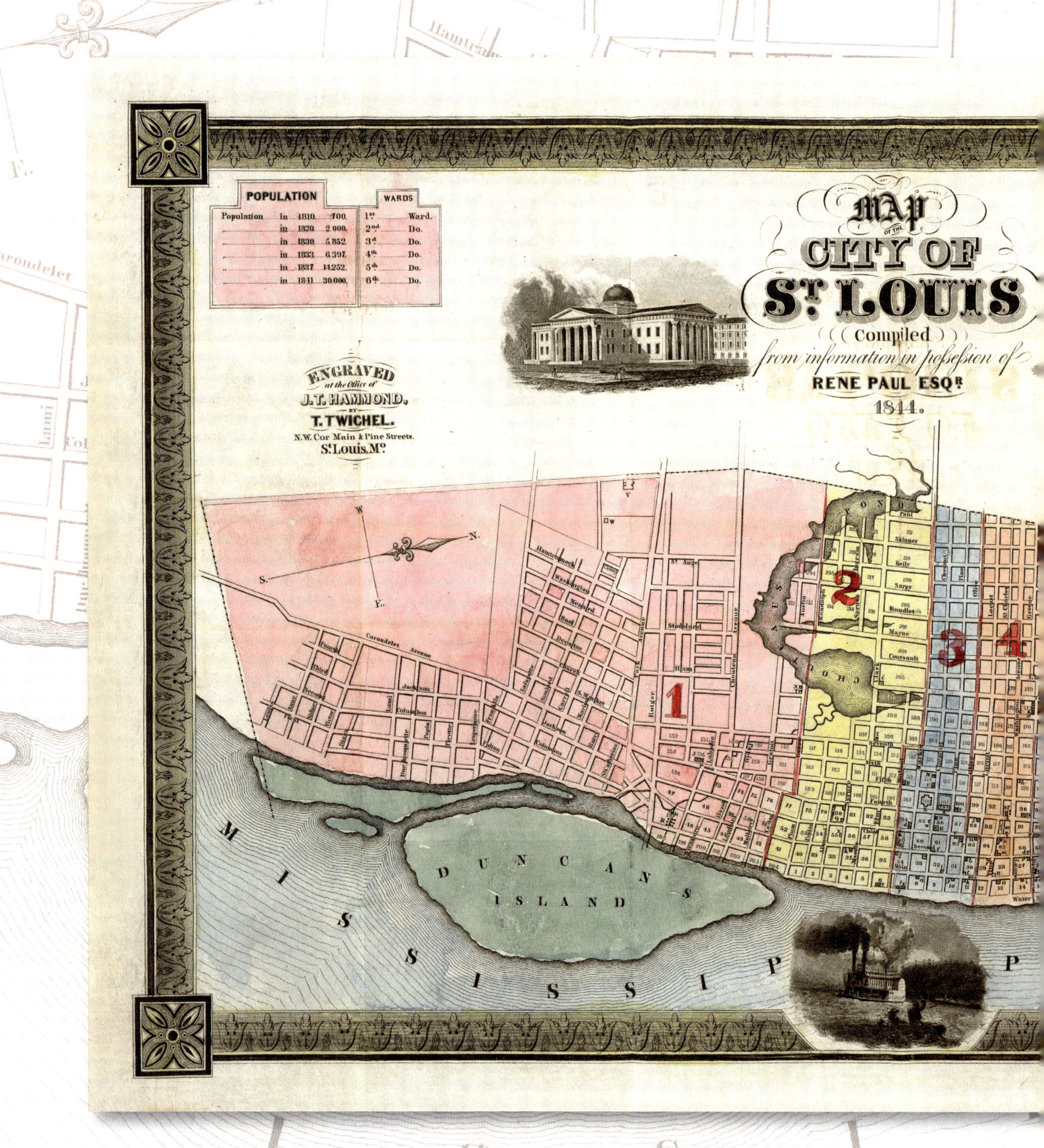
POPULATION
Population in 1810 700.
in 1820 2,000.
in 1830 5,852.
in 1833 6,397.
in 1837 14,252.
in 1841 30,000.
WARDS
1st Ward.
2nd Do.
3rd Do.
4th Do.
5th Do.
6th Do.
MAP OF THE CITY OF St. LOUIS
Compiled from information in possesion of
RENE PAUL ESQR
1844.
ENGRAVED at the Office of J. T. HAMMOND, BY T. TWICHEL.
N.W. Cor Main & Pine Streets.
St. Louis, Mo.
DUNCANS ISLAND
MISSISSIPPI
CHOUTEAU'S POND
Carondelet Avenue

1844

St. Louis Expands & Builds

Map of the City of St. Louis, Compiled from Information in the Possession of Rene Paul, Esq.

T. Twichel
(artist-cartographer)

J. T. Hammond
(publisher/printer)

Hand-colored engraving

9.4 × 15.3 inches

David Rumsey Map Collection, David Rumsey Map Center, Stanford Libraries

1844

IN 1841, the creation of new city limits expanded St. Louis from 0.75 to 4.78 square miles (480 to 3,060 acres). The City now measured an additional 20 blocks to both the north and south of the original site (as shown on the *1780 map*). The political wards are numbered and highlighted in color. Although their areas were vastly different, each ward's population was roughly the same. In addition to growing by area, St. Louis was also experiencing significant population growth. The box at the upper left details that the City doubled in population between 1833 and 1837 and then doubled again between 1837 and 1841. The "explanation" box in the upper right offers a key for locating places on the map as varied as the Big Mound and the smallpox hospital.

The title block advertises that the map was created "from information in the possession of Rene Paul, Esq." Few people knew more about the physical layout of St. Louis than Paul. Not only did he draw the *1835 map*, but as the City's official surveyor, he surveyed and laid out the new streets overlapping Chouteau's Pond on the west edge of the City. He even named one Paul Street. Paul also surveyed the first road from St. Louis to Chicago.

This map features three pictorial vignettes. There is a rather generic view of a steamboat and two detailed views of St. Louis's newest and largest buildings—the courthouse and Planter's House.

THE COURTHOUSE & PLANTER'S HOUSE

This print from 1841 shows the courthouse in the foreground and the red-brick Planter's House in the background. It is the work of artist and lithographer John Caspar Wild, who completed a series of views of St. Louis in his book, *The Valley of the Mississippi Illustrated*. The view of the courthouse in the map vignette was copied from this print.
COURTESY MISSOURI HISTORICAL SOCIETY, ST. LOUIS

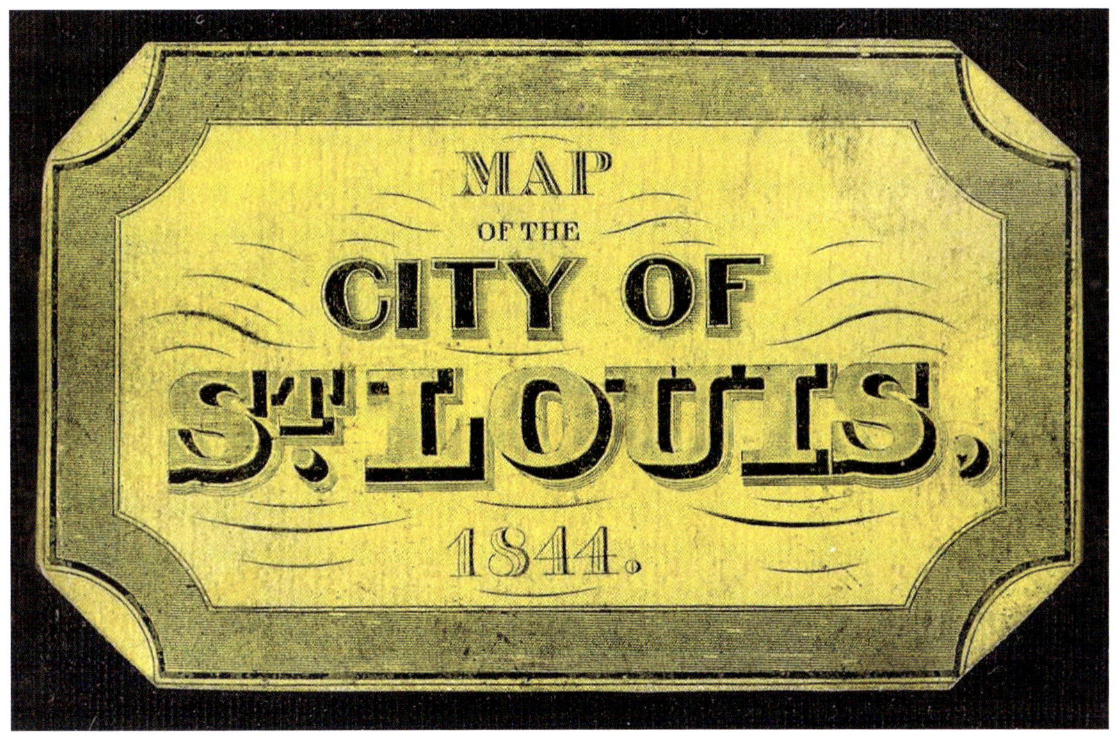

MAP OF THE CITY OF ST. LOUIS, 1844

This booklet was designed to securely store and easily transport the folded 1844 map of St. Louis. Like Google Maps on a smartphone today, the map was intended to be carried about St. Louis to help with navigation.

COURTESY DAVID RUMSEY MAP COLLECTION, DAVID RUMSEY MAP CENTER, STANFORD LIBRARIES

The courthouse is the only structure ever to have stood on the block bounded by Broadway, Chestnut, Fourth, and Market Streets. The design featured in the vignette was not actually finished when this map was printed in 1844. It was a monumental building concept for St. Louis, occupying an entire block. The design called for four wings, each faced with a Greek temple portico, meeting in a rotunda with a low dome.

Some considered it pretentious in scale, and Boston financiers refused a loan for its construction because "St. Louis was situated at too distant a point in the West to be a safe place for the investment of so large a sum." In less than 50 years, St. Louis would surpass Boston's population. Work on the courthouse would continue for the next 25 years. Through the entire construction process, the building was occupied and courtrooms were used, including during parts of the landmark Dred Scott case in 1847.

Completed in 1841, the four-story Planter's House hotel was located at Fourth and Pine Streets, removed from the traffic and pollution of the levee. The interior was lavish and detailed, with beautiful carpets and staircases. The hotel had 150 guest rooms, each with a coal-burning stove, windows fitted with Venetian shutters, and call bells linked with the front desk. Considered the finest in the West, the Planter's House was seen by city leaders as a symbol of the new St. Louis. It became the gathering place for politicians and businessmen, and its name became synonymous with luxury and good service.

Among the many famous guests was Charles Dickens, who recalled, "We went to a large hotel, called the Planter's House: built like an English hospital, with long passages and bare walls, and sky-lights above the room doors for the free circulation of air. It is an excellent house, and the proprietors have most bountiful notions of providing the creature comforts. Dining alone with my wife in our own room, one day, I counted fourteen dishes on the table at once."

However, the hotel was about the only thing Dickens liked about St. Louis.

ST ZAVIERS CH
CHRISTS CH
LIBERTY ENGINE HOUSE
COURT HOUSE
BANK OF MISSOURI
SHOT TOWER
UNION ENGINE HOUSE
PUBLIC SCHOOL
CENTENARY CH
McDOWALS MEDICAL COLLEGE
THEATRE
THE OLD MARKET HOUSE AND LEVEE
POND
WATER
DUNCANS ISLAND
MISSISSIPPI
MAP
And VIEW of ST LOUIS Mo
DRAWN ENGRAVED & PRINTED
by J. M. Kershaw
34 Second St. St. Louis.

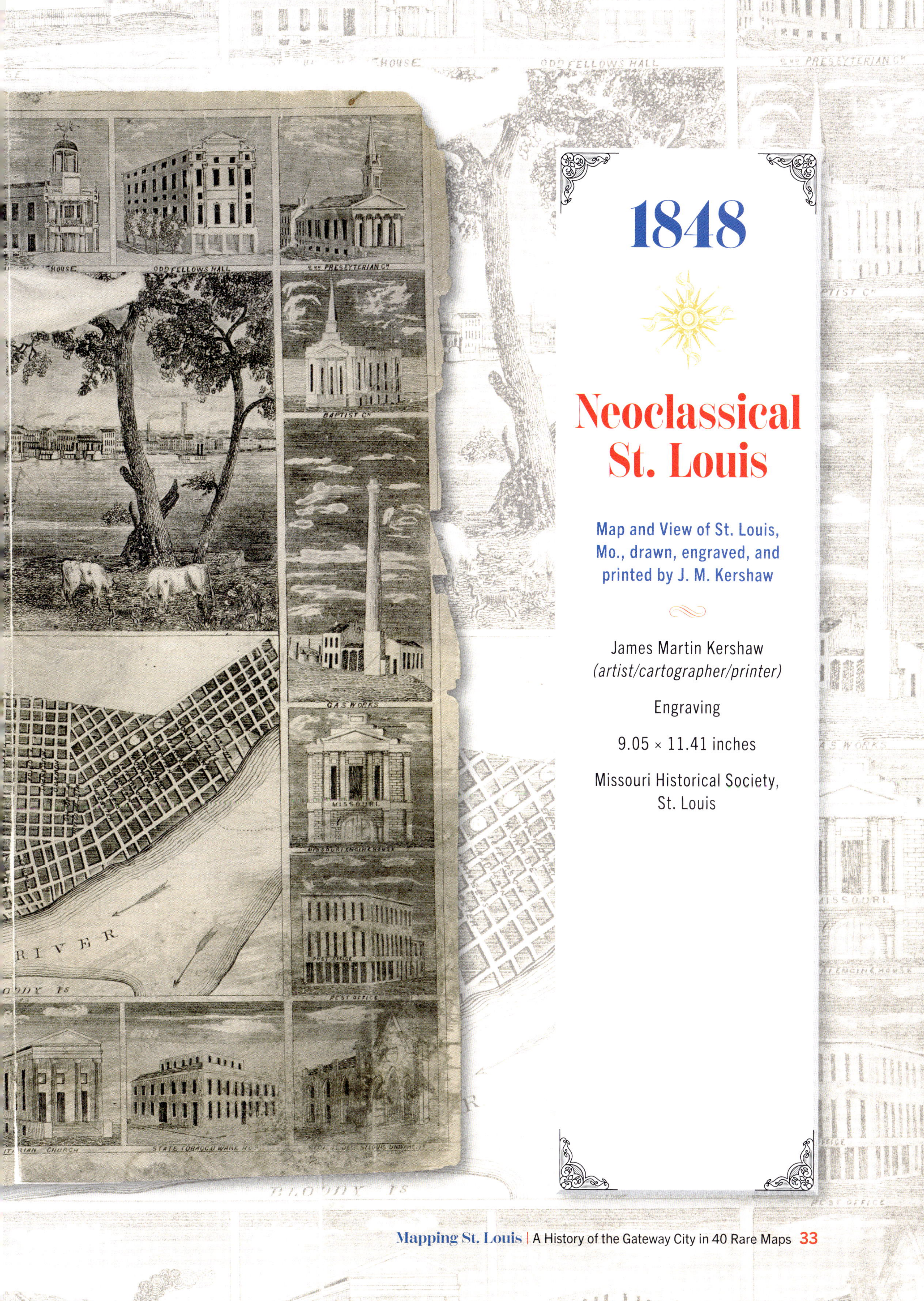

1848

Neoclassical St. Louis

Map and View of St. Louis, Mo., drawn, engraved, and printed by J. M. Kershaw

James Martin Kershaw
(artist/cartographer/printer)

Engraving

9.05 × 11.41 inches

Missouri Historical Society, St. Louis

WHEN THIS MAP and view were printed in 1848, St. Louis had become a showplace for neoclassical architecture. Columns, pilasters, and pediments proliferated in the City, as is evident by the vignettes that make up the map's border. This map and view were printed as part of the St. Louis Directory for 1848, which was advertised as "containing the names of the inhabitants, their occupations, places of business, and dwelling houses together with other useful information." The map folded out in three parts and was not a practical guide to carry around the City, but was meant to show off St. Louis.

A population explosion of more than 600 percent in just 10 years meant St. Louis required hundreds of new buildings. At the same time, exciting new technologies came to the City, including gas lights to illuminate city streets in 1847 and the telegraph in 1848.

The 22 buildings featured around the map border encompass the entire spectrum of uses: public (courthouse) and private (Bank of Missouri), secular (public school) and religious (six churches), social (Odd Fellows Hall) and industrial (shot tower).

The shot tower was, given its height, one of the most prominent structures in 1848 St. Louis. It produced small shot balls for guns by dropping molten lead from the top. Round balls are formed as they fall before being

ST. LOUIS LEVEE
This view of the St. Louis levee was the inspiration for the vignette at the bottom of the 1848 map and view. Completed by J. C. Wild in 1841, it shows the intense steamboat activity along the levee, but also the diversity of a City where Whites, Indigenous peoples, and African Americans can all be seen in action. The large red building on the left was both the market house and the town hall and was built in 1827.
COURTESY MISSOURI HISTORICAL SOCIETY, ST. LOUIS

Odd Fellows Hall, drawing by Theodor Anders.
COURTESY MISSOURI HISTORICAL SOCIETY, ST. LOUIS

SECOND PRESBYTERIAN CHURCH
Dedicated in 1840 at the corner of Fifth and Walnut Streets, the Second Presbyterian Church was an impressive building with six enormous Doric columns and a steeple that rose to a height of 175 feet. Construction cost $42,000. It was reported at the time of its completion that "a person coming from the Rocky Mountains or who had never seen any building dedicated to God, beyond a frame meeting house in the woods, would be struck by the grandeur and magnificence both exterior and interior of Second Presbyterian Church."
COURTESY CAMPBELL HOUSE MUSEUM

caught in a water pool at the bottom. Shot towers were essential for the efficient production of ammunition. It can be seen both in a vignette on the left side border and in the city view on the far right side of the skyline. The Odd Fellows Hall was a remarkable building for the sheer amount of neoclassical detailing, three-story Corinthian pilasters, and scrolled pediment. It is shown in the top right of the border.

James Martin Kershaw was responsible for the drawing, engraving, and printing of this map. His advertisement in the 1848 directory described his establishment as printing diplomas, visiting cards, wedding cards, and letterhead, and engraving jewelry and silverware.

View
of the City
of
ST. LOUIS, MO.
FOURTH
STREET
THIRD
STREET
SECOND
STREET
FIRST or MAIN
STREET
FRONT
STREET
Hospital
Cathol.
Church
Theatre
Market
ALMOND ST.
SPRUCE ST.
MARKET ST.
WALNUT ST.
CHESNUT ST.
PINE ST.
OLIVE ST.
LOCUST ST.
MISSISSIPPI RIVER
Jul. Hutawa Lith. Chesnut St. 62, St. Louis, Mo.

1849

The Great St. Louis Fire

View of the City of ST. LOUIS, MO. or The Great Fire of the City on the 17th and 18th May 1849

Leopold Gast
(artist/cartographer)

Julius Ilutawa
(publisher/printer)

Lithograph

21.5 × 17.12 inches

Missouri Historical Society, St. Louis

ON THE EVENING of May 17, 1849, the steamboat *White Cloud* caught fire at the north end of the St. Louis levee near the foot of Morgan Street. After breaking free from its moorings, the *White Cloud* drifted downriver, igniting 22 other steamboats along its path. Huge stacks of river freight stacked on the levee added fuel to the fire. The flames quickly leapt from the burning boats to buildings that lined the levee.

The entire business district of St. Louis was in the fire's path. The danger was compounded by the fact that the city reservoir quickly ran out of water. To save the City, volunteer firemen (St. Louis's first professional fire department was not established until 1857) created a fire break by filling six buildings with black powder and blowing them up. It worked, and after 11 hours, the fire was under control. It remains the largest and most destructive fire in St. Louis history.

This combination view and map was published just one month after the fire. It dramatically illustrates the flames against the evening sky as well as the path of the fire's destruction.

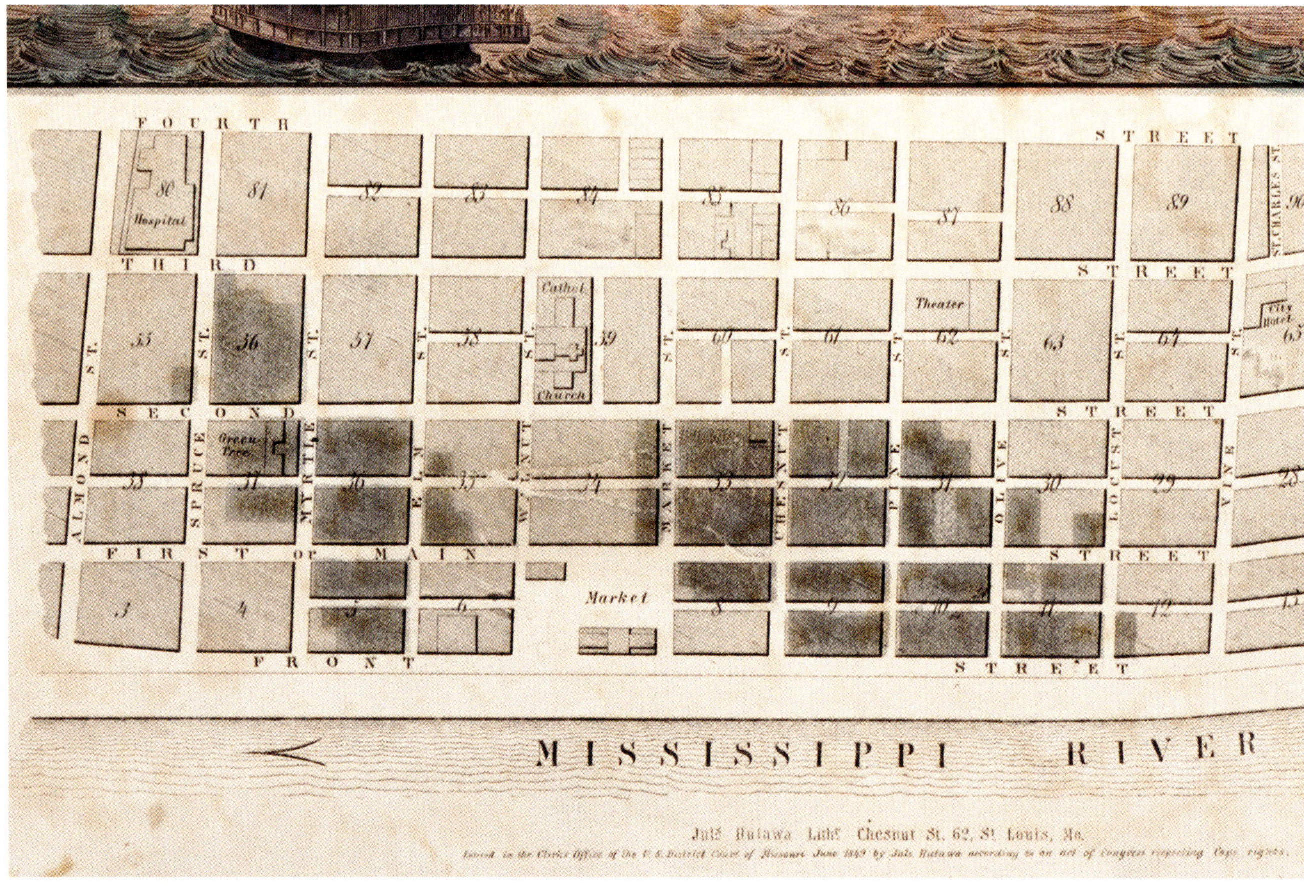

The fire quickly spread from the levee to buildings along the river and farther west. The darker gray sections of the map indicate the parts of the City destroyed by the fire. The southern arm of the fire was bounded by Front Street (the levee), and Walnut, Third, and Spruce Streets. The northern arm of the fire was larger, bounded by Front Street, Market, Second, and Locust Streets. Most of the City's newest neoclassical-style buildings were not damaged by the fire, including (as illustrated at the top of this detail, from left to right) the spires of the Catholic Church and Second Presbyterian Church, the Public Market House, the newly-built dome of the courthouse, the spire of the Episcopal Christ Church Cathedral, and the Planter's House Hotel. While the fire destroyed some of the City's oldest buildings, which were largely made of wood, it created the opportunity for substantial rebuilding. The structures that emerged following the fire were built with particular emphasis on fireproofing. They were generally four or five stories in height with heavy brick walls and were faced on the street front with stone or cast-iron facades. Most of these new buildings stood until the late 1930s, when the Jefferson National Expansion Memorial project demolished the entire area that had been impacted by the fire.

RUINS OF THE GREAT ST. LOUIS FIRE, 1849

St. Louis photographer Thomas Easterly took this daguerreotype of the fire's aftermath. It shows the total destruction of blocks of the City along the levee and one prominent building that was spared the flames: the spire of the Catholic church, today called the Old Cathedral. This is one of the earliest photographs taken of St. Louis buildings.
COURTESY MISSOURI HISTORICAL SOCIETY, ST. LOUIS

GREAT FIRE AT ST. LOUIS, MO.

Published in New York in 1849 by famous lithographer Nathaniel Currier, this print carries the caption, "23 steamboats and cargoes destroyed valued at $468,000, Value of buildings destroyed estimated at $502,290, Total amount of property destroyed estimated at $5,000,000." That's more than $180 million in today's dollars. The print vividly depicts an explosion of black powder that was used to demolish buildings in order to create the firebreak.
COURTESY MISSOURI HISTORICAL SOCIETY, ST. LOUIS

LAVENDER HILL
WILLOW
HAZEL HILL
MULBERRY HILL
WOODLAND HILL
SACRED
VALE
PRIMROSE HILL
VINE HILL
AMBROSIA HILL
VALLEY
MAGNOLIA HILL
SHRINE HILL
ALTHEA HILL
WILD ROSE VALLEY
WOODBINE HILL
TULIP HILL
FANE HILL
ASPEN HILL
WILD ROSE HILL
ROSEMARY HILL
MOUNT REPOSE
CONSECRATION DELL
LABURNUM HILL
CORDU VALLEY
VISTA HILL
OAK HILL
CREVE
EVERGREEN HILL
BELLEFONTAINE ROAD
E.W. EGLOFFSTEIN
Engraved by J.H. Fisher St. Louis Mo
Dedicated May 15th 1850
BELLEFONTAINE CEMETERY
Secretary and Treasurer
JAMES H. BACON
TRUSTEES FOR 1852
President
JOHN O'FALLON
GERARD B ALLEN
AUGUSTUS BREWSTER
WILLIAM BENNETT
HUDSON E. BRIDGE
JOHN F DARBY
JAMES HARRISON
JAMES E YEATMAN
LUTHER M KENNETT
WM M. PHERSON
JOHN R. SHEPLEY
Superintendent
A HOTCHKISS

At the bottom of this detail is the main entrance and gate to the cemetery off Bellefontaine Road. The large number of lots established in just two years show that the rural cemetery concept was popular. It was so popular that one road is marked "The Tour," which gives visitors the most scenic path through Bellefonatine's hills and valleys. The size and shape (round, oval, square, and in one case heart-shaped) of each family lot in Bellefontaine was determined by the buyer. Trees were then planted in the gaps between the plots. The names given to the roads, hills, and valleys are pastoral (Mount Repose, Hazel Hill, Willow Vale, etc.), but generic in that they bear no particular relation to the place. The topography is indicated by shading: the darker areas are ravines and the lighter areas are hilltops.

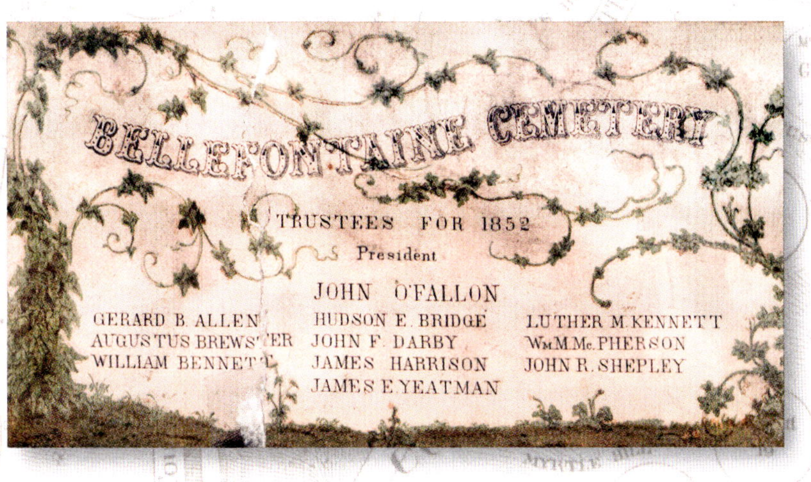

1852

Bellefontaine Cemetery

Bellefontaine Cemetery,
St. Louis, Mo.

Friedrich W. Egloffstein
(artist/cartographer)

J.H. Fisher
(publisher/printer)

Lithograph

28.5 × 21.5 inches

Bellefontaine Cemetery Association

1852

ST. LOUIS'S FIRST cemetery was the small graveyard next to the Catholic Church on third Street (illustrated in the *1822 map* section). By the 1830s, a series of cemeteries, some public but most associated with a local church, were established outside the city limits along Jefferson Avenue. Within a decade, it was clear these were becoming an impediment to the westward growth of St. Louis.

In 1849, the newly formed Rural Cemetery Association purchased the 138-acre Hempstead family farm five miles northwest of the City along the road to the old Fort Bellefontaine. Earlier that year, the City had suffered a widespread outbreak of cholera that killed possibly as many as 5,000 people over the course of the summer.

The rural cemetery movement was inspired by romantic ideas about nature, art, and a melancholy notion of death. It drew upon innovations in cemetery design in England and France, especially at Père Lachaise Cemetery in Paris. In America, rural cemeteries typically were established on elevated ground on the outskirts of larger cities. Just five years after the creation of Bellefontaine, the Catholic Church established Calvary Cemetery on an adjacent 400 acres.

Landscape architect Almerin Hotchkiss, who helped design Green-Wood Cemetery in Brooklyn, was hired to draft and implement a master plan for Bellefontaine. Hotchkiss went on to serve as

BELLEFONTAINE BIRD'S-EYE VIEW
This bird's-eye view shows the northeast corner of the cemetery, with the main gate on Bellefontaine Road, as well as the cemetery office. Today the entrance to Bellefontaine is on the west side, off Florissant Road.
COURTESY CAMPBELL HOUSE MUSEUM

superintendent of the cemetery for the next 46 years. He designed most of Bellefontaine's roadways and landscaping, and he oversaw maintenance of the grounds. The first burial at Bellefontaine took place on April 27, 1850. Over the next 20 years, not only were thousands of bodies interred here, but many family plots were established that continue to be used today.

This map includes an elaborate pictorial border that shows a view of the cemetery from across Bellefontaine Road. The sides of the border display some of the cemetery monuments, along with a list of the owners of most of the lots. Inset, inside the border, is a detailed layout of Bellefontaine's roads, buildings, and plots.

The map was drawn by Baron Friedrich Wilhelm von Egloffstein, who had come to America in 1846. In St. Louis, he established himself as a mapmaker, artist, explorer, and inventor. He was the cartographer for John C. Fremont's 1853 expedition to the Rockies, and in 1857 he helped explore the Colorado River and the Grand Canyon. The two large maps produced by Egloffstein after the Colorado expedition are considered a high point in American cartography in the 19th century.

Today, the Bellefontaine Cemetery consists of 314 acres and over 87,000 graves, including those of William Clark, Adolphus Busch, Thomas Hart Benton, Rush Limbaugh, and William S. Burroughs. Bellefontaine is home to a number of architecturally significant monuments and mausoleums, including the Louis Sullivan–designed Wainwright Tomb. The cemetery is proud of its interments, monuments, and history, regularly offering tours and programs. Bellefontaine is also a level-3 arboretum, one of only 40 in the US, as designated by ArbNet, a global network of tree professionals.

LOT 257

Robert Campbell purchased lot 257 in Bellefontaine cemetery in 1862. That same year he had the remains of five of his children moved from Christ Church Episcopal cemetery, located at Park and Jefferson avenues. He ordered the marble monument and knee-wall seen here from Philadelphia at a cost of $1,250 ($39,000 in 2024). Eventually, more than 18 members of the extended Campbell family would be laid to rest here. In the 19th century, many graves in Bellefontaine were covered in mounded ivy as seen in this 1885 photograph, a practice long since abandoned. The Robert Campbell lot is on Memory Hill in the central part of the cemetery and is unusual because the large plot contains only one monument and no individual headstones.
COURTESY CAMPBELL HOUSE MUSEUM

THE CITY OF
ST LOUIS
MISSOURI.
PUBLISHED BY J.H. COLTON & Co.
172 WILLIAM STREET.
NEW YORK.
SCALE
0 ¼ ½ Mile ¾
0 440 880 1320 Yards
The Plans of St Louis & Chicago are upon the same scale
MISSISSIPPI RIVER
Duncans Island
EXCHANGE SQ.
WASHINGTON SQUARE
CARR SQU
COURT HOUSE
POST OFFICE
RESERVOIR
GRAVE YARD
PUBLIC PARK
CITY WORK HOUSE
CITY HOSPITAL
PUBLIC GROUND
PACIFIC R.R.
ST LOUIS & IRON MT. R.R.
CITY BOUNDARY
Chouteau Avenue
Franklin Avenue
St Charles Street
Market Street
Park Avenue
Grand Avenue
St Louis Place
Front Street
Mill Creek
Rocky Branch
True Meridian
Magnetic Meridian 8° East
Entered according to Act of Congress, in the Year 1855 by J.H. Colton & Co. in the Clerks Office of the District Court of the United States for the Southern District of New York

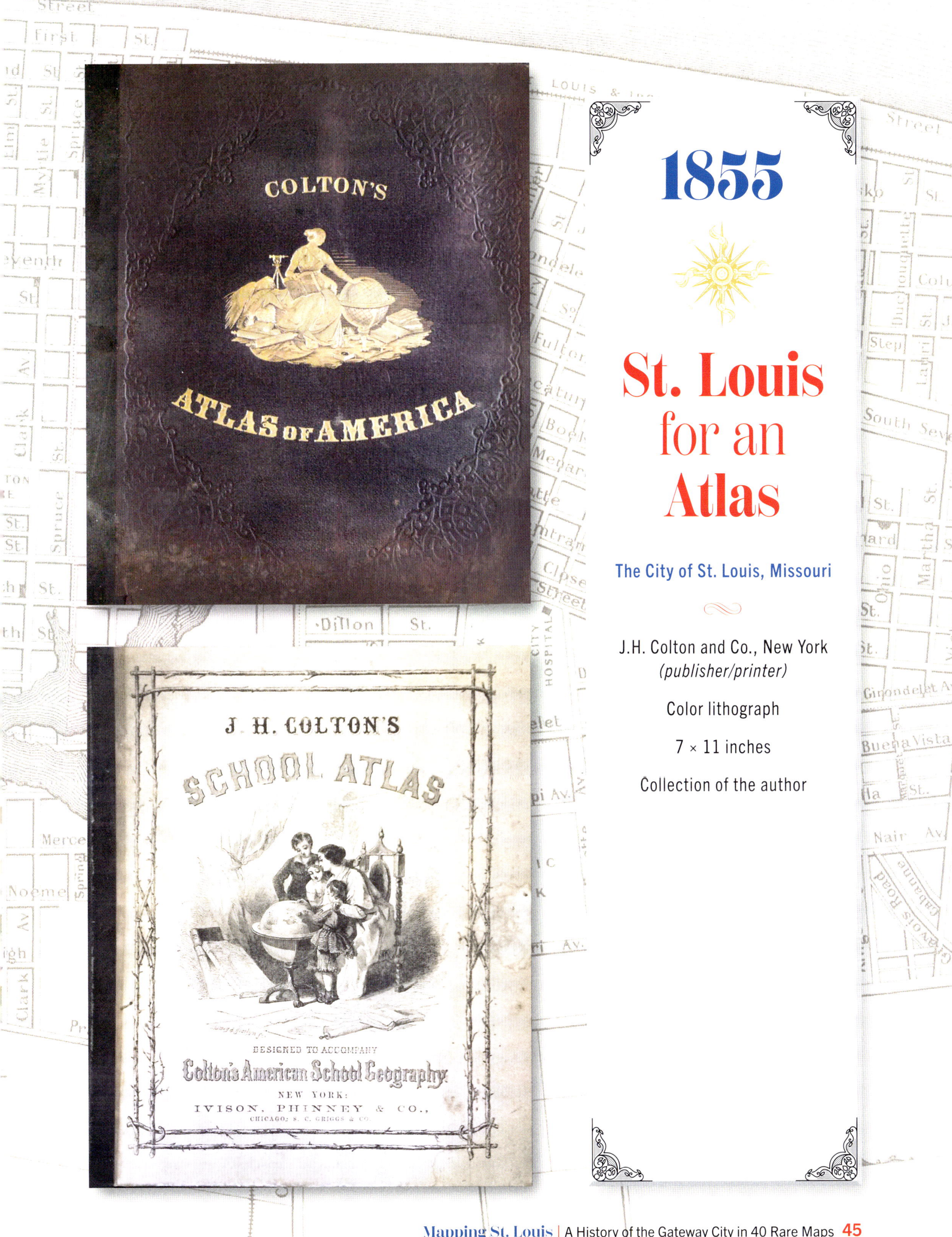

1855

St. Louis for an Atlas

The City of St. Louis, Missouri

J.H. Colton and Co., New York
(publisher/printer)

Color lithograph

7 × 11 inches

Collection of the author

1855

THIS MAP was the first of St. Louis produced specifically for an atlas. *Colton's Atlas of the World* was published in two volumes: the first (North and South America) in 1855, followed by volume two (Europe, Asia, etc.) in 1856. The atlas was one of the finest and most accurate of the period, and it had a long publishing run, remaining in print for over 30 years.

The Coltons were a prominent family firm of mapmakers. Based in New York City, they became the leaders in the American map trade in the second half of the 19th century. By 1850, the Colton firm was one of the primary publishers of immigrant guides, pocket maps, wall maps, and railroad maps. Their maps were known for the high-quality steel plate engravings with decorative borders and hand-colored detail. During the Civil War they produced a

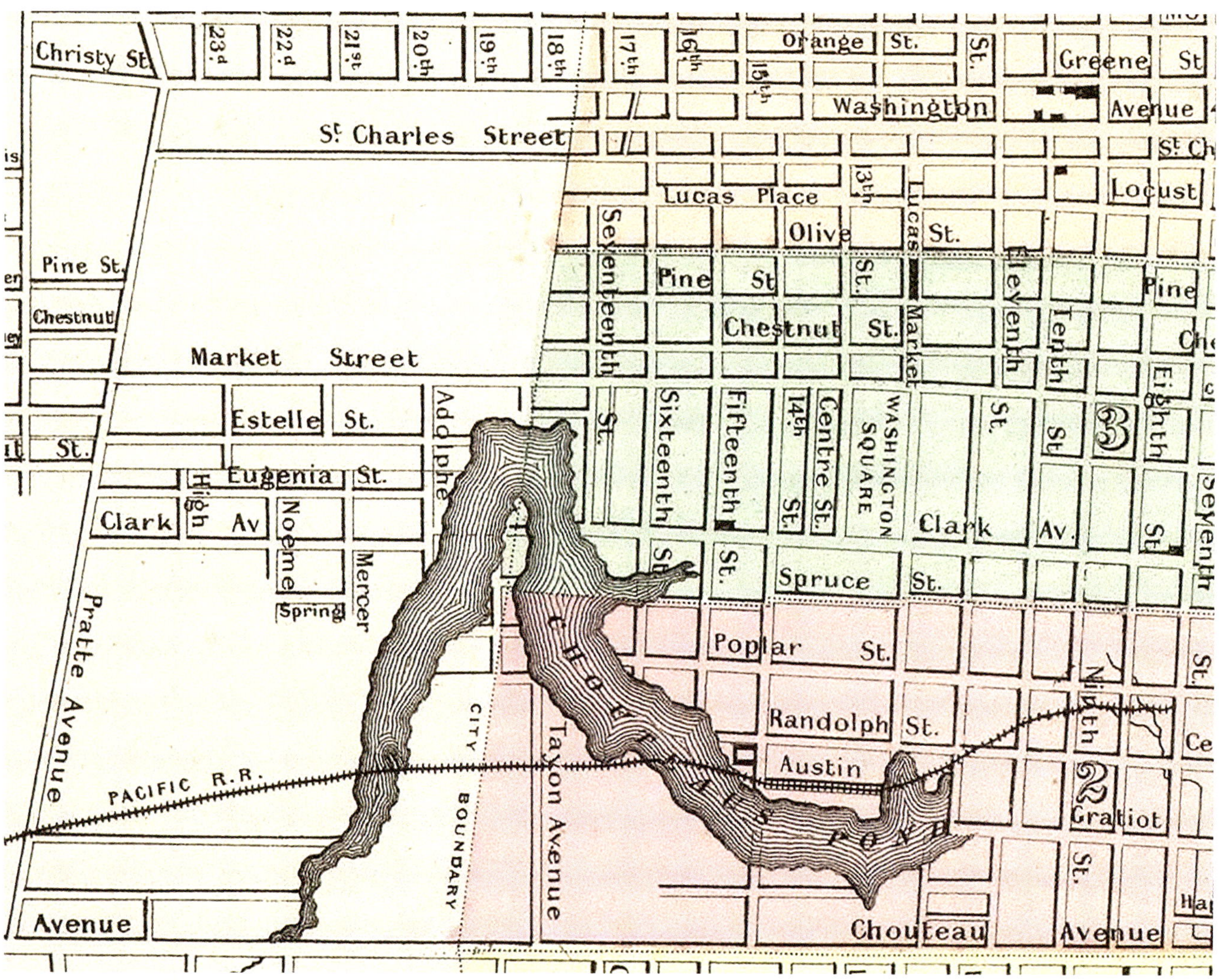

Chouteau Avenue cuts across the bottom of this detail, just south of the pond. Running north from Chouteau Avenue into the pond is Tayon Street (18th Street today). It was named for Joseph Taillon, an original St. Louis settler whose mill can be seen on the *1767 map*. Cutting across the pond is the new Pacific Railroad. Just three years before this map was published, the first train went west from St. Louis on its inaugural run of 4.5 miles to Cheltenham (today called Dogtown), where the tracks ended. Near the top of this detail is Lucas Place as it was originally established, running between 14th and 16th Streets. What the map does not show, however, is the newly created Missouri Park, which extended between Olive and St. Charles Streets, and 13th and 14th Streets. Locust Street ended at 13th Street, and Missouri Park provided the buffer between the commercialized area to the east and the new residential area of Lucas Place to the west.

CHOUTEAU'S POND DRAINED
This daguerreotype shows Chouteau's Pond after it was almost completely drained. It was taken by Thomas Easterly in the summer of 1855. The building in the background was the Collier White Lead and Oil Co. at the corner of Clark and 10th Streets. The steeple on the far left horizon is of the new First Presbyterian Church at 14h Street and Lucas Place (Locust Street). At 225 feet, the steeple was the tallest in the City. Steamboat men called it "the needle of St. Louis," as it was the first building of St. Louis they could see as they approached the City on the Mississippi River.
COURTESY MISSOURI HISTORICAL SOCIETY, ST. LOUIS

number of important maps detailing key battles.

Chouteau's Pond dominates the center of this map. This is the last time that the pond, so prominent since it was created in 1768, appears on any map of St. Louis. The pond was loved by early St. Louisans, described as "clear and cold, a great resort for boys and all the inhabitants for bathing, fishing, boating, and picnicks in the summer, and for skating in the winter." However, by the 1840s, due to St. Louis's rapid population growth, the water became polluted with sewage, creating a public health danger that came to a climax during the cholera outbreak in 1849. During the early 1850s, the pond was drained and replaced by the new Mill Creek sewer.

The disappearance of Chouteau's Pond left an unimpeded path for westward development in the second half of the 19th century, especially for St. Louis's wealthiest residents. Just to the north of the pond, Lucas Place was among the earliest developments that spread west from the center of St. Louis. Established in 1850 by siblings James H. Lucas and Ann Lucas Hunt, it is often called St. Louis's first "suburban" neighborhood.

Like the *1844 map,* the six wards of the City are tinted with color so as to easily differentiate them.

VIEW ON LUCAS PLACE, 1858
Thomas Easterly took this daguerreotype looking east down Lucas Place in about 1858. Following the Great Fire, James Lucas conceived the idea of an exclusive residential neighborhood, strictly limited to private homes and other residential services (such as churches and schools). This new neighborhood would forbid any type of industrial or commercial development. The first home was built there in 1851 and today is preserved as the Campbell House Museum. The tall steeple is the First Presbyterian Church. Because the neighborhood was in its infancy, there is a profusion of empty lots, many of which would not be filled until after the Civil War. Over time, this westward migration of private (and wealthy) residential neighborhoods would continue as people left a city they considered both too large and less healthy for family life.
COURTESY MISSOURI HISTORICAL SOCIETY, ST. LOUIS

MAP
OF
ST. LOUIS, MO.
AND ITS
FORTIFICATIONS,
1861-1865.
Joseph Mills Stanton.
May 28, 1905.
GRAND AV.
ARSENAL ST.
JEFFERSON AV.
BROADWAY
GRAVOIS AV.
FORT Nº 1
FORT Nº 2
FORT Nº 3
FORT Nº 4
FORT Nº 5
FORT Nº 6
REDOUBT
REDAN
LAFAYETTE PARK
UNITED STATES ARSENAL
IRON MOUNTAIN RAILROAD
PACIFIC RAILROAD
OLD MANCHESTER ROAD
CAMP JACKSON
LINDELL GROVE
GRATIOT ST. PRISON
GEN. FREMONT'S H'DQ'RS.
LYNCH'S SLAVE PEN PRISON
TWELFTH ST.
MARKET ST.
OLIVE ST.
FRANKLIN AV.
CHOUTEAU AV.
SOULARD ST.
MISSISSIPPI

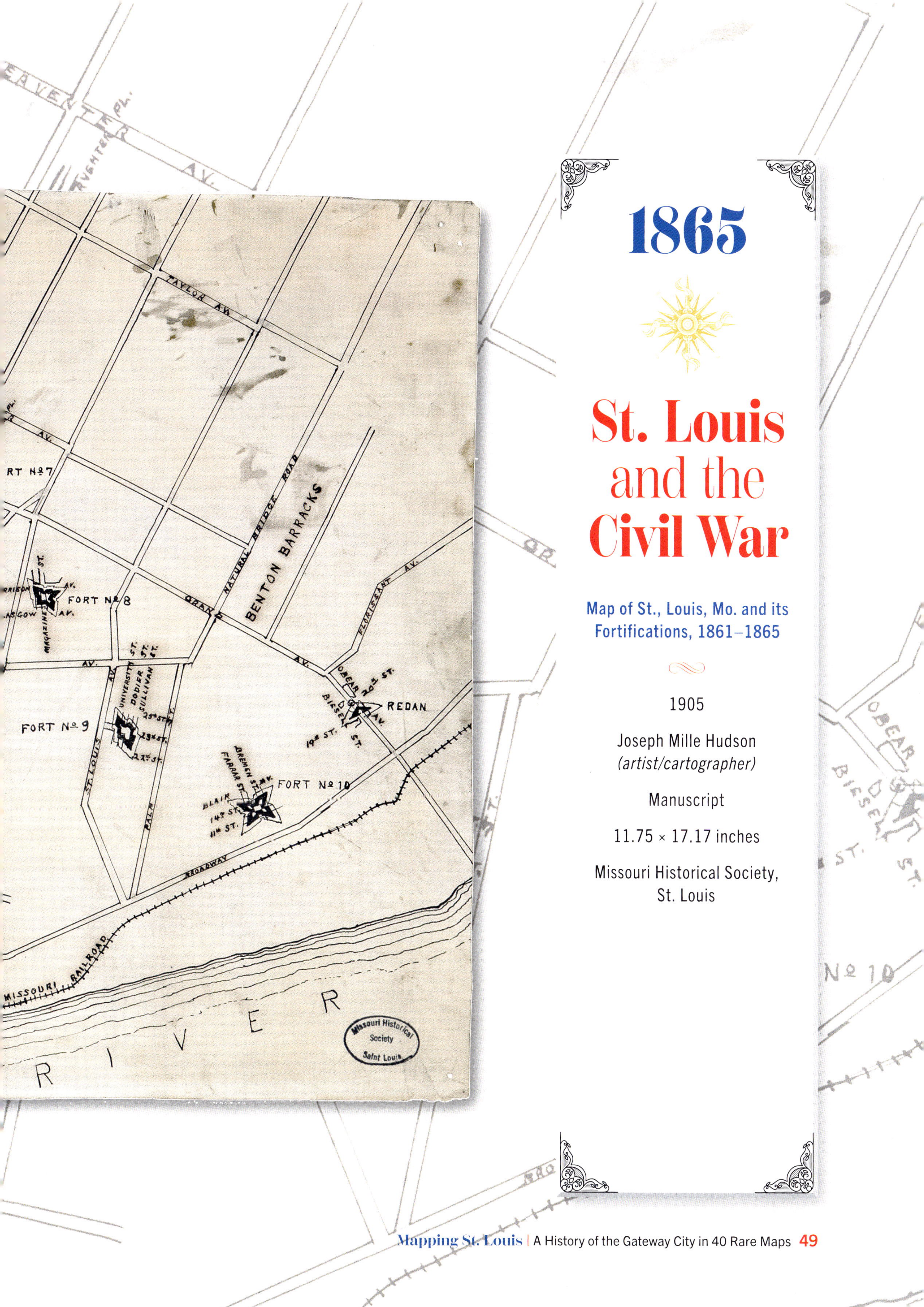

1865

St. Louis and the Civil War

Map of St., Louis, Mo. and its Fortifications, 1861–1865

1905

Joseph Mille Hudson
(artist/cartographer)

Manuscript

11.75 × 17.17 inches

Missouri Historical Society,
St. Louis

1865

ST. LOUIS WAS uniquely placed both geographically and politically when the Civil War started in April 1861. The City dominated trade on both the Missouri River and upper Mississippi River, the superhighways of their day. And in addition to being a key manufacturing center, St. Louis was also a major military site with the US Arsenal and Jefferson Barracks. Ultimately, St. Louis stayed under Union control because of a strong military presence and broad public support from loyal Germans—by far the largest percentage of volunteers to serve in the Union army. Despite the fact that slavery was legal in Missouri, it was the significant anti-slavery sentiment in St. Louis that most scholars credit with keeping Missouri in the Union.

To ensure that St. Louis and its vital port and manufacturing sites would never fall to the Confederacy, the US Army constructed and outfitted a line of earthwork forts on the western edge of the City. Compare this map to the *1780 map*, which illustrates the colonial fortifications of St. Louis.

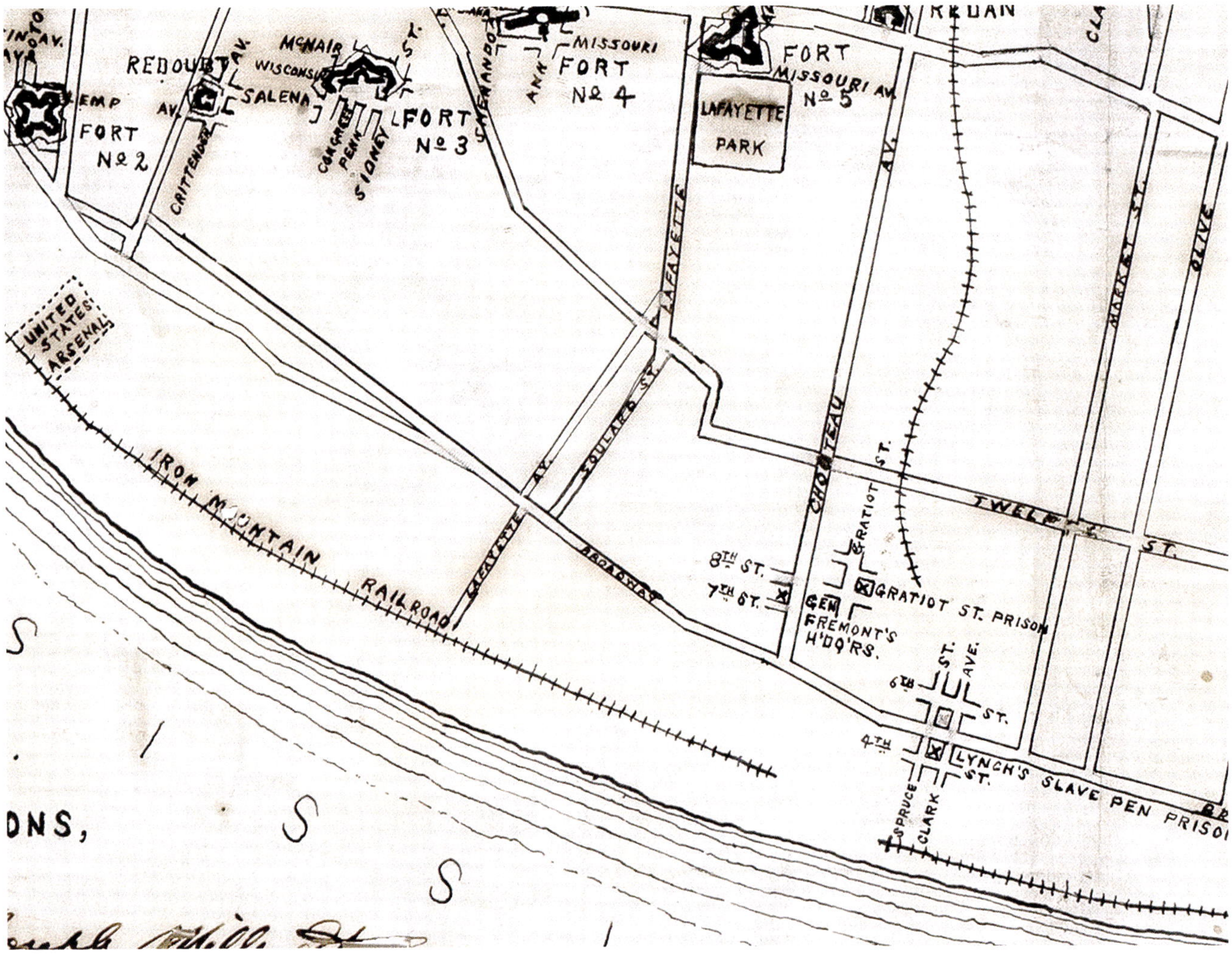

In addition to forts and redans, this map detail shows other important military sites in St. Louis. The US Arsenal was along the Iron Mountain Railroad south of the City. It was one of the largest in the nation, storing almost 40,000 guns at the start of the war. The Gratiot Street Prison at 8th and Gratiot Streets had previously been McDowell's Medical College. Its founder, Dr. Joseph McDowell, joined the Confederate Army, and consequently the college was confiscated and converted to a prison in December 1861. Through the war it housed Confederate prisoners of war, Southern sympathizers, guerrillas, spies, and federal soldiers accused of crimes. The prison's official capacity was 1,200, but at times it had 2,000 prisoners. It was used mostly as a transfer point for prisoners going to other US military prisons.

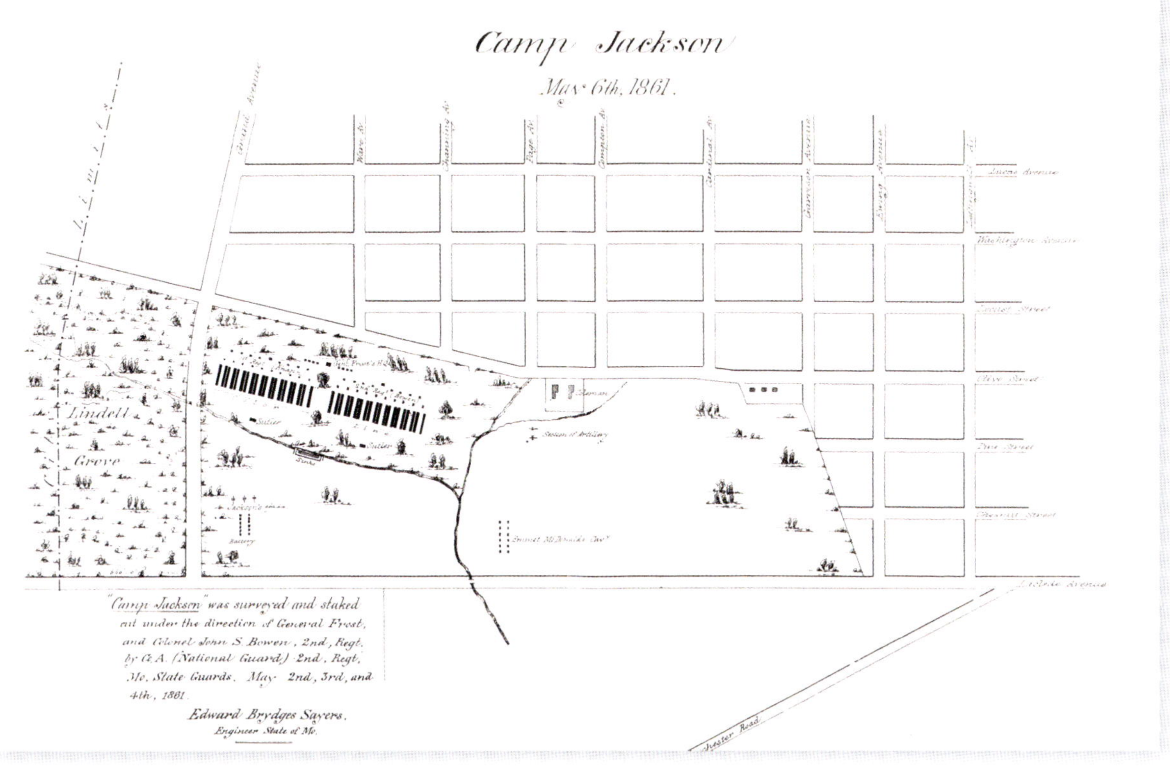

MAP OF CAMP JACKSON

The only major fighting at St. Louis during the Civil War was during the so-called Camp Jackson Affair on May 10, 1861. Camp Jackson was 4.5 miles west of the City, today the site of the campus of Saint Louis University at Grand and Lindell. Union Capt. Nathaniel Lyon led 6,000 federal Missouri Volunteers (largely German immigrants) and army regulars against the secessionist Missouri Militia that was encamped there. After the Union forces surrounded the camp, 669 of the captured militiamen were marched down Olive Street to the US Arsenal. Someone (it was never clear who) fired a shot during the march, prompting a riot. In the chaos, Lyon's unseasoned volunteers fired into the crowd, killing some 28 onlookers and wounding nearly 100 more. Eventually, the installation of martial law and the arrival of regular Army reinforcements to relieve the German volunteers would end the "affair."

COURTESY MISSOURI HISTORICAL SOCIETY, ST. LOUIS

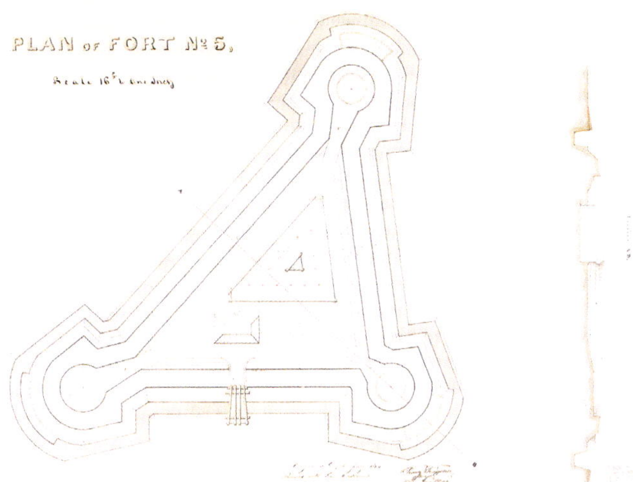

FORT NO. 5

Just west of Lafayette Park, Fort No. 5 was a trilateral earthwork that featured three large guns. This plan depicts the fort layout and, on the right, the elevation of both the fort and landscape entrenchments. Today the residential streets of Albion and Missouri avenues occupy this land.

COURTESY LIBRARY OF CONGRESS

In that map, the entrenchments run along Fourth Street. This current map illustrates how, 80 years later, the line of forts roughly creates an arc around the City from Broadway and Chippewa on the south to Broadway and Bremen on the north. In addition, there were five redans (arrow-shaped embankments) that held additional gun batteries.

This map was compiled in 1905 from 1860s maps that showed the location of the Civil War fortifications. Cartographer Joseph Hudson drew the modern streets of the City emanating from each fortification for reference. None of those streets existed in 1865.

The largest feature notated on the map is Benton Barracks. Established in August 1861, Benton Barracks was an encampment for Union troops that could house as many as 30,000 soldiers. It contained a mile of barracks, warehouses, stables, parade grounds, and a large military hospital. The hospital could serve 3,000 patients. During the summer of 1863, when St. Louis was inundated by thousands of formerly enslaved refugees, the Contraband Camp was established at Benton Barracks as a step toward resettlement.

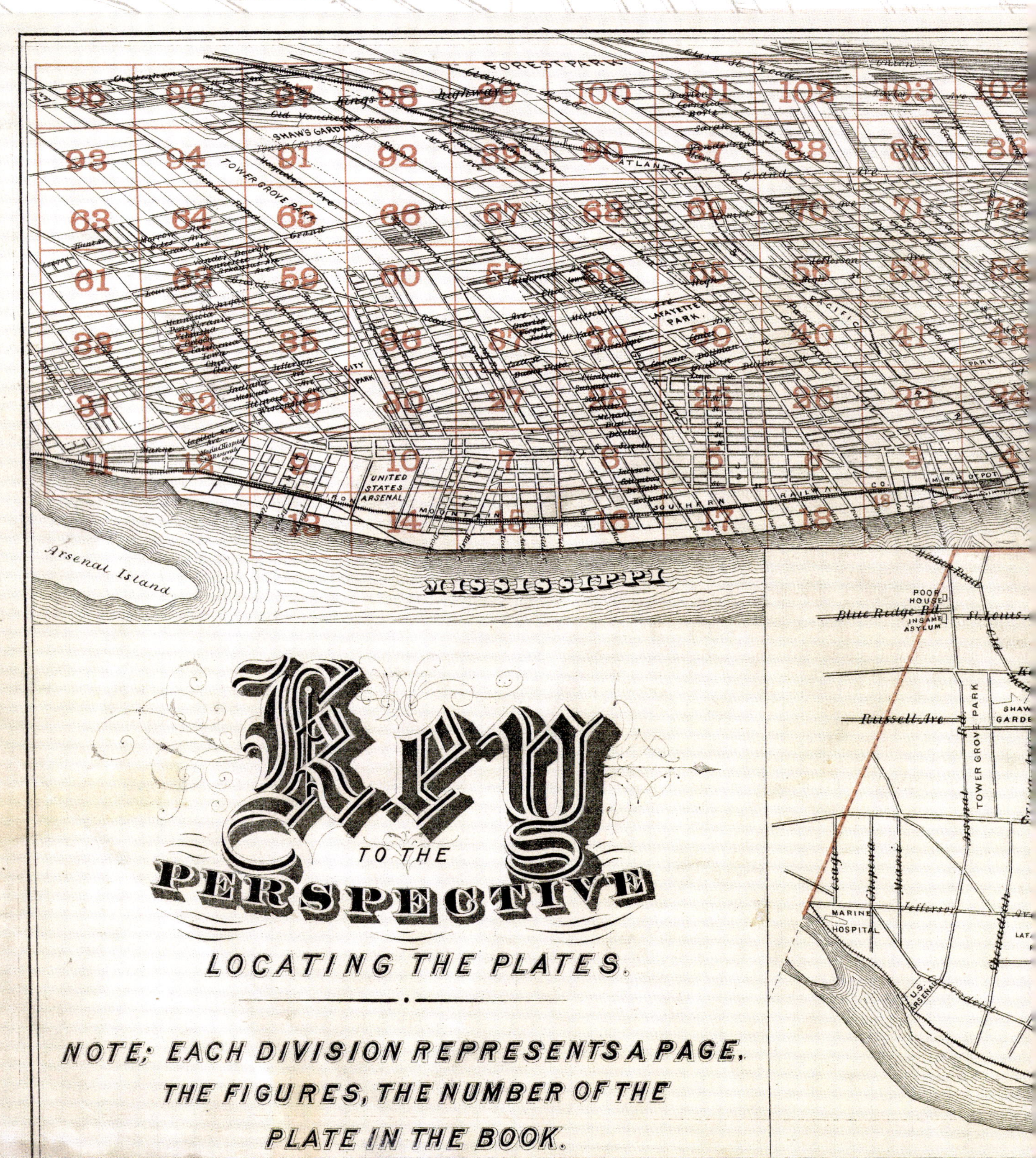
FOREST PARK
SHAW'S GARDEN
TOWER GROVE PARK
LAFAYETTE PARK.
UNITED STATES ARSENAL
Arsenal Island
MISSISSIPPI
POOR HOUSE
Blue Ridge Rd.
INSANE ASYLUM
Russell Ave
MARINE HOSPITAL
Jefferson
U.S. ARSENAL
Key
TO THE
PERSPECTIVE
LOCATING THE PLATES.
NOTE; EACH DIVISION REPRESENTS A PAGE.
THE FIGURES, THE NUMBER OF THE
PLATE IN THE BOOK.

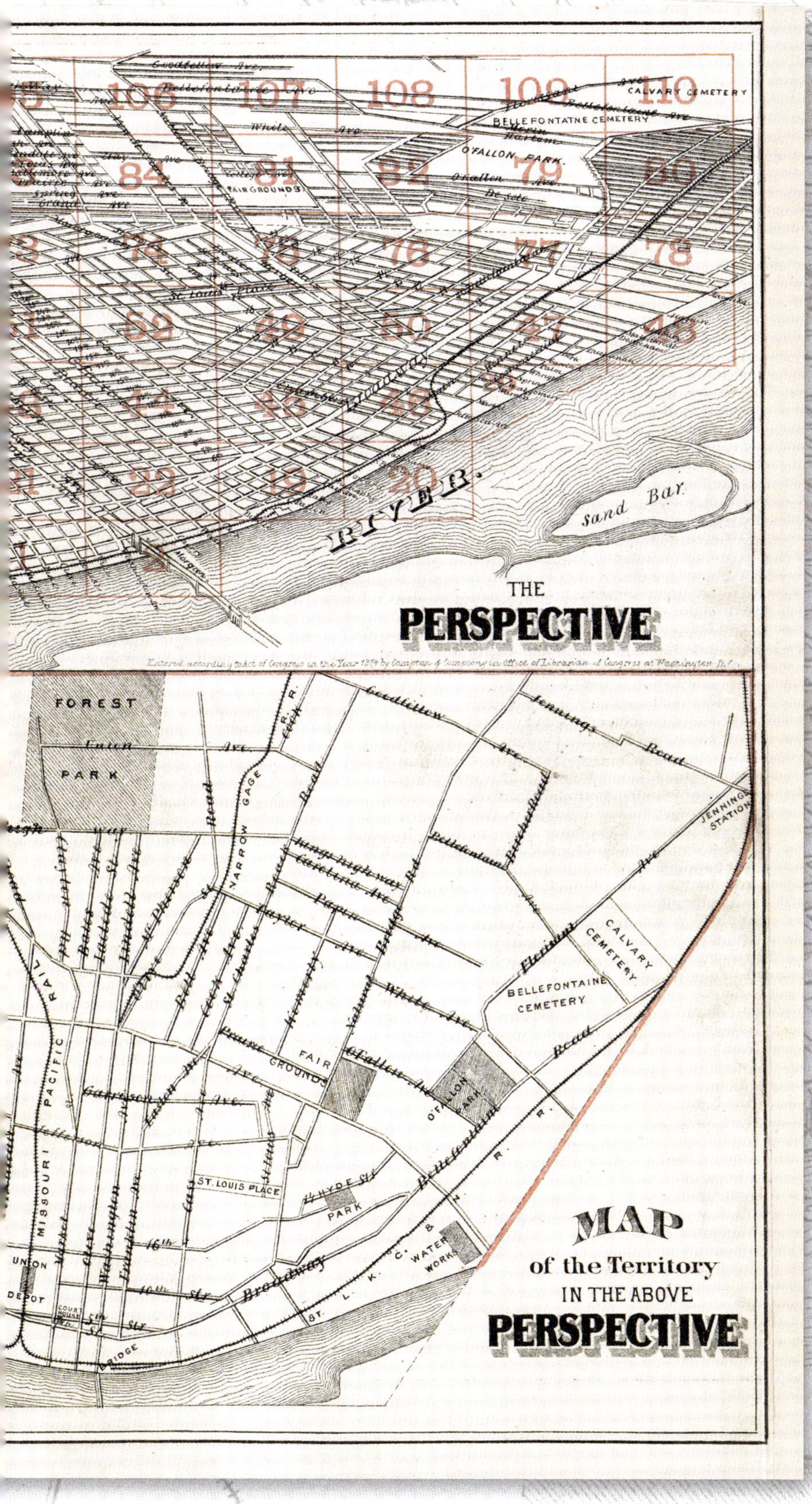

1875

Pictorial St. Louis

Pictorial St. Louis, the Great Metropolis of the Mississippi Valley: A Topographical Survey Drawn in Perspective

Richard J. Compton and Camille N. Dry
(artist/cartographer)

Compton and Co.
(publisher/printer)

Lithograph

14.5 × 20.8 inches

Campbell House Museum

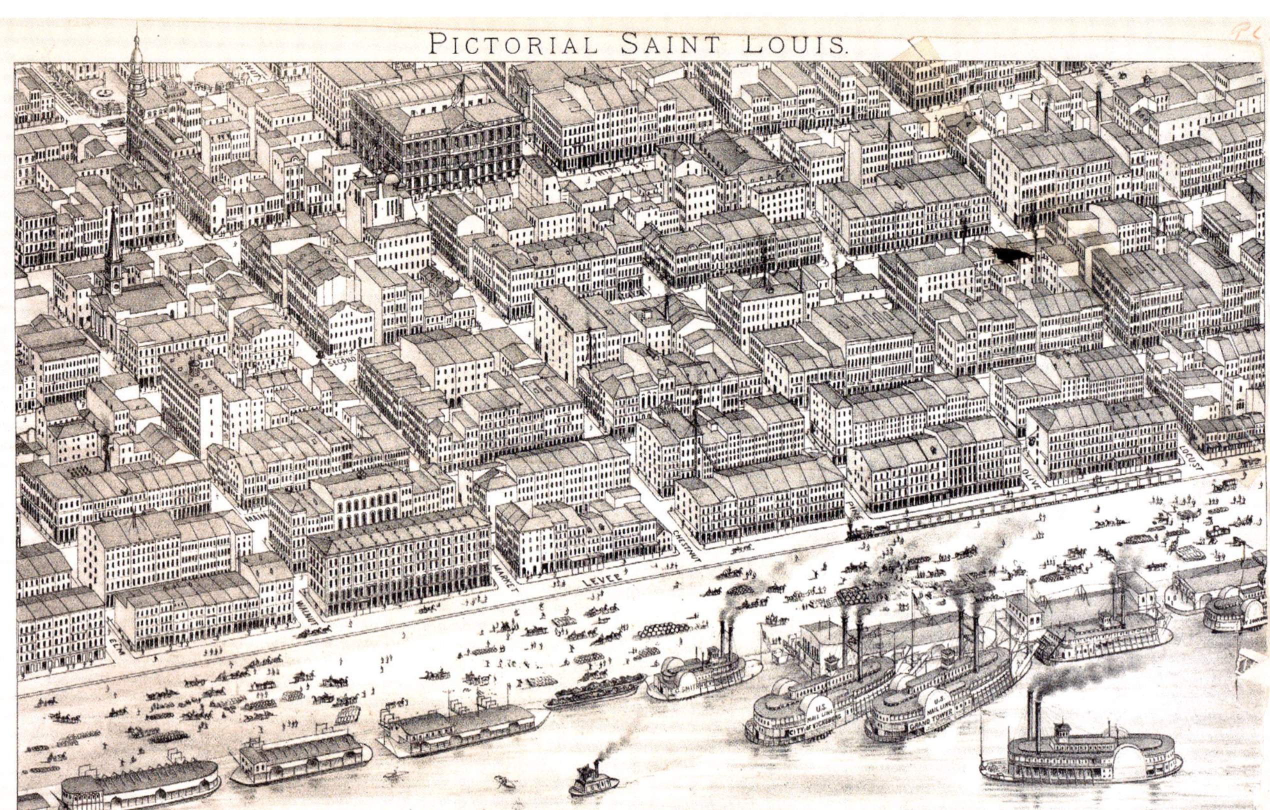

PICTORIAL ST. LOUIS 'SPECIMEN PAGE'

This specimen page was used by salesmen seeking subscriptions for the publication of *Pictorial St. Louis*. The printed text at the bottom boldly advertises, "The book will contain about one hundred and fifty pages like this, showing collectively an area of nearly seventy square miles, upon which all the buildings, and topography of unoccupied property, are accurately drawn. There will also be many pages of printed matter, descriptive of important public and private buildings, and all objects of interest . . . [which] will make the work a complete compendium of St. Louis in 1875, and the most costly and magnificent publication ever issued in the interest of any city in the world."

COURTESY CAMPBELL HOUSE MUSEUM

FOLLOWING THE Civil War, the economy and population of St. Louis grew at a pace unlike anything preceding. Because St. Louis did not see any battles during the war and because Missouri had remained in the Union, St. Louis did not struggle during Reconstruction as did some other cities. During the war, the US government had funneled more than $150 million through St. Louis to provision the Union Army. This great wealth laid the foundation for St. Louis to grow during the most prosperous era in its history—the Gilded Age. To capture the scope of St. Louis in the Gilded Age required a map as large as the City itself.

Conceived at an almost impossible scale, this work has a title to match: *Pictorial St. Louis, the Great Metropolis of the Mississippi Valley: A Topographical Survey Drawn in Perspective A.D. 1875. Pictorial St. Louis* is considered essential for viewing and understanding the St. Louis cityscape, such that it is referred to by historians (armchair and professional alike) simply by the names of its creators: Compton and Dry.

Compton and Dry is an aerial perspective map, a popular format for cities to advertise themselves as

attractive places for new people and businesses. *Pictorial St. Louis* depicts the landscape of St. Louis in precise, amazing detail, showing thousands of buildings all over the City. It uses an axonometric projection, one without vanishing points, so that city streets were shown parallel to one another rather than converging in the distance. An axonometric projection allowed for a more accurate representation of scale and eliminated the illusion of buildings disappearing into the horizon. It also produced an invaluable visual record of the City as it was in 1875.

Compton and Dry's attention to detail resulted in a map so large that it was divided into 110 individual plates bound together in an oversized, oblong book. Included is an index of businesses, churches, hospitals, and schools, many of which were numbered in the plates. Businesses paid to have their buildings identified, some even paying an additional fee to place a description on the reverse side of the plate that featured their location.

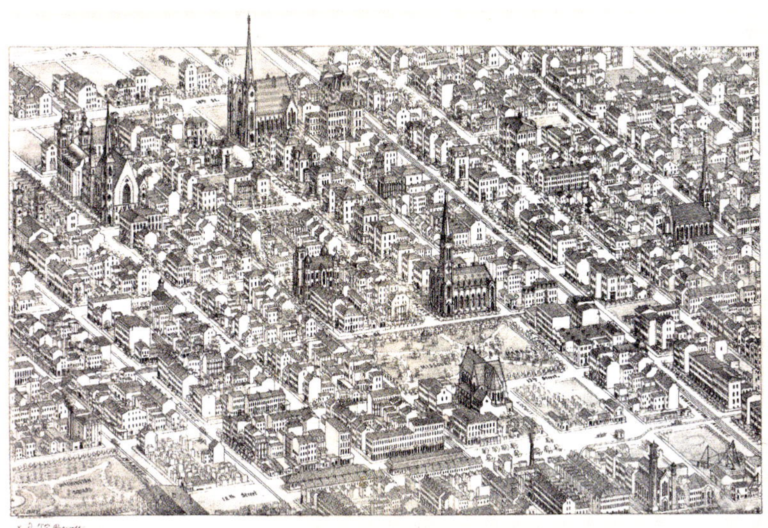

LUCAS PLACE

Compton and Dry shows the Lucas Place neighborhood at its height in 1875. Instead of the empty lots that covered the area in the *1849 map*, the street is now lined with the most expensive homes in St. Louis. In addition, new churches, Washington University, and other important buildings are listed. Lucas Place was the "Central West End" of 1870s St. Louis, and it was only after the 1904 World's Fair that mansions and many of these same amenities moved to the area around Forest Park. This is a rare alternate view of Plate 41, as it is oriented about three blocks farther to the northeast than the final printed image.

COURTESY CAMPBELL HOUSE MUSEUM

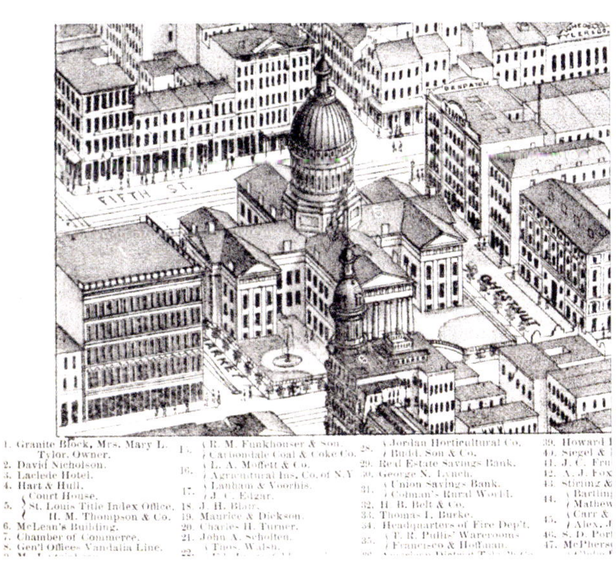

DETAIL OF PLATE 21

This small corner of plate 21 shows the extreme level of detail reproduced in *Pictorial St. Louis*. Important buildings were numbered in a key along the bottom of each plate. Landmarks shown in this detail include the courthouse (no. 5) and the Planter's House Hotel (no. 12), both also seen on the *1844 map*.

COURTESY CAMPBELL HOUSE MUSEUM

The image shown above is the key and perspective diagram for the map. At the lower right is a typical street map with a red border that outlines the large area encompassed in the view. The top half of the key illustrates the view and "how the artist transformed the ground plan of the city into a perspective grid based on an assumed viewpoint southeast of the city." Each numbered rectangle on the grid is the number of each plate in the book. The book's preface states, "after careful consideration of the subject, it was determined to locate the point of view so that the City would be seen from the southeast. Accordingly, the point of sight was established on the Illinois side of the river, looking to the northwest, and at sufficient height to overlook the roofs of ordinary houses into the streets."

When published in December 1875, *Pictorial St. Louis* cost the hefty sum of $25 ($710 in 2024). Today this rare work can sell for more than $8,000.

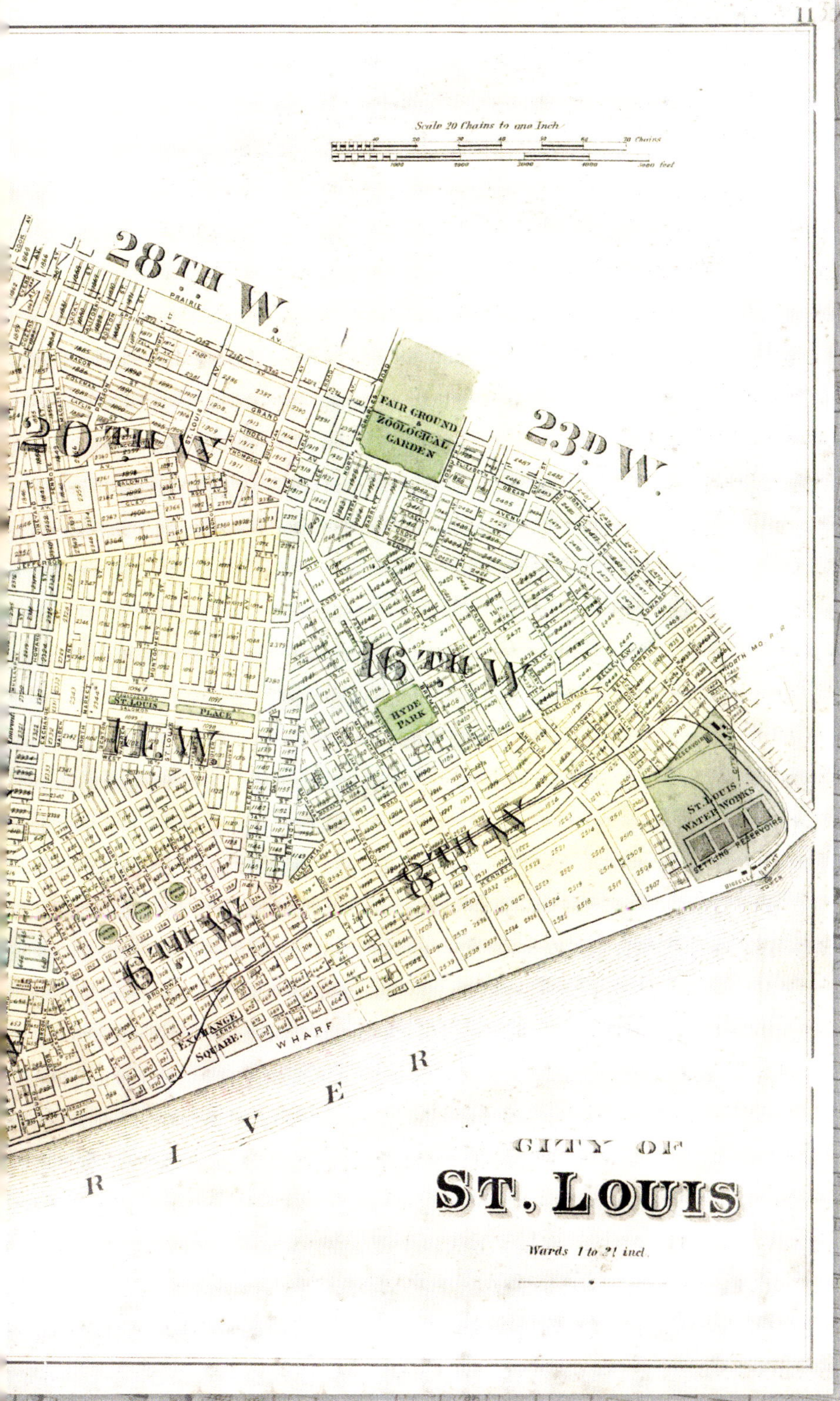

1878

The St. Louis Atlas

Pitzman's New Atlas of the City and County of Saint Louis, Missouri

Julius Pitzman
(artist/cartographer)

A.B. Holcombe & Co., Philadelphia
(publisher)

Lithograph

20.5 × 33 inches

State Historical Society of Missouri

1878

FEW IF ANY people have had a greater influence on the landscape of Gilded Age St. Louis than Julius Pitzman. Born in Prussia, Pitzman immigrated to St. Louis in 1854. With training as a surveyor, he quickly found work in rapidly growing St. Louis, where good surveyors were in the highest demand. In 1861 he quickly volunteered for the Union Army, where he served with distinction as lieutenant in the Topographical Engineers. Pitzman was responsible for the design and oversaw the construction of Fort No. 5 in St. Louis as detailed in the *1865 map*. He was later wounded at Vicksburg and mustered out of the army as a major, returning to St. Louis, where he was elected county surveyor.

In 1874 Pitzman surveyed an undeveloped tract west of the City. He then helped to convince city officials to turn the site into Forest Park. As chief engineer for the project, Pitzman played a substantial role in developing Forest Park's plan, working alongside the main designer Maximillian Kern. In private practice, Pitzman laid out most of St. Louis's finest "Places" that had arisen due to the success of

Two modern landmarks appear on this detail of Pitzman's atlas: Tower Grove Park (only 10 years old at the time this map was made) and the new Compton Hill Reservoir. By 1889, the area immediately to the left of the reservoir (blocks labeled 26 and 27) were established by Pitzman as the Compton Heights subdivision. Pitzman completely redesigned the street plan in these blocks as seen in the *1893 map*.

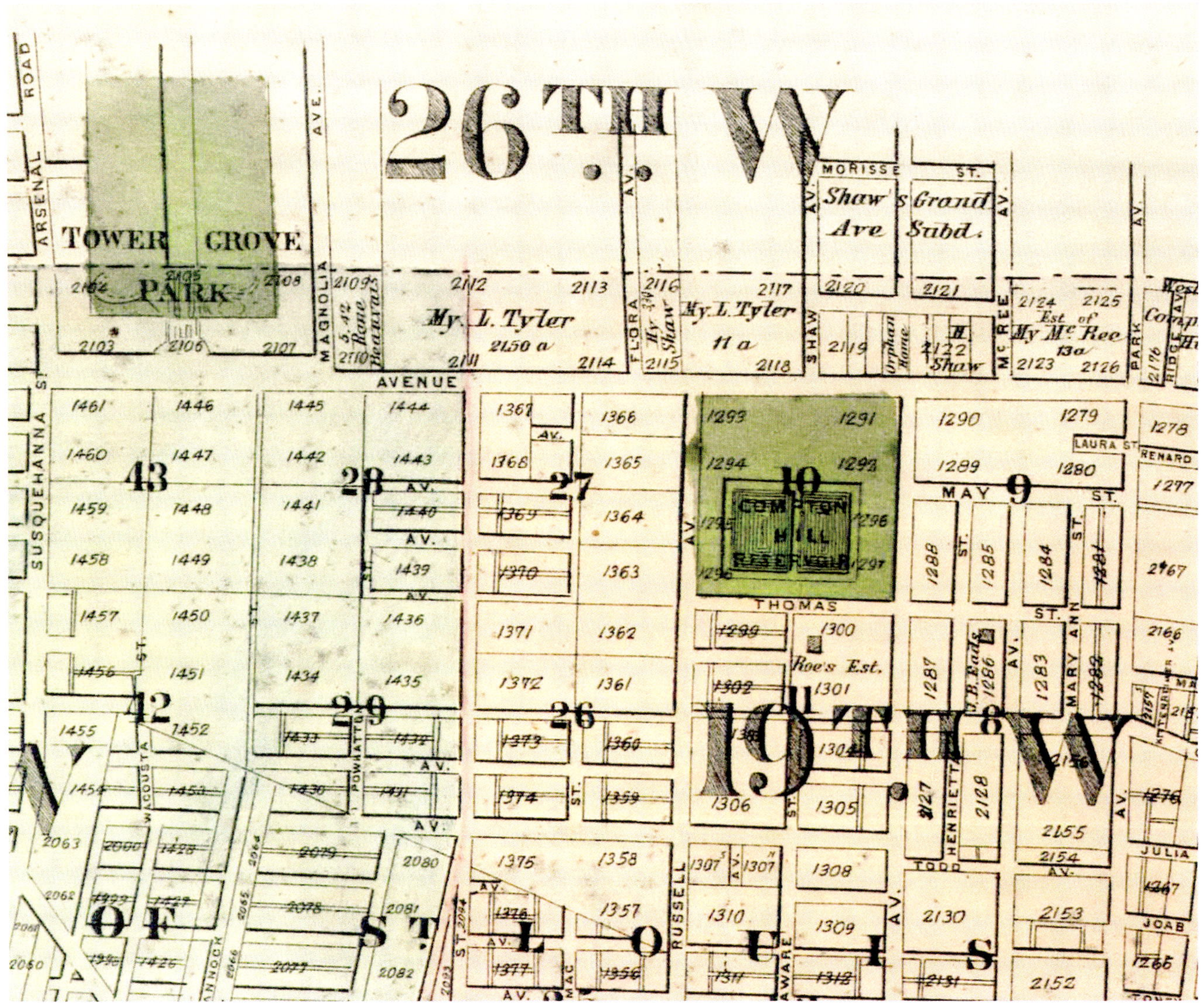

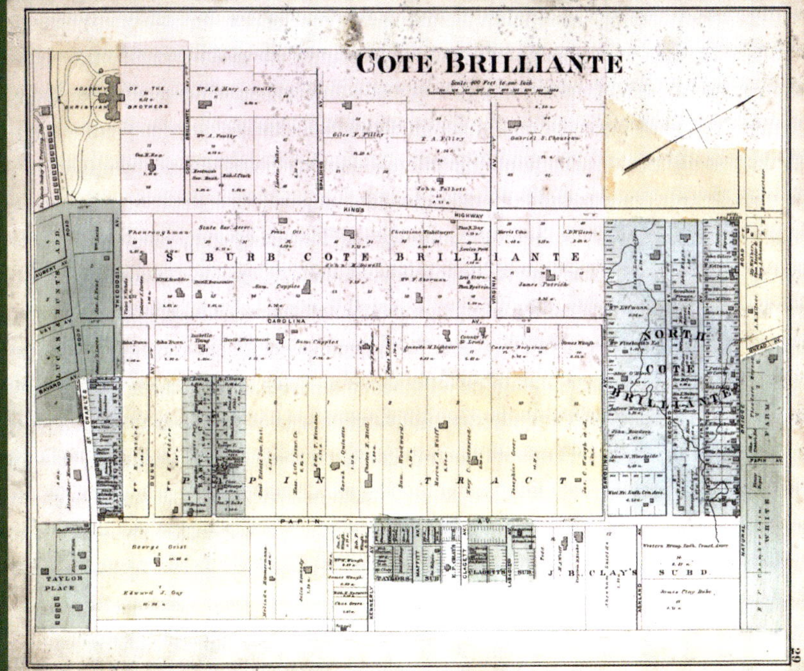

COTE BRILLIANTE

Besides the central part of St. Louis, Pitzman's atlas included detailed maps of surrounding towns and neighborhoods. Cote Brilliante, a French term meaning "bright hill" or "shining hill," is a neighborhood located near modern-day Sherman Park, close to the intersection of North Kingshighway Boulevard and Natural Bridge Avenue. 200 years ago, this site was a large, flat hill, probably built by the Indigenous peoples who also conceived Cahokia. This hill was also the site from which many explorers and emigrants left St. Louis for the West. Fur trader Robert Campbell wrote in 1825 before leaving for the Rocky Mountains, "our camp was then at Cote Brilliante, a beautiful grassy hill, six miles from the City, West of the Prairie House." Today Cote Brilliante is part of the greater Ville, a historic African American neighborhood.

COURTESY STATE HISTORICAL SOCIETY OF MISSOURI

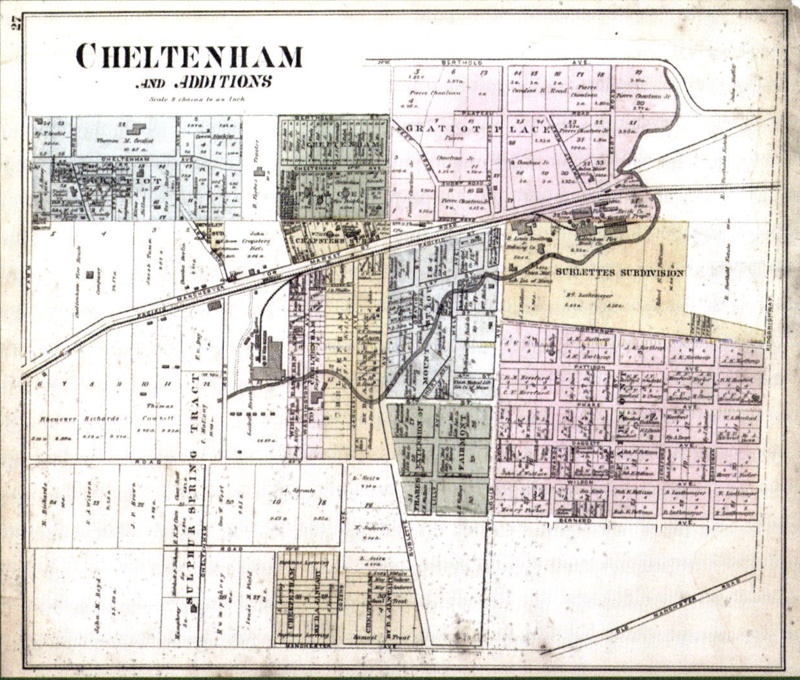

CHELTENHAM AND ADDITIONS

This map of "Cheltenham" covers what is today the Dogtown and Hill neighborhoods. The blue area at the top left shows two Dogtown institutions that still stand: the Catholic church (St. James the Greater) and the public school (the old Gratiot School, now apartments). The yellow area on the right is labeled Sublette's subdivision. This is the last remnant of legendary fur trader William Sublette's farm. Called Sulphur Springs, it once included almost all the area on the map south of Manchester Road. When Sulphur Springs became a resort in the 1830s, Cheltenham was named for the manager's birthplace, a spa town outside of Gloucestershire, England.

COURTESY STATE HISTORICAL SOCIETY OF MISSOURI

Lucas Place—Vandeventer, Portland, Westmoreland, and Flora. He later helped develop and lived in the Compton Heights neighborhood.

In 1878, this map and 30 others were issued in the form of *Pitzman's New Atlas of the City and County of St. Louis, Missouri,* which was "constructed from actual surveys and official records by Julius Pitzman, civil engineer and county surveyor of St. Louis Co." This atlas covers not only the City but all of St. Louis County. The two had separated just two years earlier in the "Great Divorce," an issue which still impacts the region today.

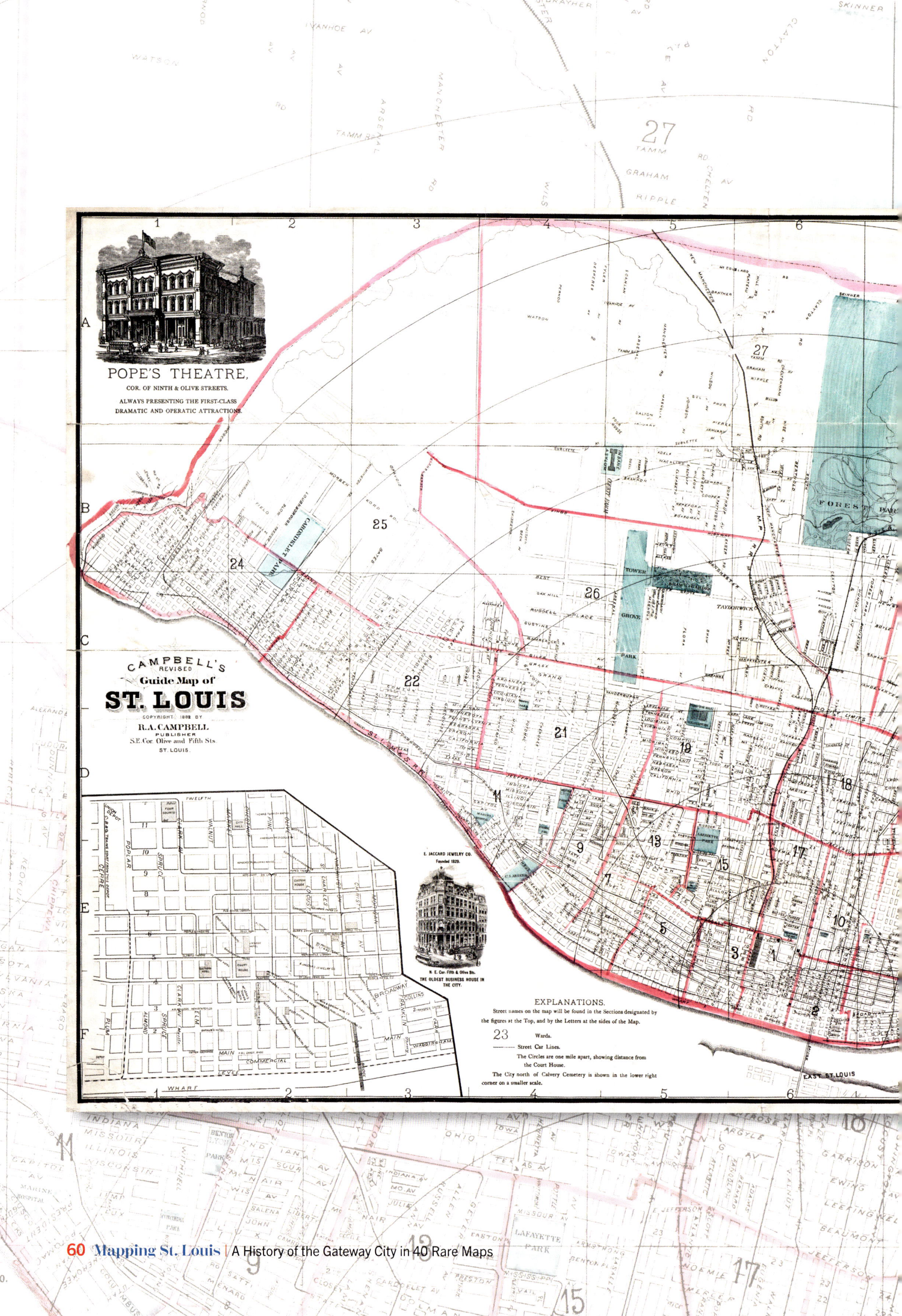
POPE'S THEATRE,
COR. OF NINTH & OLIVE STREETS.
ALWAYS PRESENTING THE FIRST-CLASS DRAMATIC AND OPERATIC ATTRACTIONS.
CAMPBELL'S
REVISED
Guide Map of
ST. LOUIS
COPYRIGHT 1882 BY
R.A.CAMPBELL
PUBLISHER
S.E.Cor. Olive and Fifth Sts.
ST. LOUIS.
E. JACCARD JEWELRY CO.
Founded 1829.
N. E. Cor. Fifth & Olive Sts.
THE OLDEST BUSINESS HOUSE IN THE CITY.
EXPLANATIONS.
Street names on the map will be found in the Sections designated by the figures at the Top, and by the Letters at the sides of the Map.
23 Wards.
Street Car Lines.
The Circles are one mile apart, showing distance from the Court House.
The City north of Calvery Cemetery is shown in the lower right corner on a smaller scale.
FOREST PARK
TOWER GROVE PARK
CARONDELET PARK
LAFAYETTE PARK
EAST ST. LOUIS

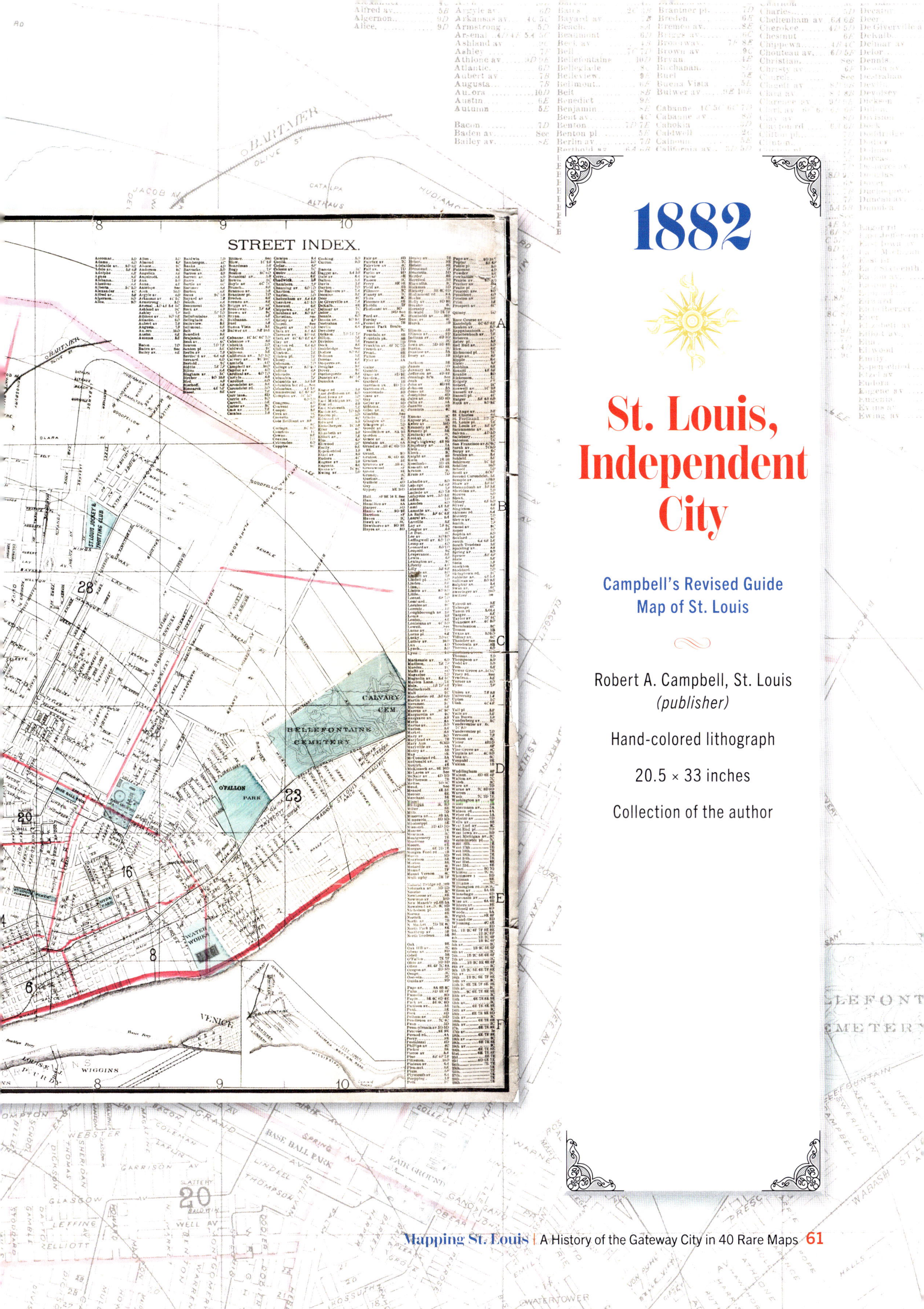

1882

St. Louis, Independent City

Campbell's Revised Guide Map of St. Louis

Robert A. Campbell, St. Louis
(publisher)

Hand-colored lithograph

20.5 × 33 inches

Collection of the author

1882

THE "GREAT DIVORCE" in 1876 separated the City of St. Louis from St. Louis County. This move was instigated by City residents who objected to, among other issues, the cost of supporting infrastructure expansion in the County. The Missouri State Charter of 1875 created the mechanism for St. Louis to become a home rule or independent city, allowing it to operate its own "county" offices. The proposed separation would set the St. Louis city limits so that no further expansion was possible. Ironic that a city whose greatest prosperity was based on westward expansion would now stop its physical growth in that very direction.

In the newspaper, supporters of separation were quoted as being happy because it "fixes permanently the city limits . . . which will never be changed, and it includes enough territory to bring the parks and cemeteries into the city." In contrast, a newspaper editorial that opposed separation issued a warning that "the days of growth and expansion are over."

After a contentious vote, residents narrowly approved the separation, making St. Louis one of the first cities in the US to limit its boundaries. Emphasizing the City's

In 1870, St. Louis annexed the village of Carondelet, expanding the City's southern border all the way to the River des Peres. Over the next few decades, Carondelet benefited from being absorbed by its larger neighbor. Carondelet Park was developed and opened on July 4, 1876 (just a few weeks after Forest Park was dedicated). Its land was once part of the Carondelet Commons. New libraries, police and fire stations, and schools were built. In 1873, Susan Blow founded the first publicly funded kindergarten in the US at Des Peres School in Carondelet. This detail shows Carondelet as an extension of the City, included in the new Wards 24 and 25.

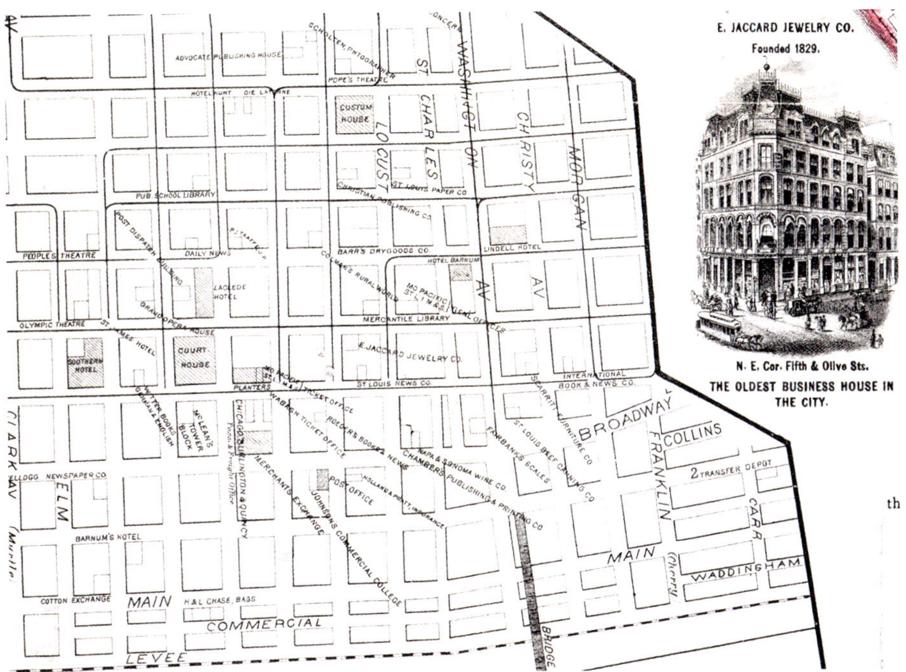

This detail allowed visitors to navigate the congested central district of St. Louis, where most of the hotels, businesses, and amusements were found. All the important government buildings and hotels are shaded in gray. Given the random nature of the labeled businesses, they were probably required to pay for the listing, including E. Jaccard Jewelry Co., whose building is illustrated in addition to being listed on the map.

newly expanded boundaries, the concentric circles on this map are one mile apart, showing the distance from the courthouse. It is just over seven miles from the courthouse to the edge of the City.

The red lines on the map are the boundaries of St. Louis's 28 wards. With the establishment of expanded city limits, additional wards were created to serve a larger area. Most of the newly created Ward 27 in the southwest part of the City was open land with very little development.

The 1880 census recorded the St. Louis population at 350,516, a staggering increase of 2,300 percent in just 50 years. Such growth brought thousands of visitors to St. Louis. *Campbell's Guide Map* was designed and produced as a pocket map that could be easily folded and used to help navigate the streets of St. Louis. Robert A. Campbell (no relation to the famous St. Louis fur trader) published this map and a number of other St. Louis–related plans and books, including the 1874 *Campbell's Gazetteer of Missouri*.

E. JACCARD & CO.
The firm of Eugene Jaccard and Co. was established in St. Louis in 1829 and quickly became the premier jeweler of the Midwest, opening stores in at least four states. Through the 19th century, Jaccard operated a watch factory in Switzerland as well as a store in Paris. Their building at 5th and Olive Streets was completed in 1870 and was crowned by a large clock in the mansard roof. Just before Christmas 1897, the Jaccard Building was completely destroyed by fire, and the firm lost $350,000 ($13 million in 2024) worth of merchandise. Within three days, Jaccard's had moved across the street to temporary quarters, and within two years they had a new, larger building at Broadway and Locust. They were later bought by St. Louis department store Scruggs, Vandervoorts and Barney.
COURTESY MISSOURI HISTORICAL SOCIETY, ST. LOUIS

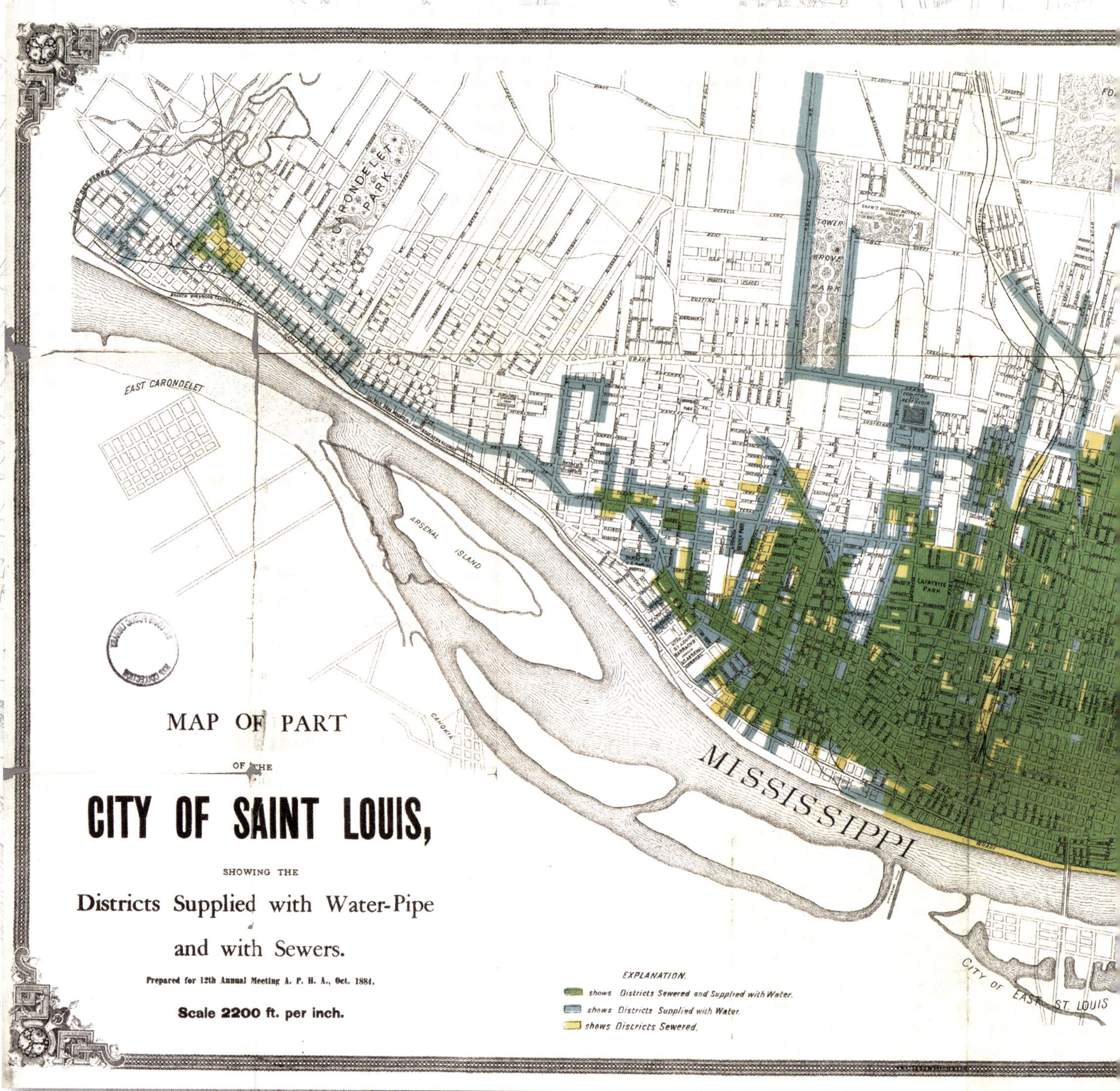
MAP OF PART
OF THE
CITY OF SAINT LOUIS,
SHOWING THE
Districts Supplied with Water-Pipe
and with Sewers.
Prepared for 12th Annual Meeting A. P. H. A., Oct. 1884.
Scale 2200 ft. per inch.
EXPLANATION.
shows Districts Sewered and Supplied with Water.
shows Districts Supplied with Water.
shows Districts Sewered.
MISSISSIPPI
EAST CARONDELET
CARONDELET PARK
TOWER GROVE PARK
ARSENAL ISLAND
LAFAYETTE PARK
CITY OF EAST ST LOUIS

Waterworks, Chain of Rocks, St. Louis, Mo.

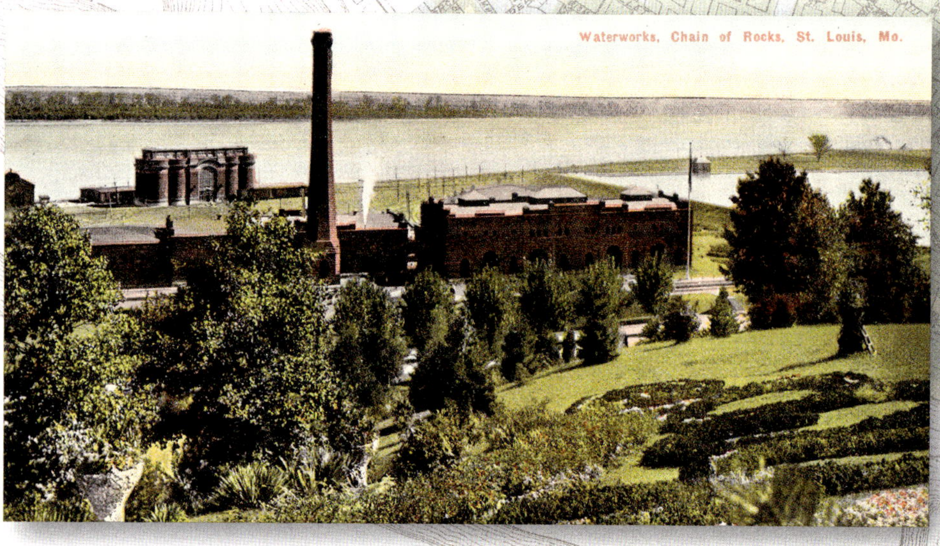

New waterworks at the Chain of Rocks.
COURTESY MISSOURI HISTORICAL SOCIETY, ST. LOUIS

Construction of the Mill Creek sewer, circa 1868.
COURTESY MISSOURI HISTORICAL SOCIETY, ST. LOUIS

1884

St. Louis Water and Sewers

Map of Part of the City of St. Louis showing the Districts Supplied with Water Pipes and with Sewers

City of St. Louis
(publisher/printer)

Color lithograph

16 × 29 inches

St. Louis Public Library

1884

ST. LOUIS IS water rich. On an average day, more than one trillion gallons flow by the Gateway Arch, almost 30 times the amount used by the entire state of California in a day. The 1871 book *Saint Louis: The Future Great City of the World* noted, "water is an important auxiliary to the growth of a great city, and the advantage is possessed by St. Louis for an inexhaustible supply." The Mississippi and Missouri rivers were, after all, the entire reason the City was founded, and the *1767 map* is not really a map of St. Louis but a survey of where the rivers meet.

The problem has always been getting water out of the river and clean enough to use. Initially people were not too concerned about how clean it looked. The same 1871 book added, "the appearance of the water is not clear, and to a stranger is rather disagreeable, yet it is nevertheless about the best river water in the world."

Since the 1830s, the City had been collecting Mississippi River water and letting the mud settle in ponds before storing it in a reservoir. The water was then pumped to public spigots and fountains spread throughout the City (the first reservoir appears on the *1837 map*). A guidebook from the 1850s described the water system: "a steam engine of considerable power draws it from the river and forces it to the reservoir. The water is taken out in the upper part of the City, above the entrance of any sewers, at a place where the river is deepest and the current is swiftest, and therefore the water taken out is the purest that can be obtained." However, St. Louis was growing so rapidly in this period that supply could barely meet demand.

In the 1860s, construction of a modern waterworks was planned for a spot on the river called Bissell Point, about four miles north of the foot of Market Street. A young engineer named Thomas Whitman was appointed the chief engineer of the waterworks and oversaw its construction. He was the younger brother of the poet Walt Whitman.

The new waterworks consisted of an intake on the river bank, a pumping station, settling basins, a standpipe (what most people call a water tower), and a storage reservoir on Compton Hill. The new waterworks had a capacity

Just north of downtown St. Louis stood the Bissell Point Water Works. Its four large settling ponds are shown in this detail. The long branching blue lines show the reach of water service and reflect the way that the pipes were laid in the street. Today the Bissell Point Water Works site is a wastewater treatment facility run by the Metropolitan St. Louis Sewer District. The current waterworks were built six miles farther north at the Chain of Rocks in 1915.

of 32 million gallons per day and went into operation in 1871.

As illustrated on this map, by 1884 St. Louis boasted 238 miles of water pipe, with more being laid every day. At the same time, there were some 223 miles of public sewers, along with 58 miles of private sewers. The areas of the map colored green were supplied with both water and sewers, blue areas were only supplied with water, and yellow areas sewered only. Interestingly, the streets adjacent to the waterworks in 1884 did not have water.

This map was initially published for the 12th annual meeting of the American Public Health Association, held in St. Louis in October 1884. At this meeting, "special committees composed of active and eminent sanitarians" reported on the management of epidemics, vital statistics, compulsory vaccination, and necrology.

GRAND AVENUE WATER TOWER

Completed in 1869, the Grand Avenue Water Tower is technically a "standpipe"—a large cylindrical tower used to maintain a consistent water pressure throughout the entire system. Without standpipes, the pumps that create the water pressure would create a phenomenon called a "water hammer," a loud banging of pipes. There are only 12 standpipes from the 19th century still standing in the US, three of which (Grand Avenue Tower, Bissell Street Tower, and Compton Hill Tower) are in St. Louis.
COURTESY MISSOURI HISTORICAL SOCIETY, ST. LOUIS

The Bissell Point Water Works was completed in 1871. As shown in this postcard from about 1900, it was just as beautiful as it was practical, with gardens and walking paths. In the background of this image is the Merchant's Bridge.
COURTESY MISSOURI HISTORICAL SOCIETY, ST. LOUIS

GRAND
PEOPLES RY.
4TH ST. CABLE
AND
GRAND AVENUE
AVE. ELECTRIC RY.
COMPTON HILL
COMPTON HILL RESERVOIR
PARK
BLOCK 1367
BLOCK 1366
BLOCK 1365
BLOCK 1368
BLOCK 1369
BLOCK 1364
BLOCK 1370
BLOCK 1363
BLOCK 1371
BLOCK 5015
BLOCK 1362
BLOCK 1372
BLOCK 1361
BOULEVARD
AVENUE
ARKANSAS AVE.
TENNESSEE AVE.
LOUISIANA AVE.
LOUISIANA AVE.
BLOCK 1299
VIRGINIA AVE.
BLOCK 1301
BLOCK 1302
COMPTON
AVENUE
BLOCK 1373
BLOCK 1374
BLOCK 1359
BLOCK 1360
BLOCK 1306
BLOCK 1303
BLOCK 1304
MICHIGAN AVE
BLOCK 1305
HAWTHORNE
LONGFELLOW
LONGFELLOW
SHENANDOAH
AVENUE
COMPTON HEIGHTS DIVISION
BLOCK 1375
BLOCK 1376
MILTON AVE
ACCOMAC
BLOCK 1357
RUSSEL
BLOCK 1310
ALLEN
BLOCK 1307
GEYER AVE.
BLOCK 1308
PENNSYLVANIA AVE.
BLOCK 1309
LAFAYETTE
AVENUE
NEBRASKA
AVENUE
BLOCK 1377
ACCOMAC ST.
BLOCK 1356
BLOCK 1311
BLOCK 1312
OREGON
AVENUE
BLOCK 1378
BLOCK 1355
CALIFORNIA
UNION DEPOT ELECTRIC ROAD
AVENUE

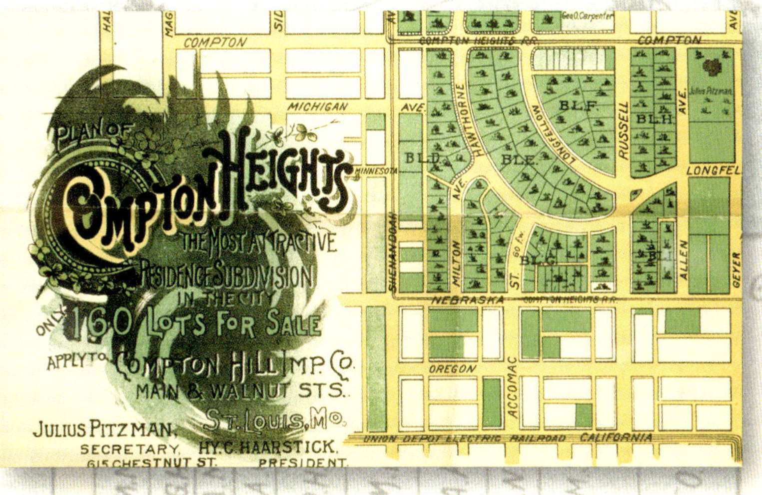

BUY NOW!

THIS IS YOUR OPPORTUNITY

TO BUY LOTS IN

COMPTON HEIGHTS

EAST OF GRAND AVENUE, BETWEEN TOWER GROVE PARK AND COMPTON HILL RESERVOIR PARK.

FOURTH STREET CABLE runs on north and west line of the property. PINE STREET ELECTRIC CARS run within two blocks of the east line of the property. LINDELL RAILROAD, Compton Heights Division, runs along Nebraska Avenue and Compton Avenue, and the new GRAND AVENUE ELECTRIC LINE furnishes rapid transit to the West End.

The character of the surrounding neighborhood and the high location make it the most desirable residence district in the City of St. Louis.

NO DUST! NO SMOKE! NO SOOT!

FRESH BREEZES; all the ADVANTAGES of the country in the heart of the city. This Property is now fully improved with SEWERS, GAS AND ELECTRIC LIGHT, WATER, TELFORD PAVEMENTS, GRANITOID SIDEWALKS, CURB and GUTTER. Every lot is above grade of street. Agents are authorized to sell at prices that will insure a GOOD PROFIT in the near future.

IF YOU WANT A HOME LOT, IF YOU WANT TO BUY ON SPECULATION, SEE AT ONCE OUR AGENTS, OR

JULIUS PITZMAN, Secretary, 615 CHESTNUT STREET. OR HY. C. HAARSTICK, Prest. of Compton Hill Imp. Co., 101 SOUTH MAIN STREET.

SEND OR CALL FOR PLAT.

Longfellow Blvd. in Compton Heights.
COURTESY OF MISSOURI HISTORICAL SOCIETY, ST. LOUIS

1895

Compton Heights

Plan of Compton Heights, The Most Attractive Residence Subdivision in the City

Julius Pitzman
(cartographer/artist)

Buxton and Skinner, St. Louis
(printer/publisher)

Color lithograph

21 × 15 inches

Missouri Historical Society, St. Louis

1895

THE FIRST inhabitants of St. Louis lived in the original city blocks laid out along the river. By the 1840s, new neighborhoods had been built surrounding the old village site, which was quickly becoming commercialized. In the 1850s, new streets like Lucas Place on the western edge of the city limits were developed exclusively for residences. In the decades that followed, St. Louis's wealthiest citizens moved even farther west, following the expanding city limits and into St. Louis County.

During the 1870s, the area around the new Compton Hill Reservoir at Grand and Russell avenues became a popular spot for large "country" houses. Here, removed from the congested city core, the ground was high and the air clear. Among the early residents were two German immigrants who had great success in America, Henry Haarstick and Julius Pitzman. Haarstick made a fortune in river transportation. After the Civil War, he operated the largest barge line on the river. Pitzman was a civil engineer and surveyor (see *1878 map*), and given the nature of his business, he no doubt also speculated in land.

In 1885, work began on the Grand Avenue Viaduct, which would connect the area south of Chouteau Avenue to the central corridor of the City. In 1888, Saint Louis University moved from Ninth Street to a new campus at Grand and Lindell. That same year, the Compton Hill Improvement Company was incorporated. Its president and secretary were Haarstick and Pitzman, respectively. In 1889 the *Globe-Democrat* reported, "Several months ago workmen under the supervision of Julius Pitzman, civil engineer, were put to work grading, and there are now 600 men and 300 teams plowing, shoveling, digging, and hauling away." The goal of this earthmoving was to redesign the roads in the new Compton Heights subdivision to a graceful

Price List "Compton Heights"

MAY 1ST, 1895.

SUBJECT TO CHANGE WITHOUT NOTICE.

BLOCK "A"

	Lot.	Average Front.	Per Foot.
Block No. 1366	1—Grand Ave.	118 feet,	$150 00
	2— "	100 "	125 00
	3—Longfellow Boulv'd,	113 "	90 00
No. 1365	5— "	101 "	125 00
	7— "	97 "	120 00

BLOCK "B"

	Lot.	Average Front.	Per Foot.
Block No. 5015	3—Hawthorne Boulev'd,	97 ft.	$106 00
	5— "	100 "	102 00
	7— "	100 "	98 00
	8— "	95 " 4 in.	96 00
	16— "	100 "	90 00
	17—Longfellow Boulv'd,	100 "	90 00
	18— "	90 " 4 in.	86 00
	19— "	88 " 8 in.	88 00
	21— "	93 "	90 00
	24— "	96 "	94 00
	25— "	102 " 8 in.	96 00
	26— "	99 " 8 in.	98 00
	27— "	99 "	100 00
	28— "	98 "	102 00
	29— "	101 " 8 in.	104 00
	30— "	98 " 8 in.	106 00

Building Restrictions.

No flats.

Not more than one dwelling to be erected on each lot.

All buildings in these blocks must conform to building line as per official plat.

No building can be erected within 10 feet of the dividing line between lots, except for porte cochere.

No dwelling of less value than $8,000 to be erected, unless plans and specifications are submitted and approved by Executive Committee of the Company.

The 1895 "Price List" for Compton Heights details the cost of each lot based on street frontage per foot. The prices vary from $150 to $50 per foot. The price was determined by the desirability of the block and, generally, the closer to Grand, the more expensive the lot. Also specified is the banning of multi-family dwellings, a minimum construction cost of the home to be erected, and finally, rules dictating the placement of buildings on each lot. A careful look at the map will reveal a dotted line near the front of each lot for sale. This is the "building line" and for each new house it was required that the front facade be placed on this line.
COURTESY MISSOURI HISTORICAL SOCIETY, ST. LOUIS

Taken in about 1897, this view looking east on Hawthorne Boulevard from Grand Avenue shows the signature curved streets of Compton Heights. The second house on the left side of the street is the Bollman residence at 3435 Hawthorne.
COURTESY MISSOURI HISTORICAL SOCIETY, ST. LOUIS

curve, setting it apart from the City street grid. The first building permits for Compton Heights were issued in the summer of 1890.

The map shows the newly laid-out streets of Hawthorne and Longfellow. The dark green areas highlight the lots being offered for sale, while blocks 1303 and 1362 show Pitzman's and Haarstick's homes, both of which predate the subdivision.

An 1895 Compton Heights "Price List" advertised the benefits of this new subdivision: "The boulevards are built along graceful, curved lines adapted to the undulations of the land, and the lots are planted in park style with the finest varieties of trees and shrubs; It is the highest ridge in close proximity to the City; healthier and better sewered than any other district; No smoke vitiates the atmosphere, because it is south of the central manufacturing district; Permanent restrictions are imposed, preventing the use of lots for anything but first-class homes, surrounded by trees, light and air."

Compton Heights became a bastion for German American immigrants—Haarstick and Ptizman were both German by birth. In 1895, 22 of the 24 heads of household in Compton Heights were first- or second-generation Germans. The map shows lots purchased by the Lemps, Greisediecks, and even Adolphus Busch, who purchased three adjoining lots numbered 1, 2, and 31 in block 5015.

BOLLMAN RESIDENCE, 3435 HAWTHORNE (1895)
Designed by the short-lived architectural partnership of Link, Rosenheim, and Ittner, this house contained one of the larger rooms in Compton Heights—a 47 × 23-foot music salon built with art-glass windows designed with musical motifs. The house was built for Emily and Otto Bollman, who with his brother operated Bollman Brothers, one of the finest music and piano galleries in St. Louis. The windmill behind the house is a testament to the fading rural landscape of Compton Heights.
COURTESY MISSOURI HISTORICAL SOCIETY, ST. LOUIS

MAP
SHOWING THE PATH OF
CYCLONE
Wednesday, May 27, 1896
Map
SHOWING
Location of the Principal
RESIDENCE DISTRICTS
IN
ST. LOUIS
FOREST PARK
CLIFTON HEIGHTS
REBER PLACE
TOWER GROVE PARK
TOWER GROVE
COMPTON HEIGHTS
SOUTH SIDE
SOUTH ST. LOUIS
CARONDELET
UNION STATION
EXPOSITION
Mississippi
JAS. C. TRAVILLA, RIALTO BLDG.

1896

The Great Cyclone

Map Showing the Path of the Cyclone, Wednesday, May 27, 1896

James C. Travilla
(cartographer/artist)

Engraving

11.25 × 16 inches

Missouri Historical Society,
St. Louis

On May 27, 1896, a massive tornado tore east through the center of St. Louis. At the time, this was one of the most concentrated areas of population in the US. The path of destruction was more than 18 blocks wide. Even today, the 1896 St. Louis tornado is the costliest and third-deadliest tornado in American history.

The tornado was a catastrophe that created big news and big business. In its aftermath, newspapers, magazines, and book publishers made fortunes printing photos and accounts of the destruction. This map was hastily produced to satisfy the public's appetite for information about the catastrophe. The map's creator, James Travilla, used the existing map titled "Location of Principal Residence Districts in St. Louis" as the base map to which he added a new red title and a red overlay outlining the tornado's path. One of the newest residential districts was Compton Heights, where many of the homes were severely damaged.

May 27, 1896, began warm and muggy, but by midafternoon a storm front approached, blanketing the St. Louis area with thick clouds. At about 5 p.m., the storm erupted with torrential rain, thunder, and lightning. According to news reports, "in but a few minutes the savings of a lifetime were scattered to the four winds of heaven. Many were thankful to escape with their lives, absolutely penniless. Death, destruction and desolation went hand in hand, and together brought about a reign of sadness and mourning, such as modern or ancient history but rarely records." It was all over in 20 minutes.

The St. Louis tornado killed at least 305 people, injured over 1,000 others, and caused more than $10 million in damage (equivalent to $365 million in 2024). More than 5,000 people were left homeless. The hardest-hit areas were Lafayette Square, Compton Heights, Mill Creek Valley, Soulard, and LaSalle Park. Every tree in

TORNADO'S PATH

The path of the 1896 storm through St. Louis was about seven miles long. The tornado touched down near the western edge of the City at what is now Hampton Avenue. Two initial narrow paths of damage joined at Grand Avenue as the storm gathered strength. The destruction was worst from 12th Street to the river. After wrecking steamboats, the tornado crossed the Mississippi River and destroyed the eastern approach to the Eads Bridge. "Nearly half of East St. Louis was wrecked," according to *The Great Cyclone*, a book published from newspaper accounts just weeks after the event.

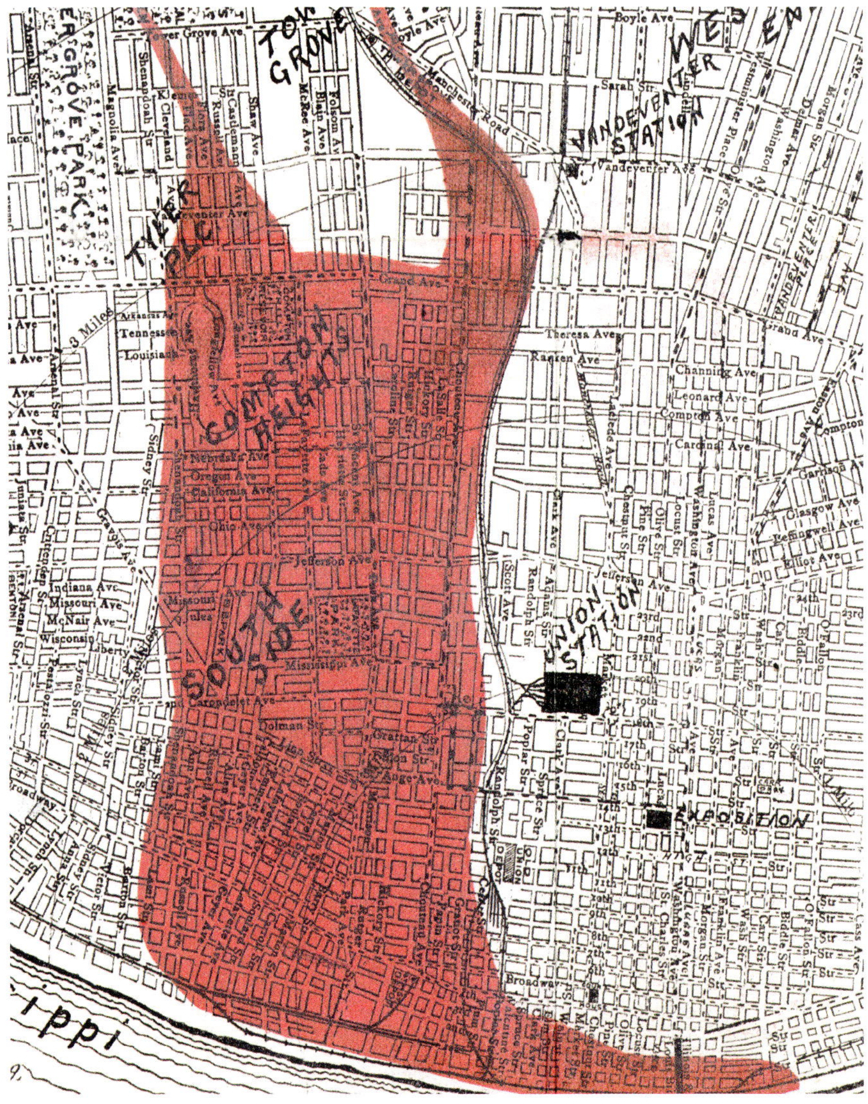

THE GREAT TORNADO AT ST. LOUIS

This dramatic depiction shows the 1896 tornado as it crossed the river into East St. Louis. On the far right, the eastern approach to the Eads Bridge was blown off its supports. The dome of the courthouse can be seen in the distance. This view is the center image of a large print that includes 18 other scenes of tornado destruction. It was published in Chicago just two weeks after the storm by the famed printing house of Kurz and Allison.
COURTESY LIBRARY OF CONGRESS

Lafayette Park was damaged, and most were cut down after the storm. Downtown St. Louis narrowly escaped any major damage.

St. Louis's location in the Mississippi River valley, although strategically placed for economic and resource benefit, brought with it the risk of these types of weather patterns. St. Louis would suffer two more destructive tornadoes: in 1927 and again in 1959. Both followed a similar path to the 1896 storm; however, the building destruction and death tolls were much lower, with 78 fatalities in 1927 and 21 in 1959.

Less than three weeks after the tornado hit, St. Louis played host to the 1896 Republican National Convention. There was speculation that it might be impossible to hold the convention, but after a concentrated cleanup effort, the event went ahead as planned. This map of downtown was produced by the Ringen Stove Co. as a guide for conventioneers. Illustrated is the temporary wood convention hall. It lost part of its roof in the storm and is marked with a large orange square on the map. It was built in 60 days at a cost of $60,000 on the lawn south of city hall. William McKinley, the former governor of Ohio, was nominated for president here on the first convention ballot on June 18, 1896.
COURTESY MISSOURI HISTORICAL SOCIETY, ST. LOUIS

Samuel B. Wiggins.
COLLECTION OF THE AUTHOR

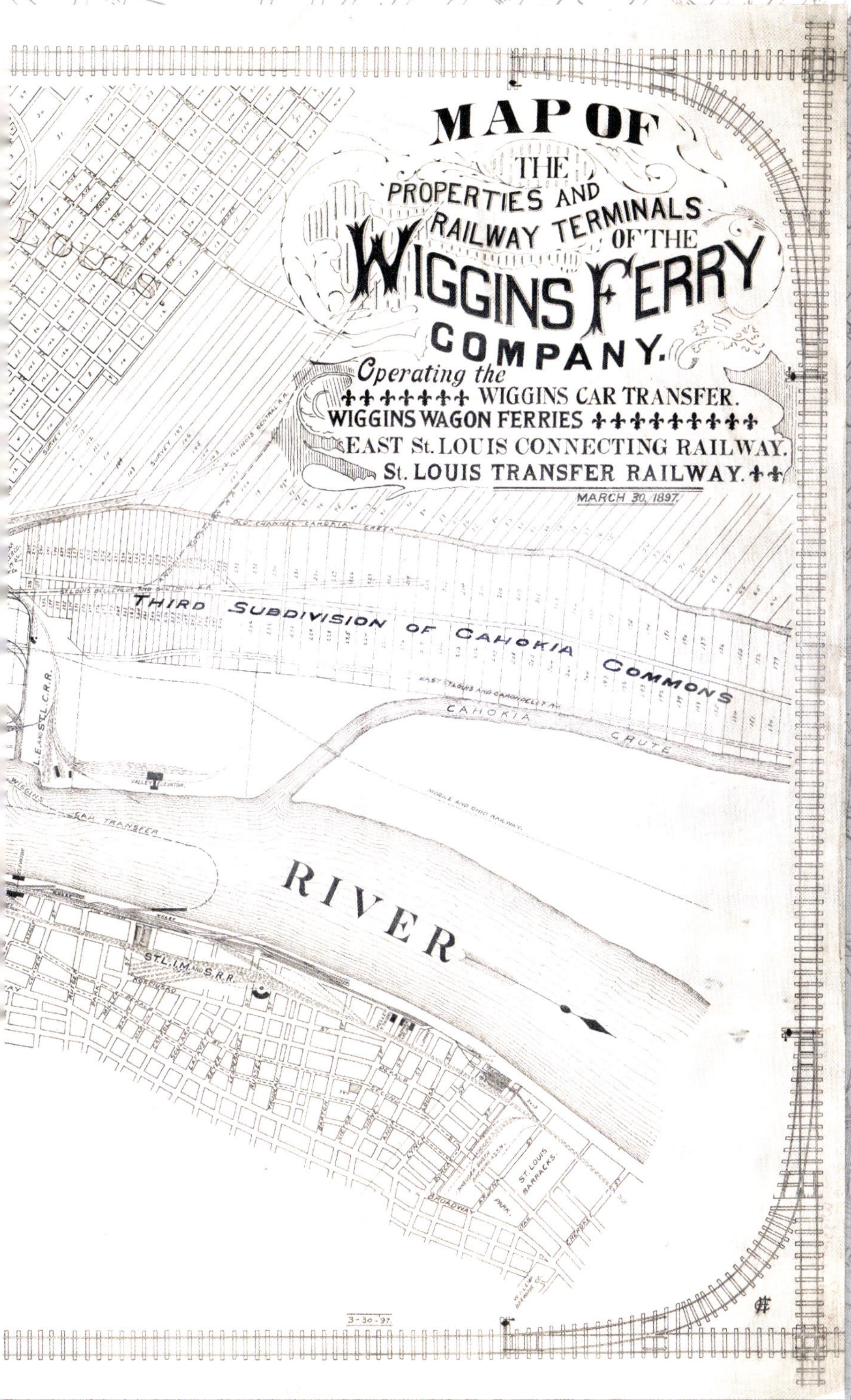

1897

Wiggins Ferry, St. Louis & East St. Louis

Map of the Properties and Railway Terminals of the Wiggins Ferry Company

Wiggins Ferry Co.
(publisher/printer)

Lithograph

25 × 42 inches

St. Louis Mercantile Library at the University of Missouri–St. Louis

1897

THE MISSISSIPPI RIVER has historically been at the center of St. Louis's economy. The City was founded at the confluence of the Mississippi and Missouri rivers because they were a nexus of fast and relatively cheap transportation. However, a river is an imposing obstacle for those who simply want to cross from one side to the other. When John Darby moved to St. Louis in 1818, he recalled that it took three days to ferry his family and all their possessions from the east to the west side of the river. Darby was elected mayor in 1835, and he spearheaded the effort to rescue the St. Louis harbor from silting as detailed in the *1837 map*.

In 1818, William Wiggins founded the Wiggins Ferry Company. By the mid-1820s, Wiggins had a fleet of ferry boats with imposing names—*Sea Serpent*, *Rhinoceros*, and *Antelope*—and in 1828 Wiggins upgraded to steam power, with the boats *St. Clair* and *Ibez*. In 1839, winter river crossings became easier with the new boat *Icelander* and its ice-smashing iron hull. Despite some setbacks, including an 1851 ferry explosion and the loss of four boats to an 1864 ice floe, the Wiggins Ferry Company kept expanding along with St. Louis.

As the company grew, Wiggins acquired about 900 acres of land along the Illinois banks of the Mississippi directly across from St. Louis. In the coming decades, Wiggins not only ran a ferry business, but also operated extensive yards, depots, warehouses, elevators, and, eventually, railroad tracks. The Wiggins Ferry Company

This map detail illustrates the more than 20 railroad companies operating in St. Louis and East St. Louis in 1897. The Illinois side has more than a dozen rail terminals where freight was loaded and unloaded, or entire railcars were moved onto ferries. Rail companies like the Illinois Central, Baltimore and Ohio, and Missouri Pacific were quite large and operated across the country. However, most of the railroads drawn here were either regional or operated just in the area of St. Louis, including the Venice and Carondelet Railroad and the St. Louis, Belleville and Southern Railway.

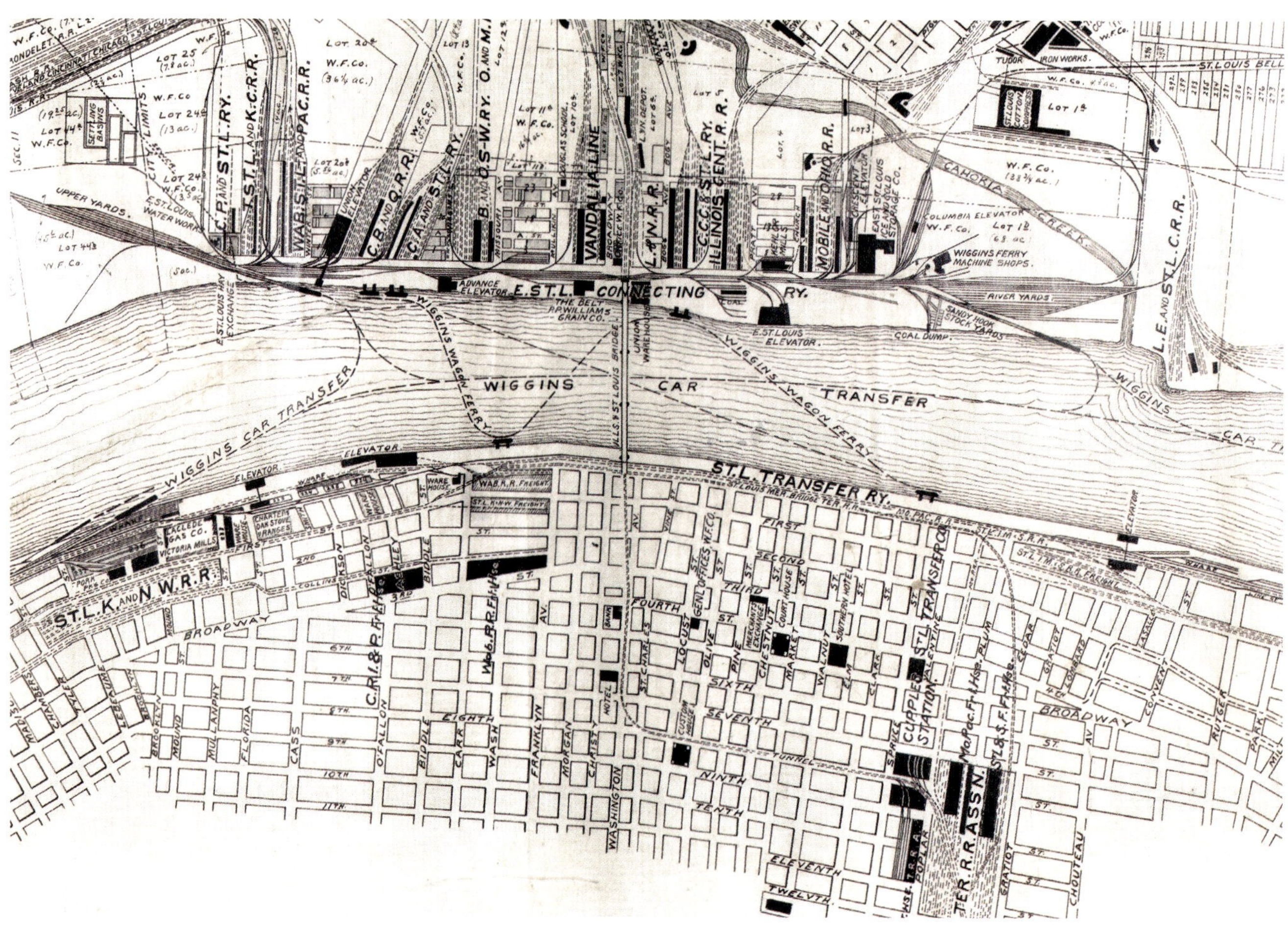

became a major connecting point for the many railroads terminating at East St. Louis and St. Louis. By 1870, Wiggins had established a railcar ferry system to move rail traffic over the Mississippi. After the Eads Bridge opened in 1876, the company reduced its ferry rates by half, undercutting the bridge tolls. The tactic worked, allowing the company to operate for another 50 years.

In 1893, the company was sold to the Terminal Railroad Association, a collective made up of St. Louis's largest rail companies. They kept the still-profitable ferry going, but the ferry business was surviving on borrowed time. When the Municipal (later MacArthur) Bridge opened in 1917 as a toll-free route across the Mississippi River, Wiggins was doomed. The last of the Wiggins ferryboats, the *Julius S. Walsh*, stopped running in the 1930s.

This photo shows a Wiggins ferry boat docked on the Illinois side of the river around the year 1905. Every Wiggins ferry landing had two docks, one for loading and the other for unloading. This allowed for quick and efficient transfers. In the background on the right is the Eads Bridge, which gave the ferries stiff competition for freight and passengers.
COURTESY MISSOURI HISTORICAL SOCIETY, ST. LOUIS

When this map was created in 1897, there were only two bridges over the Mississippi at St. Louis—the Eads Bridge (called the Illinois and St. Louis Bridge on the map) and the Merchants Bridge farther north. The river was a choking point for rail traffic. To satisfy the need to get rail cars across the river, Wiggins operated 10 ferry terminals on the river at downtown St. Louis. This map stands out for its distinctive railroad track design border.

RATES
OF THE
ST. LOUIS AND ST. CLAIR
FERRY
REDUCED.

All Children under 10 years of age, crossing with their Parents or Guardians, and Drivers, - - - FREE.

Each foot passenger, - - $0 6¼
Each man and horse, - - 0 20
Each 1 horse wagon, gig or sulky, - 0 50
Each 2 horse do. or carriage, - 0 62½
Each 3 horse do. do. - 0 75
Each 4 horse do. do. - 0 87½
Each 5 horse wagon or carriage, - $1 00
Each 6 horse do. do. - 1 12
Each 8 ox team and wagon, - 1 25
Each led horse, or stock cattle, - 0 12½
Each head of hogs and sheep, - 0 5

MARKET WAGONS & CARTS,
oaded with the produce or manufacture of the States of Illinois and Missou and returning, within 10 days after crossing, empty:

Each 1 horse wagon or cart, each way, - - 18¾ cts. $0 37½
Each 2 horse do. do. do. 31¼ " 0 62½
Each 3 horse do. do. do. 37½ " 0 75
Each 4 horse do. do. do. 43¾ " 0 87½
Each 5 horse do. do. do. 50 " 1 00
Each 6 horse do. do. do. 50 " 1 00
Each 8 ox team and wagon, 62½ cts. $1 25
Each barrel (or sack) of salt, pork, beef, flour, cider, &c., - - 0 6¼
Each barrel of whiskey, wine, brandy, or other spirits, - - - 12½
Each 100 *lbs.* merchandise, - - 0 6¼
Each 100 feet lumber, - - - 0 8

MERCHANTS' WAGONS AND CARTS,
Loaded one way, & crossing empty the other, returning within 10 days after crossing:

Each 1 horse wagon or cart, each way, - - 25 cts. $ 50
Each 2 horse do. do. do. 37½ " 75
Each 3 horse do. do. do. 50 " 1 00
Each 4 horse do. do. do. 62½ cts. 1 25
Each 5 horse do. do. do. 68¾ " $1 37½
Each 6 horse do. do. do. 68¾ " 1 37½
Each 8 ox team and wagon, 81¼ " 1 62½

MERCHANTS' WAGONS, LOADED BOTH WAYS:

Each 2 horse wagon, each way, - - 50 cts. $1 00
Each 3 horse do. do. do. 62½ " 1 25
Each 4 horse do. do. do. 75 cts. 1 50
Each 5 or 6 horse wagon, do. 87½ "
Each 8 ox team do. do. $1 "

PLEASURE CARRIAGES,
Crossing and returning within 10 days after crossing:

Each 1 horse gig, sulky or Dearborn over and back, - - - - - - - $0 62½
Each 2 horse carriage, over and back, - - - - - - - 0 87½
Each 3 or 4 horse carriage, over and back - - - - - - - 1 00

N. B. The old rates will be charged when the Ice runs in the river.

July 4, 1842. WM. C. WIGGINS, Collector.

RATES OF THE ST. LOUIS AND ST. CLAIR FERRY

This poster advertises the rates of the Wiggins Ferry for July 1842. The ferry charges were equivalent to today's bus fare or highway toll. In 1842 a single ferry passenger fare was $.06 ($1.95 in 2024), while an eight-ox team and wagon cost $1.25 each way ($40). By the 1870s, Wiggins Ferry was transporting on average 1,500 passengers each day, along with 10,000 bushels of coal and 750 wagons.
COURTESY MISSOURI HISTORICAL SOCIETY, ST. LOUIS

The trees of Forest Park before the fair.
COURTESY MISSOURI HISTORICAL SOCIETY, ST. LOUIS

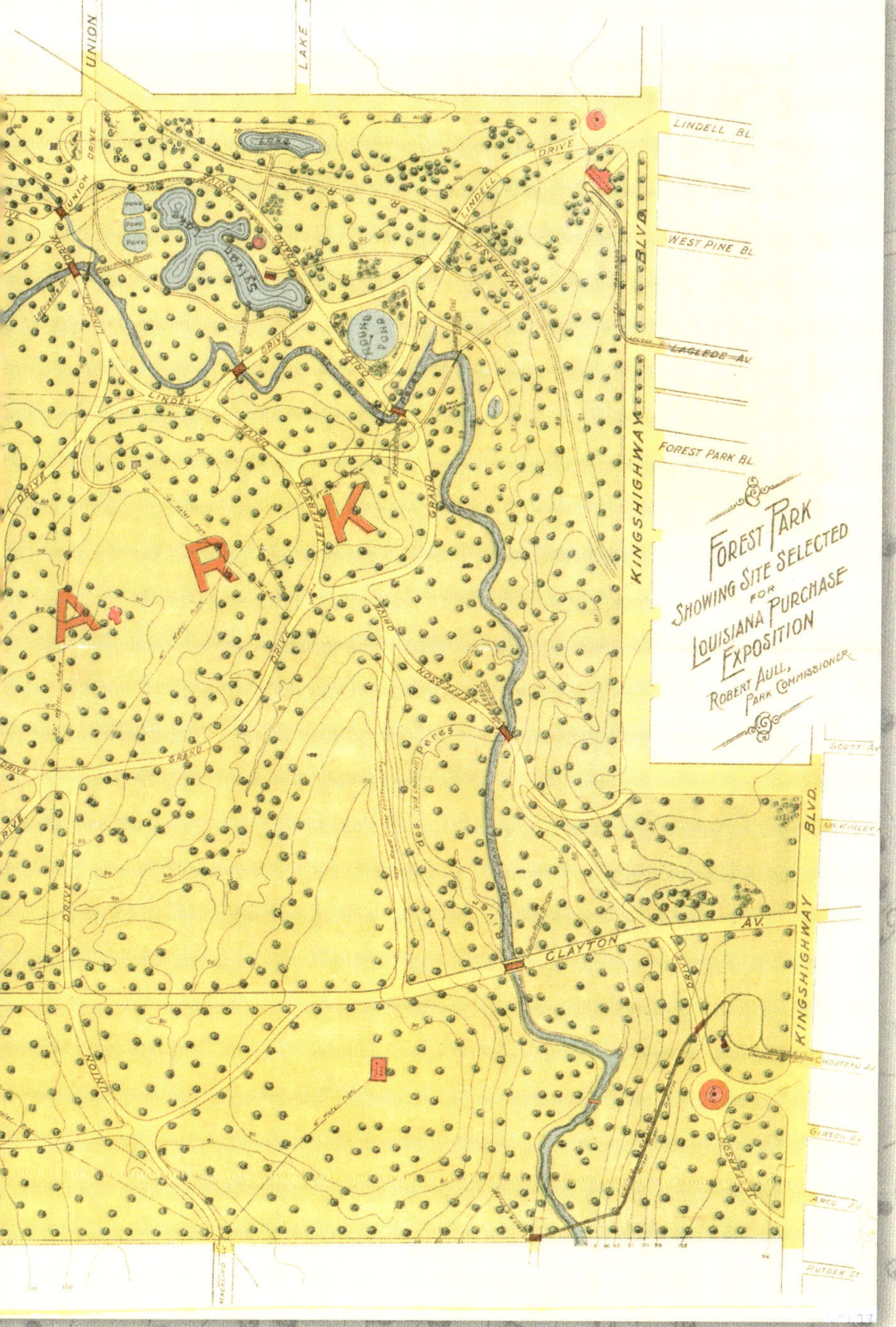

COURTESY MISSOURI HISTORICAL SOCIETY, ST. LOUIS

1904

Forest Park Welcomes the World

FOREST PARK BEFORE THE FAIR, showing site selected for the Louisiana Purchase Exposition

St. Louis Parks Department
(artist/cartographer)

Woodward and Tiernan Printing
(publisher)

Lithograph

33.85 × 18.11 inches

State Historical Society of Missouri

ON JUNE 24, 1876, 1,371 acres of land at the western edge of the newly established St. Louis City limits were dedicated as Forest Park. Previous developed green spaces like Lafayette, Missouri, and Washington parks were considerably smaller. Forest Park was twice the size of all those parks combined, and ever since has been the spot where the people of the St. Louis region go to enjoy the outdoors, visit the Zoo, or experience a museum.

But just having a place for recreation is not enough. St. Louis had hosted an annual exposition since the mid-1870s in order to highlight new inventions, display fine art, perform concerts, stage horse races,

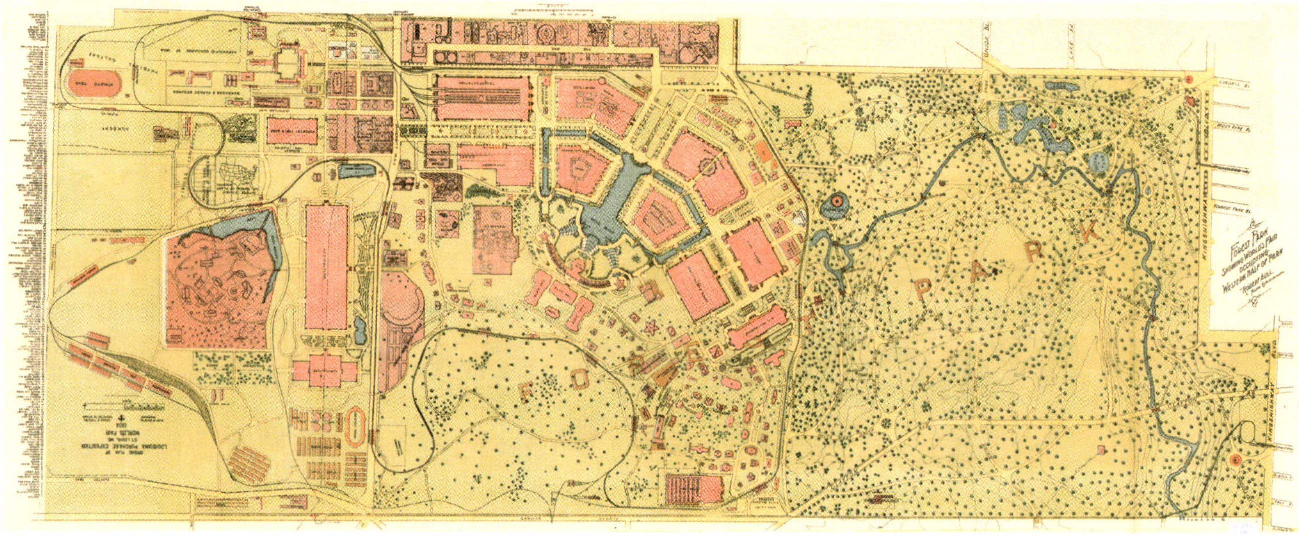

FOREST PARK DURING THE FAIR

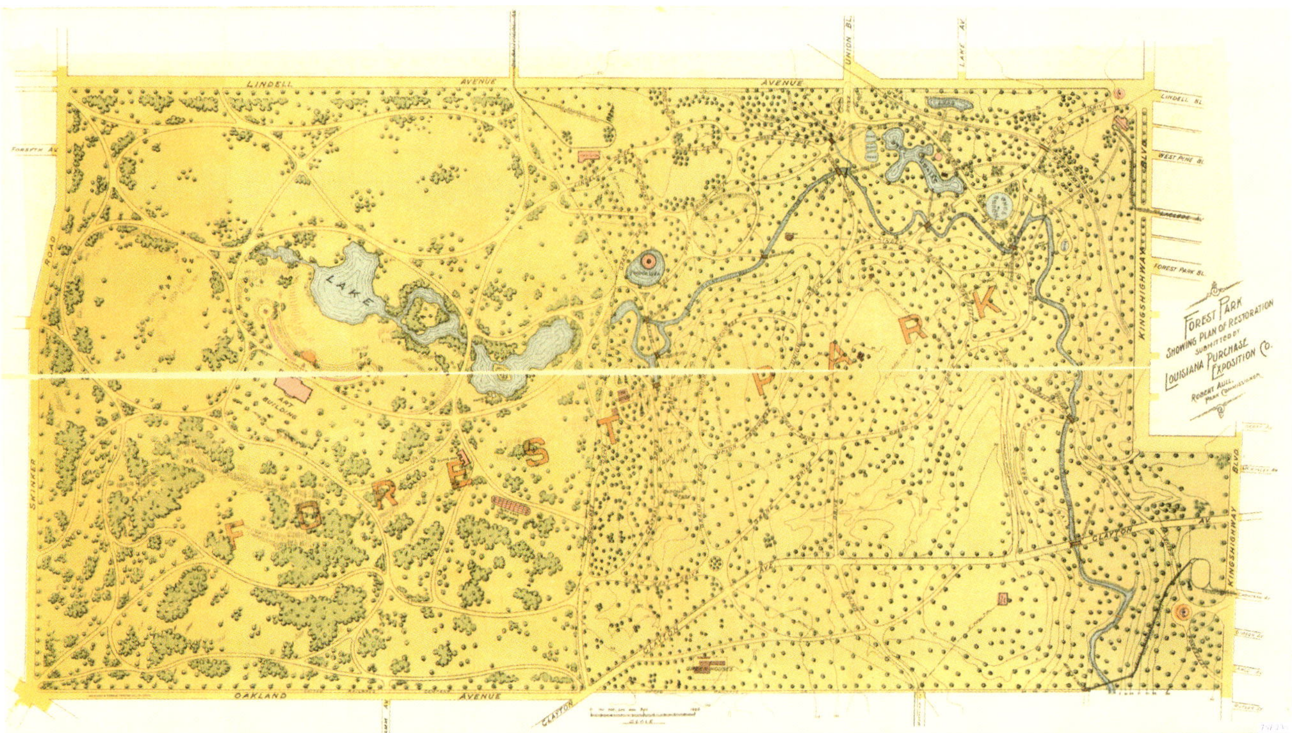

FOREST PARK AFTER THE FAIR

and attract visitors. Initially, these expositions were held at Fairgrounds Park, and later the St. Louis Exposition and Music Hall was built on the site of the old Missouri Park.

But as the Gilded Age came to a close and St. Louis reached the zenith of its wealth and prestige, the city fathers wished to celebrate that prosperity by hosting a (literally) world-class event in honor of the 100th anniversary of the Louisiana Purchase. That would require a much larger venue and would need to be carried out on a scale to match similar exhibitions held elsewhere. Twenty-eight years after its dedication, Forest Park was chosen as that venue. The entire world would be invited to visit the Louisiana Purchase Exposition, or as it is popularly known, the 1904 World's Fair. This series of maps documents Forest Park via three maps—before, during, and after the Fair. They were produced in 1904 under the auspices of the St. Louis Parks Department and its commissioner, Robert Aull.

The Forest Park before the fair shows that before the Fair, the western half of the park (left side of the map) was heavily wooded, while the eastern half contained almost all of the park's structures—

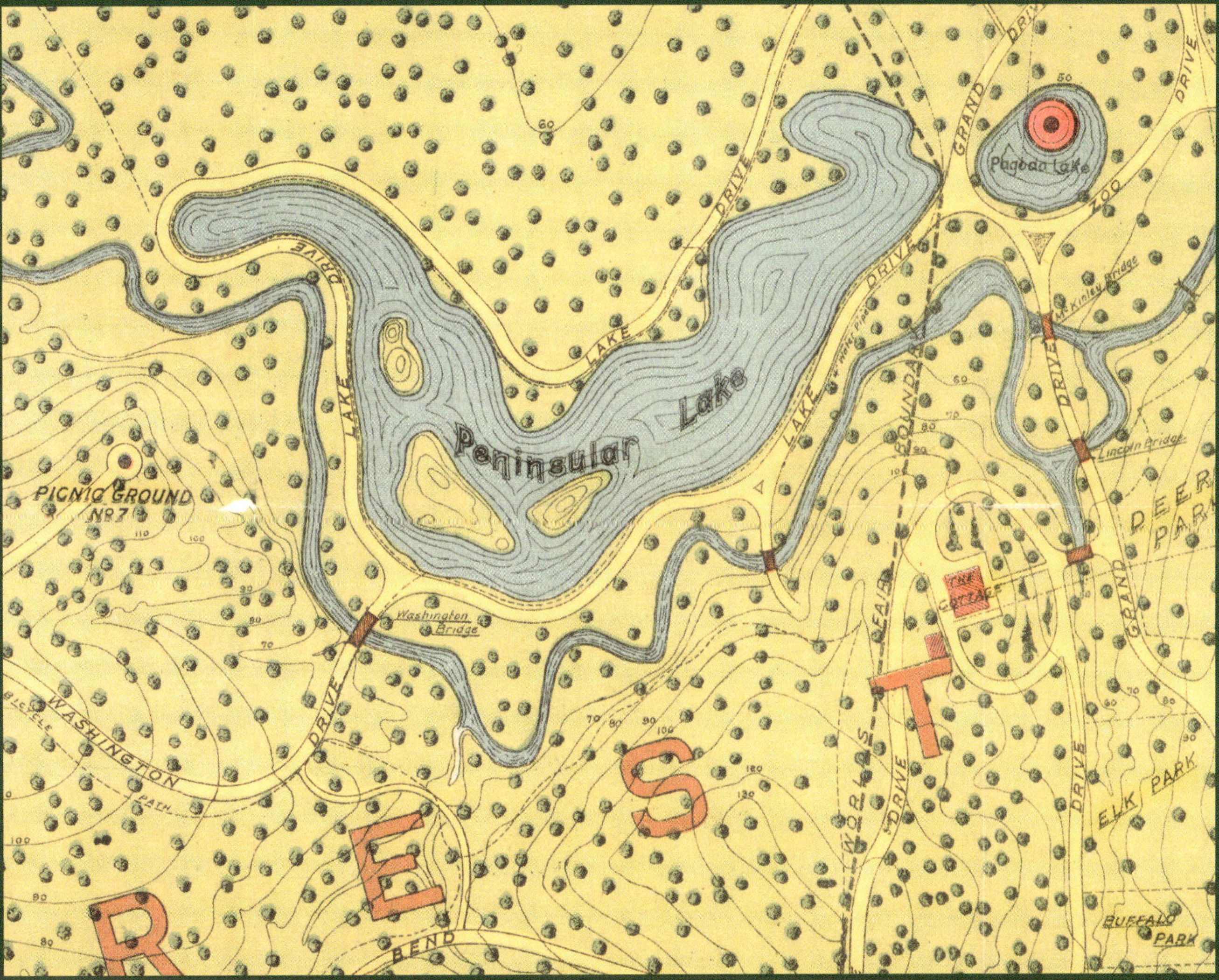

FOREST PARK BEFORE THE FAIR
Before the Fair, the central part of Forest Park was dominated by Peninsular and Pagoda lakes, both of which were created by diverting water from the River des Peres, which flows alongside them. The River des Peres was the dominant feature of the park. Flowing into the northwest corner, it bisected the entire park before exiting the southeast corner. As a natural stream, the river was initially seen as an asset; however, in later years, it was called a sewer. The *1929 map* tells the story of the River des Peres.

BEFORE THE FAIR

This image was taken by renowned St. Louis photographer Emil Boehl in 1902 looking east up Lindell Boulevard from where it ends at Skinker Road. The large dark area of trees at the right shows just how heavily wooded Forest Park was before the Fair. The cleared area in the foreground is the beginning of the new campus for Washington University.

COURTESY MISSOURI HISTORICAL SOCIETY, ST. LOUIS

pavilions, greenhouses, bridges, statues, and the police station. Carefully noted are the elevation contour lines indicating that the highest part of the park was at the southwest corner near the intersection of Oakland Avenue and Skinker Road, while the lowest elevation was in the northeast corner, near the intersection of Kingshighway and Lindell.

Planning for the centennial celebration of the Louisiana Purchase began in 1899. Within a year, $15 million in public and private funds had been raised to support the effort. On June 25, 1901, (25 years and a day after Forest Park's opening in 1876) it was announced by the Louisiana Purchase Exposition Company that Forest Park was the unanimous selection as the site for the Fair. Other sites considered included Carondelet Park, O'Fallon Park, a southwest site (St. Louis Hills), and two sites in North St. Louis along the city limits.

What seems to be an obvious choice today was

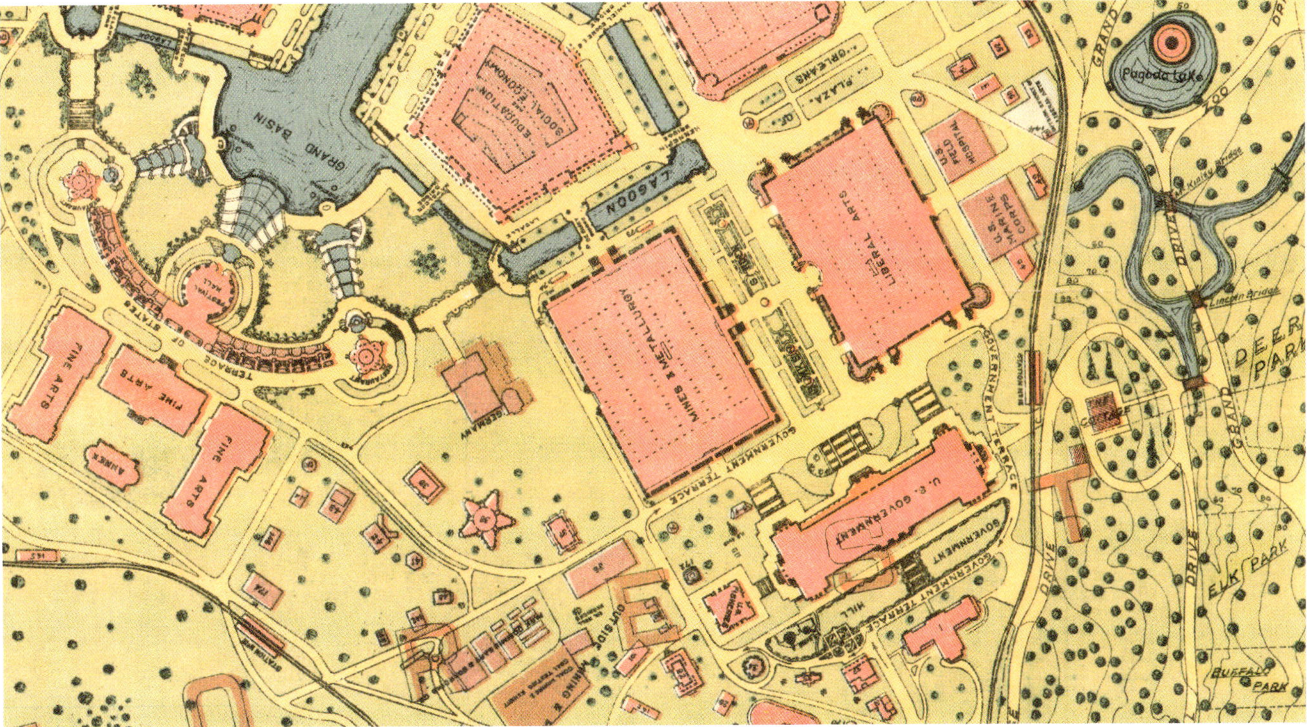

FOREST PARK DURING THE FAIR

During the Fair, Peninsular Lake was transformed into the Grand Basin. Pagoda Lake (on the far right) sat just outside of the fairground fence and was left untouched. Just below Pagoda Lake are areas labeled "Deer Park," "Elk Park," and "Buffalo Park." These are the predecessors to the Saint Louis Zoo as explained by the *1919 map*.

FESTIVAL HALL & THE CASCADES

The centerpiece of the Fair was the Grand Basin crowned by the large dome of Festival Hall atop a crescent-shaped hill. The hill was adorned with an elaborate series of waterfalls called the Cascades, made famous by Scott Joplin's rag of the same name. Immediately behind Festival Hall was the Palace of Fine Arts. The St. Louis Art Museum was part of the Palace of Fine Arts, as detailed in the *1915 map*.
COLLECTION OF THE AUTHOR

actually considered quite controversial at the time. There was outrage among many St. Louisans, some of whom were quoted in the *St. Louis Globe-Democrat* as saying , "my heart bleeds at the thought of destroying Forest Park" and "charges ought to be brought against a man who would want to chop down Forest Park's trees, and he should be sent to the penitentiary." But it was hard to argue that Forest Park wasn't ideal for the Fair: it was already served by the city water and sewer systems, it was centrally located along the main axis of the City's population, and it was well connected to rail and streetcar lines. A city ordinance approved the use of Forest Park for the Fair with many conditions, including that the Fair commissioners return the park in the condition they found it.

After the announcement, city officials reminded the people of St. Louis that the Fair was only going to use the western half of Forest Park, leaving more than 700 acres undisturbed. Following this announcement, however, it quickly became clear that half of Forest Park simply would not be big enough to accommodate what was planned. So the commissioners leased an additional 657 acres to the west and north of Forest Park (across Skinker Road

FOREST PARK AFTER THE FAIR

Removing the buildings from the Fair was only the first step in restoring the park. Laying out new streets reconnected the two halves. This new street pattern is still in use today.

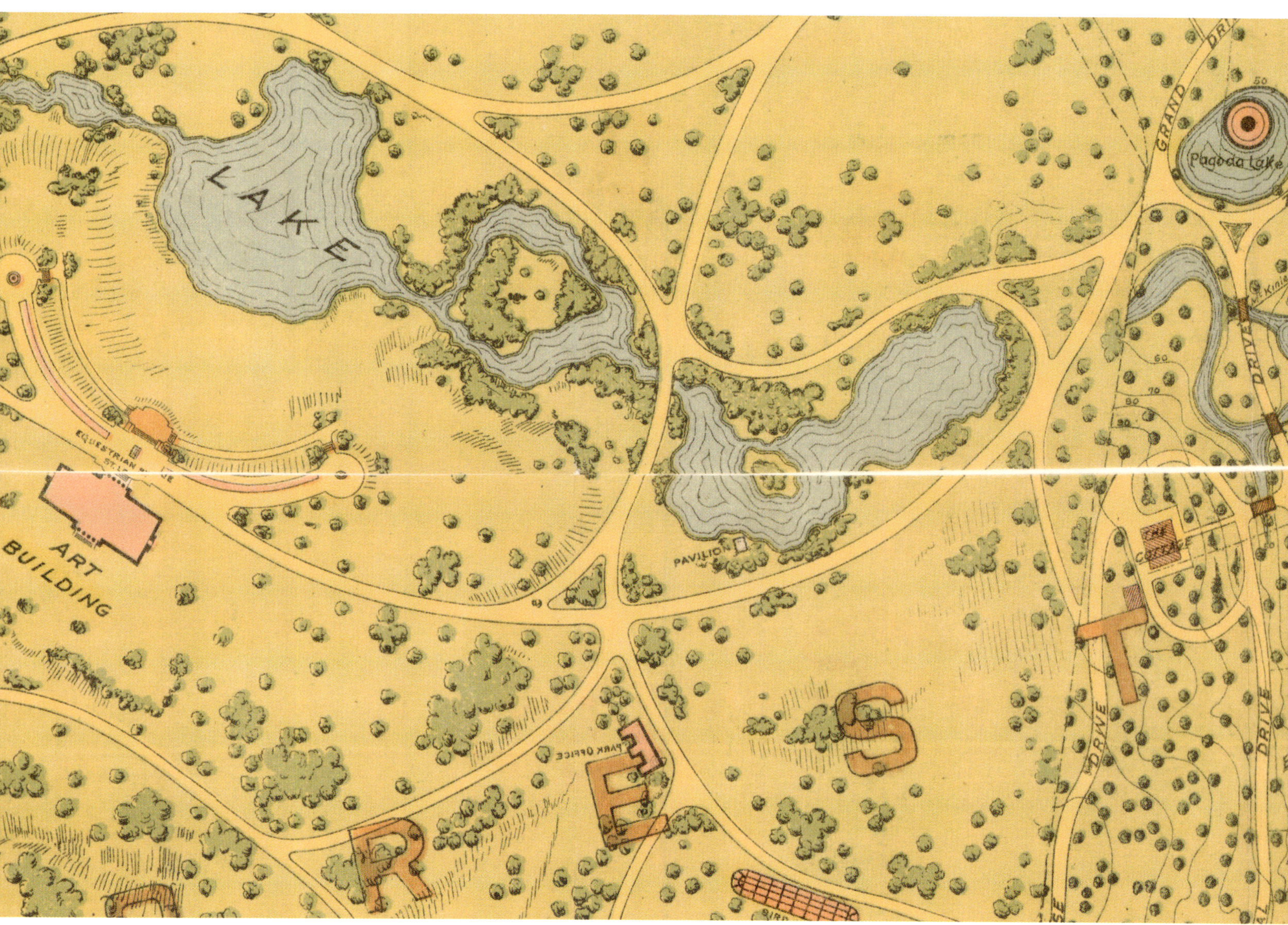

THE PAGODA
The pagoda in the middle of Pagoda Lake was completed the year the park was dedicated. Of "Syrian" design, it cost $7,000 to construct and was demolished in 1911. It was one of the few structures to both predate and postdate the Fair in Forest Park. Today the Nathan Frank Bandstand is on the same island as the pagoda, opposite the Muny.
COLLECTION OF THE AUTHOR

and Lindell Avenue), bringing the total acreage of the Fair to 1,272.

On the Forest Park during the fair map, the scale of the Fair is apparent. With the extensions across Skinker and Lindell, the site measured an impressive 1.75 by 1.05 miles and included 1,576 buildings, all served by 17 streetcar stations. The entire site was enclosed by an eight-foot iron fence. Over the course of seven months, the Fair welcomed 19 million visitors—30 times the population of St. Louis in 1904. While the Fair promoted the City around the world and celebrated American and European artistic and technological advances, many of its displays reinforced racist stereotypes of non-White cultures.

In the Forest Park restoration map, plans to return the park to its pre-Fair state are drawn. A few features from the Fair remain—the Art Museum, Flight Cage, and the Grand Basin. On the disused fairgrounds, trees were planted in clusters with open meadows. Today, in the meadows above the lake, is the Forest Park Golf Course, consisting of three nine-hole courses.

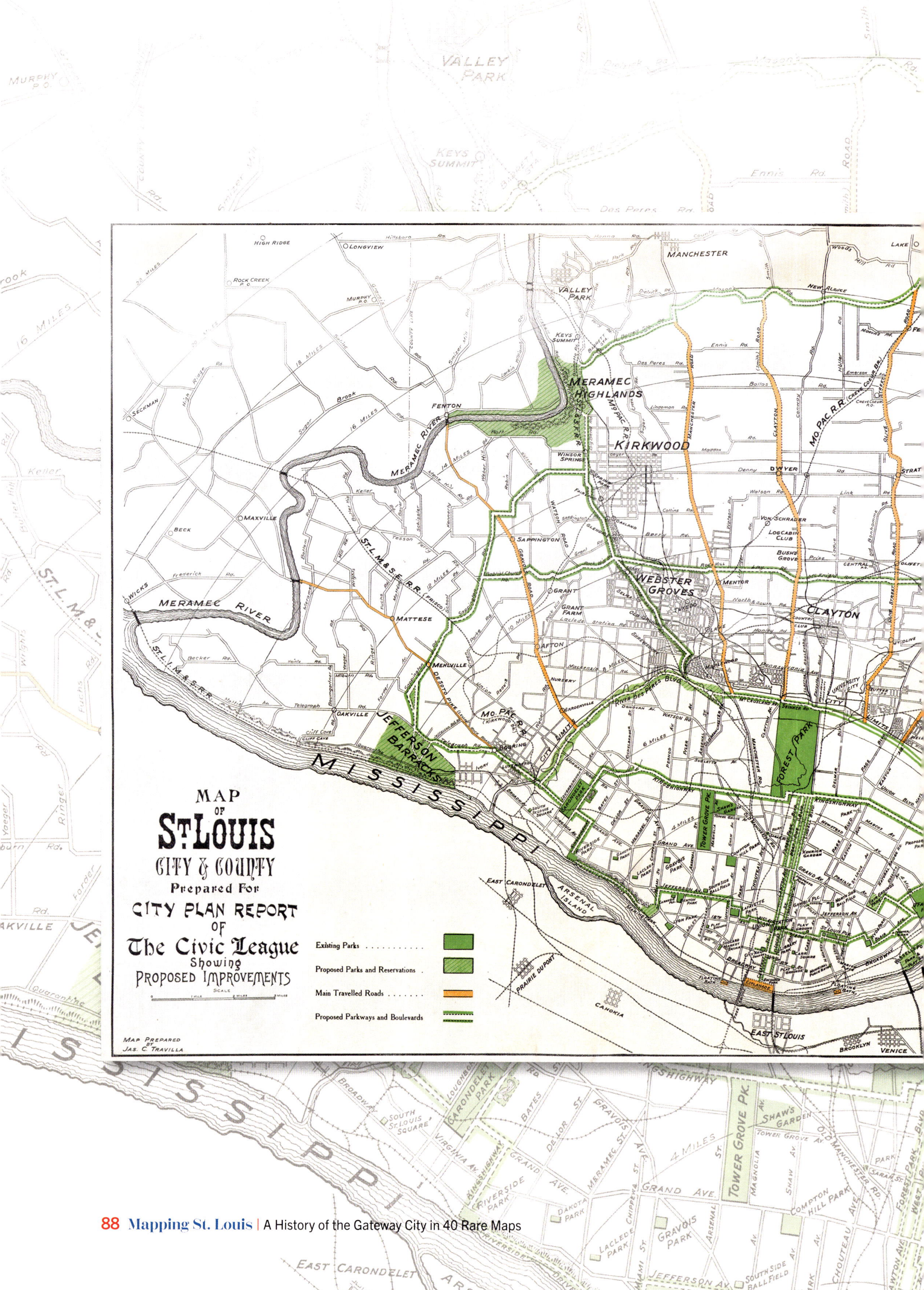
MAP OF ST. LOUIS
CITY & COUNTY
Prepared For
CITY PLAN REPORT
OF
The Civic League
Showing
PROPOSED IMPROVEMENTS
Existing Parks
Proposed Parks and Reservations
Main Travelled Roads
Proposed Parkways and Boulevards
MAP PREPARED BY JAS. C. TRAVILLA

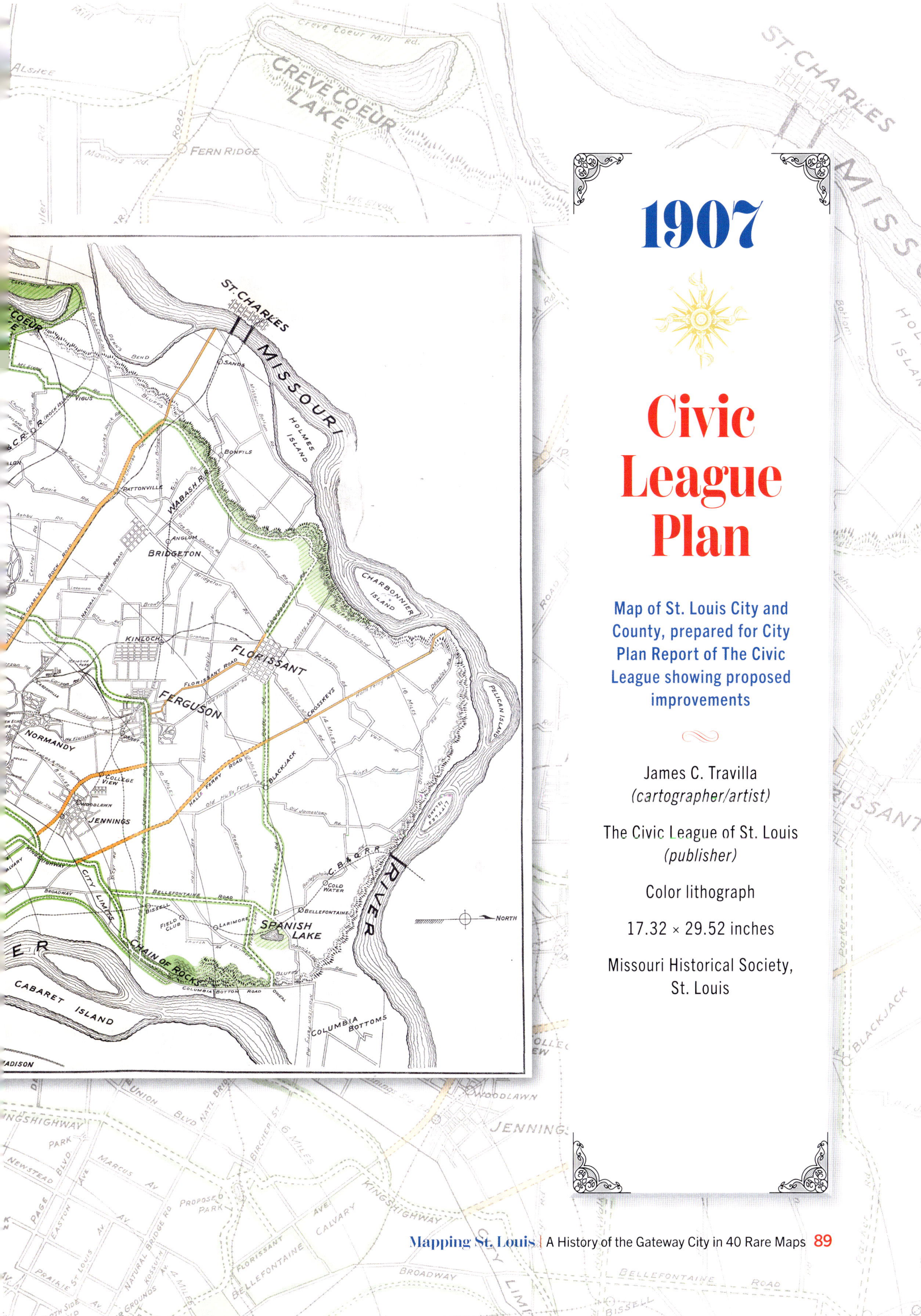

1907

Civic League Plan

Map of St. Louis City and County, prepared for City Plan Report of The Civic League showing proposed improvements

James C. Travilla
(cartographer/artist)

The Civic League of St. Louis
(publisher)

Color lithograph

17.32 × 29.52 inches

Missouri Historical Society, St. Louis

THE 1904 World's Fair marked a transition from the Gilded Age to the Progressive Era in St. Louis. The optimism of the Fair generated new dreams and new plans for the City.

This map was produced as part of the 1907 report, *A City Plan for St. Louis*. This visionary document was commissioned by the Civic League of St. Louis as the first comprehensive plan for *any* American city and is widely studied by urban planners today. The Civic League was formed in 1901 and played a central role in the citywide cleanup campaign before the start of the 1904 Fair. After the Fair, the Civic League drafted this plan, which presented a strategic vision for the future development and improvement of St. Louis.

The plan was drafted by six committees, each working on specific issues—municipal buildings, parks and boulevards, civic centers, street improvements, public art, and finally, the legislation necessary to implement plans in all these areas. The

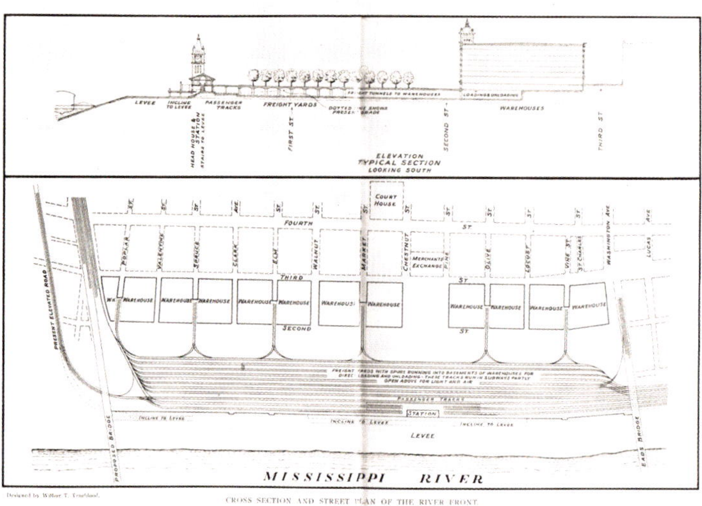

CROSS SECTION AND STREET PLAN OF THE RIVERFRONT

The esplanade along the river was designed to conceal the commerce moving underneath while presenting an attractive entranceway to St. Louis. A passenger station is surrounded by freight tracks with spurs that run into the basements of a new row of 12 warehouses, each the size of a city block.

COLLECTION OF THE AUTHOR

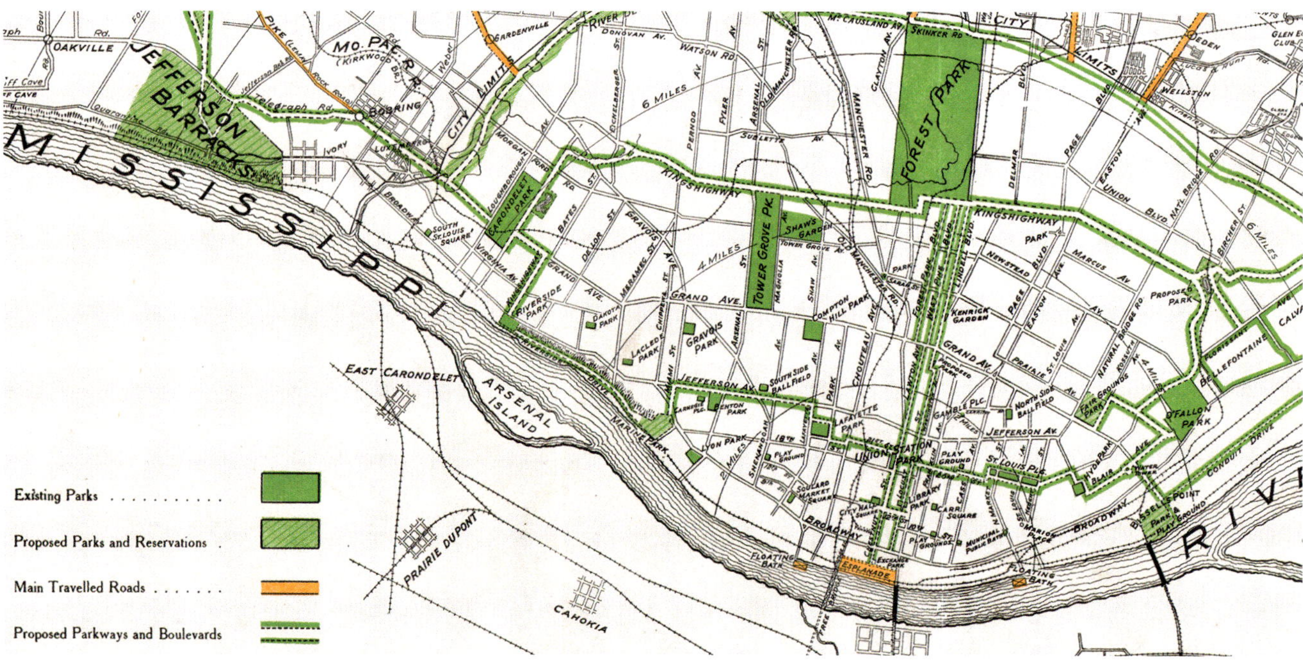

A proposed esplanade at the riverfront is highlighted in orange at the bottom of this detail. Long before the Jefferson National Expansion Memorial, the esplanade was an idea for the redevelopment of the riverfront to accommodate rail traffic, both passenger and commercial. Three parkways were proposed to run north and south across the City: River des Peres/Skinker, Kingshighway, and Jefferson. These tree-lined parkways would not only accommodate more traffic, but also would connect green spaces like Forest and O'Fallon parks. This concept closely mirrors the work of the 21st-century nonprofit Great Rivers Greenway.

THE RIVERFRONT AS IT SHOULD BE
One proposal of *A City Plan for St. Louis* called for an esplanade along the levee, what was called in the plan a "national entranceway unique among American municipalities." This broad, open plaza concealed railway tracks and a passenger station underneath. Building this plaza would have required the destruction of dozens of historic buildings along the riverfront. This eventually did happen in the 1930s and 1940s as part of the Jefferson National Expansion Memorial project. The illustration also shows an additional Mississippi River bridge at the south end of the levee at Poplar Street. The Poplar Street Bridge was built 60 years later in 1967.
COLLECTION OF THE AUTHOR

plan noted the importance of acting quickly for the betterment of St. Louis: "a city cannot maintain a high commercial standing unless it maintains, at the same time, a high civic life. . . . [I]f one city makes itself more inviting than its neighbor it is bound to attract more people."

Illustrated on this map are existing roads and proposed parkways. The orange lines are the "main traveled roads" that link St. Louis City and St. Louis County: DeSoto Pike (Lemay Ferry), Gravois, Manchester, Clayton, Olive, St. Charles Rock Road, Florissant, and New Halls Ferry. The green lines are proposed parkways that were intended to connect the City's existing parks and a series of proposed parks, such as Jefferson Barracks, Meramec Highlands, and Creve Coeur Lake. A series of concentric rings emanating from the levee measures the distance from downtown at increments of two miles (compared to the one-mile increments on the *1882 map*), and extending just past High Ridge at 22 miles. This map was drafted by James Travilla, a member of the plan's street-improvement committee and the superintendent of the street department. A cartographer of some skill, he also drafted the *1896 map*.

Many of the proposals outlined in the 1907 plan were considered by the new city plan commission, a branch of St. Louis government that was established by city ordinance in 1911 and is still in operation today.

One of the main focus areas of *A City Plan for St. Louis* was park and street improvements. This detail is taken from a map in the plan that outlines improvements to the north end of Kingshighway Boulevard. The widening and improvement of this street was not only practical as a means to create a better connection between the north and south ends of the City, but it also enhanced the landscape with new trees and green spaces.

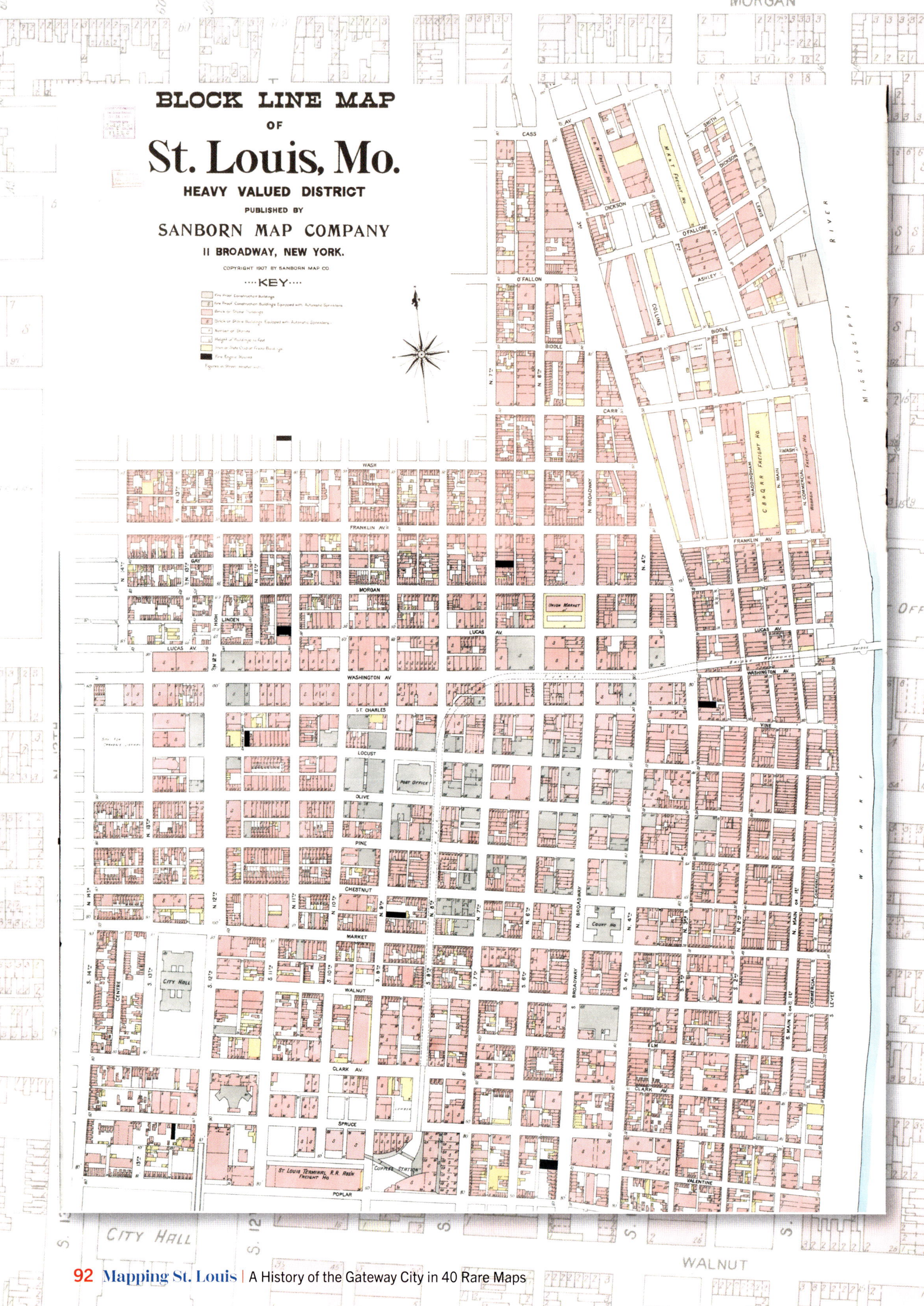
BLOCK LINE MAP
OF
St. Louis, Mo.
HEAVY VALUED DISTRICT
PUBLISHED BY
SANBORN MAP COMPANY
11 BROADWAY, NEW YORK.
COPYRIGHT 1907 BY SANBORN MAP CO.
····KEY····
MORGAN
OFFICE
CITY HALL
WALNUT
CASS
O'FALLON
BIDDLE
CARR
WASH
FRANKLIN AV.
LUCAS AV.
WASHINGTON AV.
ST. CHARLES
LOCUST
OLIVE
PINE
CHESTNUT
MARKET
CLARK AV.
SPRUCE
POPLAR
POST OFFICE
UNION MARKET
COURT HO.
CUPPLES STATION
ST. LOUIS TERMINAL R.R. ASS'N FREIGHT HO.
N. BROADWAY
S. BROADWAY
MISSISSIPPI RIVER
WHARF

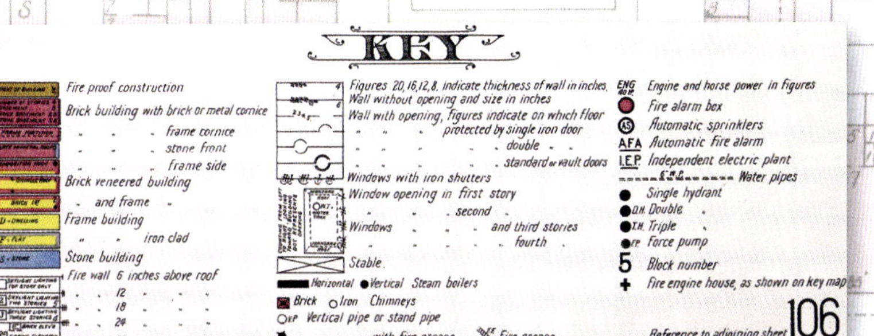

Fire engine at Engine House No. 32, 1903.
COURTESY MISSOURI HISTORICAL SOCIETY, ST. LOUIS

1907

Fire Insurance Maps

Block Line Map of St. Louis, Mo., Heavy Valued District

Sanborn Map Co.
(publisher)

Lithograph

40 × 50 inches

Library of Congress

1907

A LARGE POPULATION and thousands of buildings required extensive insurance to ensure stability and profitability. In the mid-19th century, a new kind of map was developed that detailed individual buildings for fire insurance companies. As cities like St. Louis rapidly grew, it became increasingly difficult for insurance underwriters to personally inspect property to determine risk. Specialty mapmakers developed atlases that documented the size, shape, and construction material of houses, commercial buildings, and factories, as well as fire walls, locations of windows and doors, sprinkler systems, and types of roofs. These atlases also display street widths and names, property boundaries, location of fire hydrants, building use, and house and block numbers.

Using these new maps, insurers had accurate details of structures and neighborhoods that provide invaluable information in determining the insurability of a property. The earliest available St. Louis fire insurance map was produced by A. Whipple & Co. in 1870. Later, Sanborn Map Co. became the publishing standard. The maps are invaluable research tools, not only for the wealth of detail they provide, but as a research tool to track the evolution of a street and its buildings.

Printed in 1907 by the Sanborn Map Co., this map is one of hundreds the company produced of St. Louis. Sanborn Map Co. was founded in New York in 1866 and by the 1890s was a major producer of fire insurance maps. They developed and copyrighted a key of specialized map symbols that are still in use today. The company also developed the use of "pasters" or corrections that updated building information by pasting new information on to maps in bound atlases This enabled customers to keep maps up to

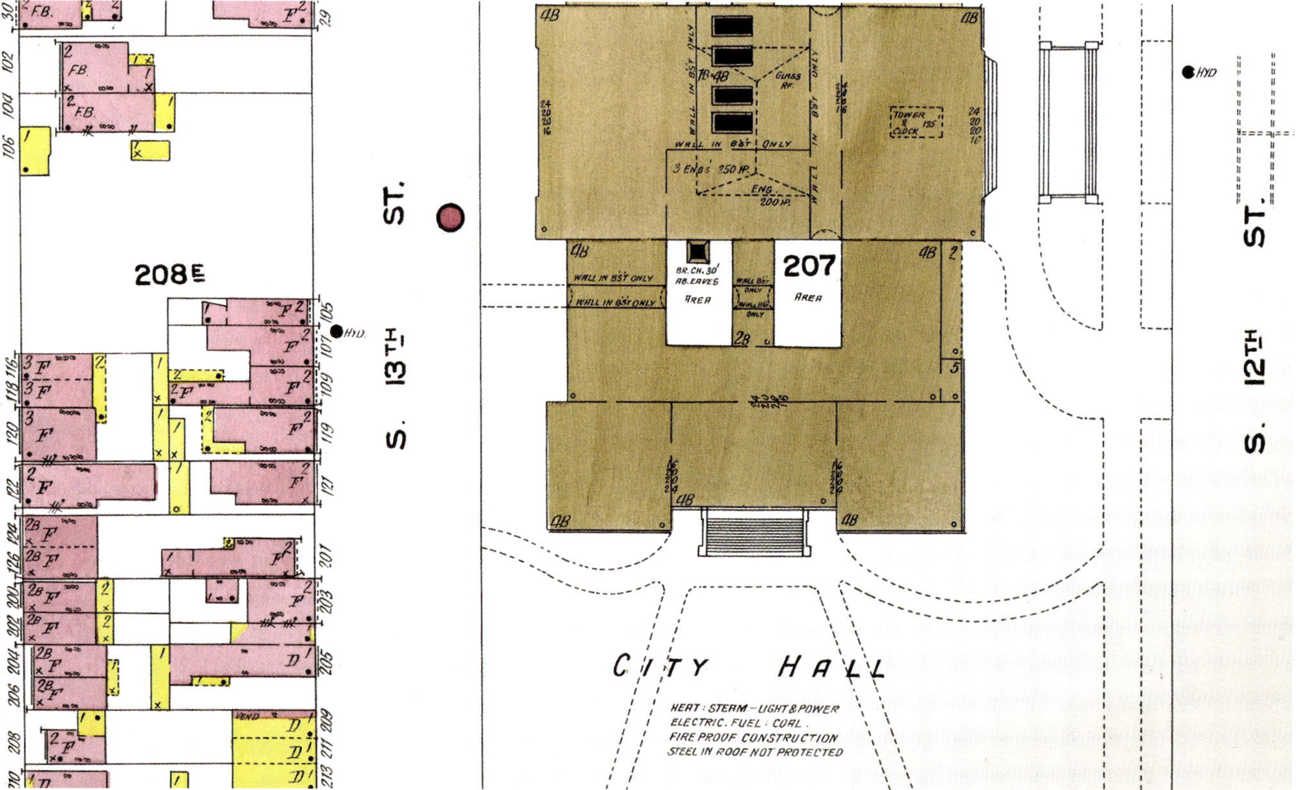

The large footprint of City Hall contrasts with those of its neighbors. These small buildings colored in pink (indicating brick or stone construction) were built as residences in the 1860s and 1870s. The number in front of each building is its address. The parts of the buildings highlighted in yellow are built of wood and usually indicate porches, sheds, and privies. The black dots are fire hydrants, while the pink dots outlined in black are fire alarm boxes—used to call in a fire alarm before the widespread use of telephones.

THE NEW CITY HALL

George Richard Mann, of the firm Eckel & Mann in St. Joseph, Missouri, won the design competition for the new St. Louis City Hall. His plans were chosen from 37 national entries. Mann's French-style design was inspired by the Hotel de Ville or City Hall of Paris; with ornamental dormer windows and towers, it was a natural choice for a city with such strong French heritage. As evident in this photo, the first story is Missouri pink granite that contrasts with pink-orange Roman brick on the upper floors and buff color sandstone trim located around the window openings and dormers. Today, the buff color sandstone is heavily stained due to decades of coal soot pollution in St. Louis. The distinctive 80-foot-tall tower was removed in 1936 because of corrosion. The public was outraged at its removal, and the mayor promised to replace it when funds became available. The funds never materialized.
COURTESY MISSOURI HISTORICAL SOCIETY, ST. LOUIS

Shown here is a fire insurance map detailing city blocks 208 and 207. Block 207 was originally occupied by Washington Park, which was later selected as the site of the St. Louis City Hall. In 1889, an ordinance was passed authorizing the City to seek designs and bids for a new city hall at a cost not to exceed $1 million. The building design commission noted the precise number of square feet required by each city department. It also required the new building be "fire-proof throughout." Construction began in July 1890 and would take 14 years to finish. No bond issue or special tax was used to finance construction, resulting in construction taking more than a decade to complete. Funds came from general revenue and the sale of city property. Every year or two, the City would authorize an average of $110,000 to continue construction. In 1893, the construction budget was increased to $2 million. The building was officially completed on November 5, 1904, when Mayor Rolla Wells held an open house for the residents of St. Louis. This map detail was issued in Sanborn's atlas *1909 St. Louis Fire Insurance Maps*, Volume 2, page 12.

date without having to purchase complete, re-issued volumes. Sanborn Map Co. is still in business today and is a leader in the geospatial mapping industry. Over the past 150 years, the company has made fire insurance maps for over 13,000 American towns.

This map shows the St. Louis "heavy valued district"—the core of downtown with the greatest concentration of buildings and businesses. The map's key highlights buildings in gray as fireproof construction; pink indicates brick or stone buildings; and yellow shows construction of iron or slate clad. Lastly, the black buildings are fire stations; there are eight noted on the map. The large gray building at the lower left occupying an entire block is the new city hall, completed in 1904.

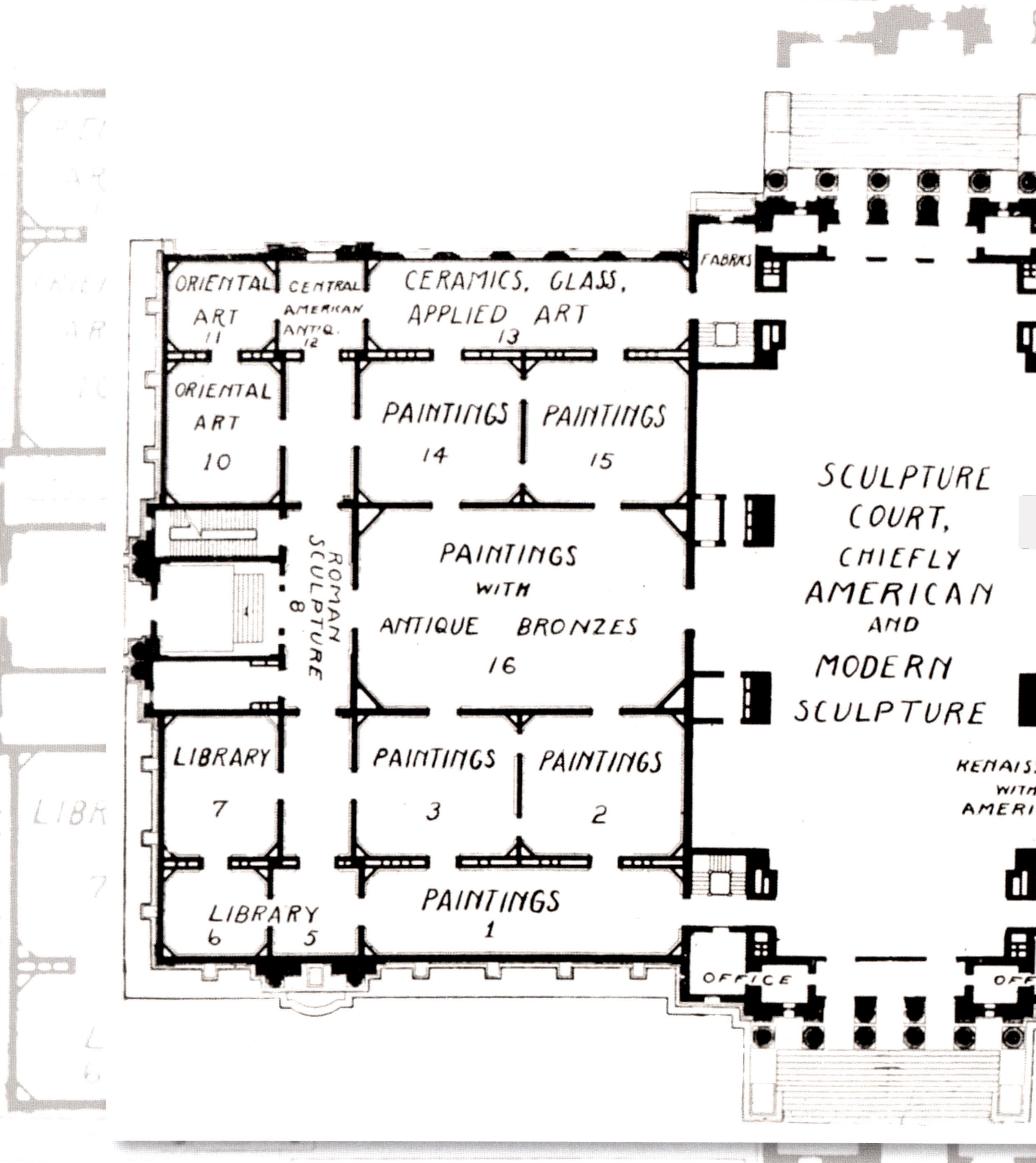
ORIENTAL ART 11
CENTRAL AMERICAN ANTIQ. 12
CERAMICS, GLASS, APPLIED ART 13
FABRKS
ORIENTAL ART 10
PAINTINGS 14
PAINTINGS 15
SCULPTURE COURT, CHIEFLY AMERICAN AND MODERN SCULPTURE
ROMAN SCULPTURE 8
PAINTINGS WITH ANTIQUE BRONZES 16
LIBRARY 7
PAINTINGS 3
PAINTINGS 2
LIBRARY 6 5
PAINTINGS 1
OFFICE

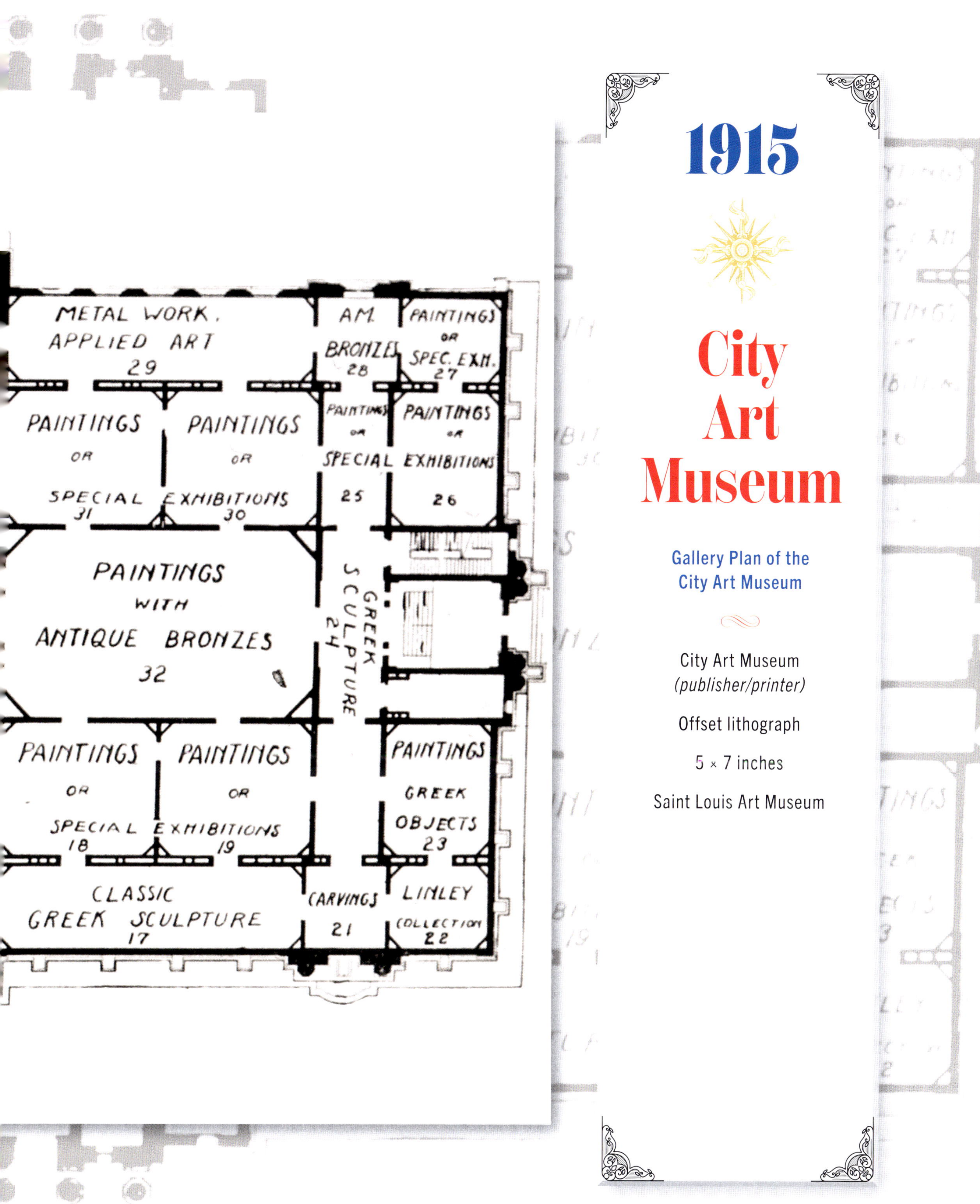

1915

City Art Museum

Gallery Plan of the City Art Museum

City Art Museum
(publisher/printer)

Offset lithograph

5 × 7 inches

Saint Louis Art Museum

Gilbert's grand and elegant design was modeled on the ancient Baths of Caracalla in Rome. The construction of the Art Museum building was completed in less than a year. In 1915, Gilbert submitted plans and cost estimates for an expansion of his original design, which would have expanded the gallery space tenfold, but it was considered too expensive.
COURTESY MISSOURI HISTORICAL SOCIETY, ST. LOUIS

THE FIRST museum in St. Louis was William Clark's display of objects from the Lewis & Clark Expedition, including a fine array of Indigenous artifacts. Later, the annual St. Louis Exposition (initiated long before the 1904 World's Fair) always included a display of fine arts featuring local, national, and international artists.

In 1880, St. Louis's first permanent fine art museum opened. The St. Louis Museum of Fine Arts and School, part of Washington University, was located at 19th Street and Lucas Place. Artist Halsey Ives was its director. Ives would go on to help organize the art departments at the 1893 Columbian Exposition in Chicago and the 1900 Exposition Universelle in Paris. At the 1904 St. Louis Fair, Ives was the head of the art department and oversaw the Palace of Fine Arts.

The St. Louis Art Museum in Forest Park was designed by renowned American architect Cass Gilbert for the 1904 Fair. Originally the central section of the Palace of Fine Arts, the Museum was the only building from the Fair intended to be a permanent structure, the one material monument of the Exposition. In 1906, the Museum of Fine Arts on Lucas Place moved into the Palace of Fine Arts building at Forest Park.

In a bold proposal, Ives introduced the idea for an art tax to support the new Art Museum. It was approved by city voters by a nearly 4-to-1 margin. This was the start of the Museum's maxim "free to all." However, the City's controller refused to distribute the tax revenue to the Museum, as it was not a municipal entity and so had no right to funds from taxes. This resulted in the formal separation of the Museum of Fine Arts from Washington University in 1909. As a result, the Museum of Fine Arts became the City Art Museum. Washington University agreed to lend its collection for display and for Halsey Ives to continue to direct it.

A visit to any large museum or gallery is made much more enjoyable with the help of a floor plan or map. This gallery floor plan was published in the April 1915 *City Art Museum Bulletin*. It shows the building's 32 galleries on the main floor. The gallery numbering scheme was the same used during the Fair, but the collection description for each gallery would change "[as]necessitated by

HALSEY C. IVES BY ANDERS ZORN
When it opened on Art Hill in 1906, the Art Museum was led by director Halsey C. Ives (1847–1911). Swedish artist Anders Zorn completed this portrait of Ives in 1895. The two were close friends. This painting was later exhibited at the 1904 World's Fair as an outstanding example of modern portraiture. In 1981, it was donated to the Saint Louis Art Museum by Ives's descendants and is frequently on display.
COURTESY SAINT LOUIS ART MUSEUM

special exhibitions and other demands." The 1915 *Bulletin* noted that "antique bronzes are installed decoratively in various galleries."

Galleries 5, 6, and 7 are labeled "library." The Richardson Memorial Library was the first major gift to the Art Museum. Funds were bequeathed by Mary Richardson in memory of her husband. This public research library opened in 1915 and is still a valuable resource, although it has since been relocated to a different part of the building.

The basement and second level of the Museum were not as large as they are today and only displayed small parts of the collection. The bulletin describes the print collection as installed on the second floor and the basement galleries displaying the "Egyptian, Assyrian, and modern Indian handiwork" collections.

While staircases have been moved and elevators added, the gallery plan is little changed and the galleries marked 12 and 8 lead into the Museum addition designed by architect David Chipperfield, completed in 2012.

Galleries 32 and 16 were the largest in the City Art Museum in 1915. This postcard image shows the north wall of gallery 32. As noted on the floor plan, this gallery was filled with bronzes and paintings. The largest painting shown is titled *Mlle. de Sombreuil.* It was painted by American artist Julian Story in 1887 and was acquired by the Museum in 1914. The 13 × 16.5–foot oil-on-canvas depicts a scene from the French Revolution. It was later deaccessioned by the Museum and its whereabouts are unknown.
COLLECTION OF THE AUTHOR

During 1915 the United Railways transported 356,814,595 passengers—of th
The average fare per passenger therefore w

TOURIST'S TROLLEY MAP OF ST. LOUIS AND ENVIRONS

CLUBS

AUTOMOBILE, 115 North Fourth. **Olive, Laclede, Market, Fourth or Broadway car.**

CITY, 915 Locust. **Hodiamont or Olive car.**

COLUMBIAN, Vandeventer and Lindell. **Vandeventer or Olive car.**

ELKS, 3617 Lindell. **Olive or Grand car.**

LIEDERKRANZ, Grand and Magnolia. **Grand or Fourth car.**

MERCANTILE, Seventh and Locust. **Hodiamont or Olive car.**

MISSOURI ATHLETIC, Fourth and Washington. **Compton, Park, Page, Fourth or Broadway car.**

NOONDAY, Fourth and Locust. **Hodiamont, Olive or Fourth car.**

RACQUET, Kingshighway and McPherson. **Olive-University car.**

ST. LOUIS, 3633 Lindell. **Olive or Grand car.**

SUNSET INN, Gravois road, 3 miles west of city limits. **Cherokee car to terminus and take bus.**

UNIVERSITY, Grand and Washington. **Grand, Page or Olive car.**

ASSOCIATIONS

Y. M. C. A., Grand and Franklin Avenues. **Page, Hodiamont or Grand car.**

Y. W. C. A., Locust near 14th St. **Olive, Page, Park or Compton car.**

R. R. Y. M. C. A., 20th. and Eugenia Sts. **Market, Laclede, Manchester or Chouteau car.**

Y. M. H. A., 3645 Delmar Avenue. **Olive, Page or Grand car.**

CONVENTION HALLS

COLISEUM, Jefferson, Washington to Locust—seats 10,000 persons. **Jefferson, Page or Olive car.**

ODEON, Grand and Finney—seats 2,000. **Grand, Page or Hodiamont car.**

ARMORY, Grand and Market—seats 4,000. **Market, Manchester or Grand car.**

MOOLAH TEMPLE, Lindell, near Spring—seats 2,250. **Olive or Vandeventer car.**

VICTORIA THEATER, Delmar, just west of Grand—seats 1,800. **Page, Grand or Hodiamont car.**

HOTEL DIRECTORY

AMERICAN, Seventh and Market. **Market, Laclede, Manchester or Cass car.**

AMERICAN ANNEX, Sixth and Market. **Market, Laclede, Manchester, Broadway or Cass car.**

BEERS, Grand and Olive. **Olive or Grand car.**

BENTON, 819 Pine. **Olive, Chouteau-Southampton, Market, Laclede, Manchester, Tower Grove, Bellefontaine, or Cherokee car.**

BLUE GRASS, 4038-4044 Olive. **Olive or Sarah car.**

BUCKINGHAM, Kingshighway and West Pine. **Laclede car.**

1. Union Station
2. Coliseum
3. Municipal Buildings
5. Court House
6. Sportsman's Park
7. Robison Field
8. Fairground Park
9. O'Fallon Park
10. Art Museum
11. Jefferson Memorial
12. Zoo
13. Washington University
14. Delmar Garden
15. Forest Park Highlands

The ratio of fatalities in 1915 was one fatality to 89 million Passengers. A ST

UNITED RAILWAYS PRINT SHOP

)43,205 were free transfer passengers.
cents.

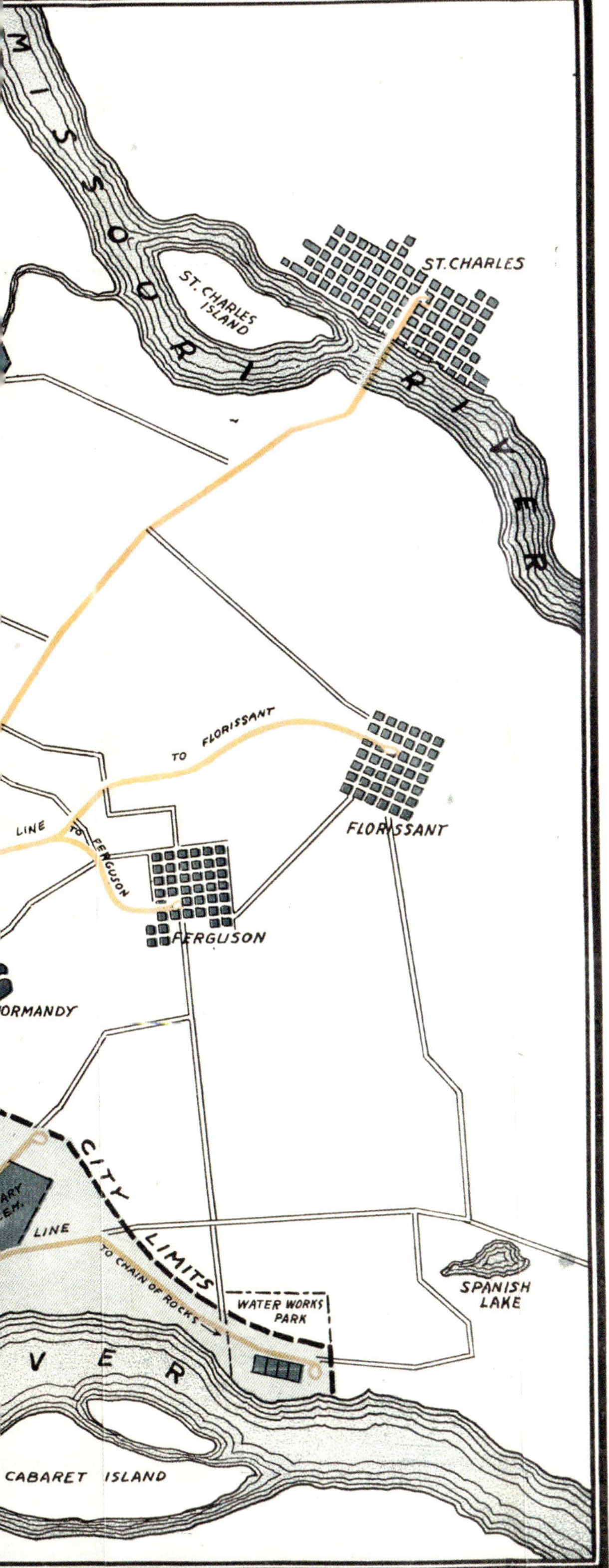

HOTELS. (Continued)

BLUM, 14th and Chestnut. **Market, Laclede, Manchester, Bellefontaine, Chouteau-Southampton or Olive car.**

BREVORT, 412 Pine. **Olive, Wellston, Chouteau - Southampton, Broadway or Fourth car.**

HAMILTON, Hamilton and Maple. **Hamilton or Hodiamont car.**

JEFFERSON, 12th and Locust. **Hodiamont or Olive car.**

LACLEDE, Sixth and Chestnut **Market, Laclede, Manchester, Broadway or Cass car.**

LaSALLE, Broadway and Chestnut. **Market, Laclede, Broadway, Cass or Manchester car.**

LELAND, 1414 Market. **Market, Laclede, Manchester or Bellefontaine car.**

MAJESTIC, 11th and Pine. **Market, Laclede, Manchester, Chouteau-Southampton, Tower Grove, Bellefontaine or Olive car.**

MARQUETTE, 18th and Washington. **Park, Compton, Belt or Page car.**

MARYLAND, Ninth and Pine. **Olive, Chouteau-Southampton, Market, Laclede, Manchester, Tower Grove, Bellefontaine or Cherokee car.**

METROPOLE, 12th and Morgan. **Page, Wellston or Belt car.**

NEW REGENT, 14th and Chestnut. **Market, Laclede, Manchester or Chouteau-Southampton car.**

NEW ST. JAMES, Broadway and Walnut. **Broadway, Market, Laclede or Manchester car.**

PLANTERS, Fourth, Pine to Chestnut. **Laclede, Market, Olive, Fourth or Broadway car.**

PLAZA, Olive and Leonard. **Olive car.**

PONTIAC, 19th and Market. **Market, Laclede, Manchester, Park, Compton or Belt car.**

PORTLAND, 1817 Market. **Market, Laclede, Manchester, Park, Compton or Belt car.**

REGENT, 14th and Chestnut. **Market, Laclede, Manchester or Chouteau-Southampton car.**

R. R. Y. M. C. A., 20th Street, opposite Union Station. **Market, Laclede, Manchester or Chouteau-Southampton car.**

ST. REGIS, Broadway and St. Charles. **Broadway, Hodiamont, Page, Park or Compton car.**

STRATFORD, Eighth and Pine. **Olive, Chouteau-Southampton, Cherokee, Tower Grove, Bellefontaine, Market, Laclede or Manchester car.**

TERMINAL, Union Station. **Market, Laclede, Manchester, Chouteau-Southampton, Park, Compton or Belt car.**

WARWICK, 15th and Locust. **Olive, Page or Hodiamont car.**

WASHINGTON, Kingshighway and Washington. **Olive-Delmar or Olive-University car.**

WELLINGTON, 715 Pine. **Olive, Tower Grove, Cherokee, Bellefontaine, Market, Laclede, Chouteau-Southampton or Cass car.**

WEST END, Vandeventer and West Belle. **Hodiamont or Vandeventer car.**

CAR IS A PRETTY SAFE PLACE.

1915

Tourist's Trolley Map

Tourist's Trolley Map of St. Louis and Environs

United Railways
(publisher/printer)

Color lithograph

14.7 × 20.5 inches

St. Louis Mercantile Library at the University of Missouri-St. Louis.

1915

A GROWING CITY needs to move large groups of people across large distances in a safe manner. In 1843, Erastus Wells began operating the first regular horse-drawn omnibus service in St. Louis. By the 1890s, cable cars and electric trolleys operated on almost 100 miles of track across the City. By 1907, the consolidation of nearly 10 smaller streetcar lines formed the St. Louis United Railways Co.

During the first two decades of the 20th century, streetcars were the primary mode of transport for most St. Louisans. The top of the map boldly announces that in 1915 the United Railways transported 365,814,595 passengers, more than 3.5 times of the entire US

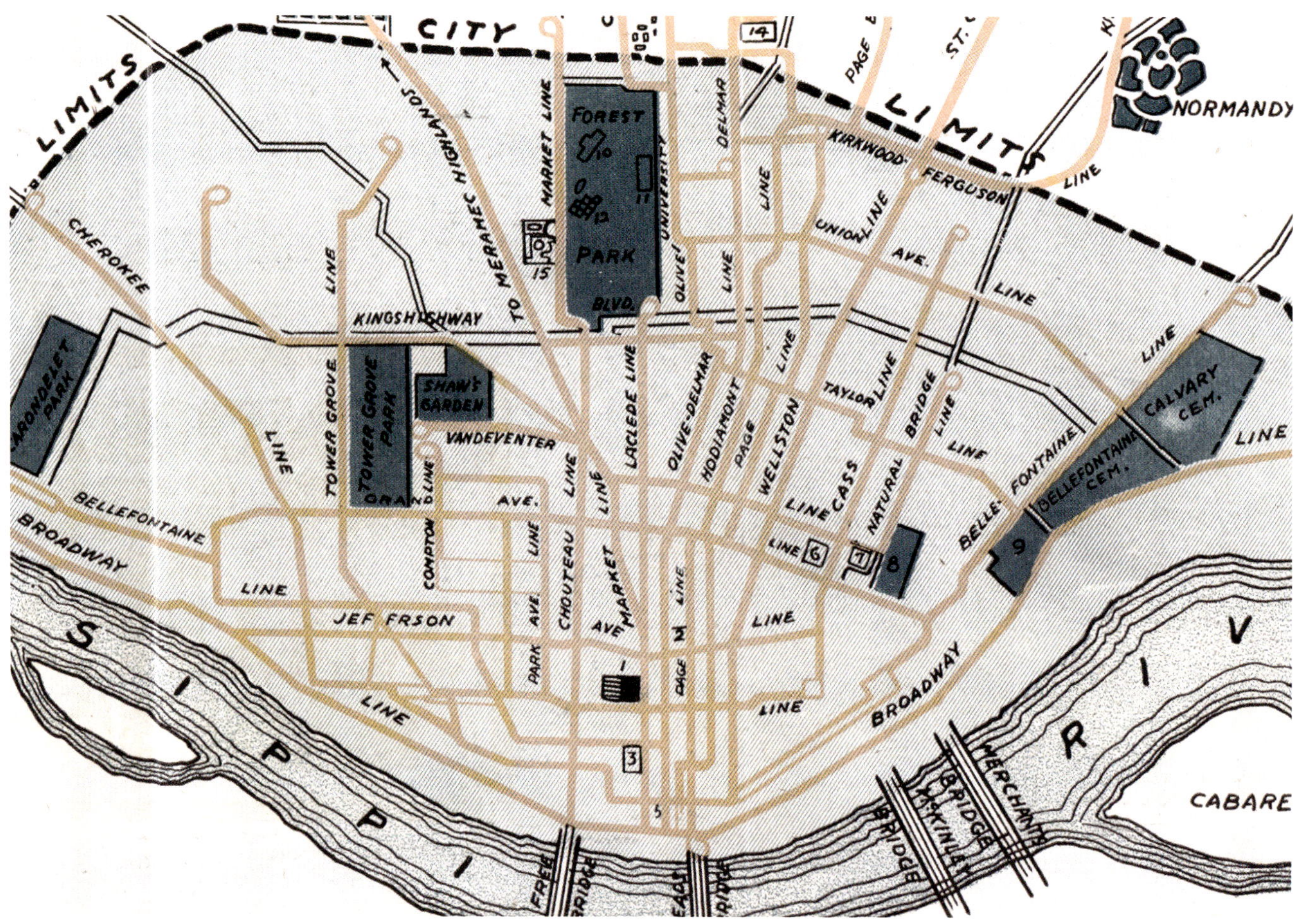

Before the formation of the United Railways Co., St. Louis was served by a network of competing street car companies:

1. National Railway (operated the Natural Bridge, Cass, Wellston, and North Broadway lines)
2. Union Depot Railroad (operated the Bellefontaine and Tower Grove lines)
3. Lindell Railway (operated the Market, Page, Hodiamont, and Taylor lines)
4. Southern Electric Railway (operated the South Broadway line)
5. St. Louis and Suburban Railway (operated the Meramec Highlands and Kirkwood-Ferguson lines)
6. Missouri Railroad (operated the Chouteau, Jefferson, and Vandeventer lines)
7. Peoples Railroad (operated the Park and Compton lines)

Each company built and maintained their own rails, cars, and fare schedule. On this detail, 15 important places are numbered, including the City's professional ballparks: Sportsman's Park (numbered 6) and Robison Field (numbered 7). From 1893 until 1920, the St. Louis Cardinals (National League) played all their home games at Robison Field. The St. Louis Browns (American League) played at Sportsman's Park from 1902 until 1953, when they were sold and became the Baltimore Orioles. Between 1920 and 1953, both the Browns and the Cardinals played at Sportsman's Park, which became Busch Stadium after the Browns left. The Cardinals continued there until the club relocated to the new downtown Busch Stadium in 1966.

SAFETY FIRST

In an effort to educate the public about safety, United Railways Co. published this advertisement in the November 12, 1911, edition of the *St. Louis Star* newspaper. Safety was a real concern, as dozens of St. Louisans were injured or killed in streetcar accidents every year. In 1915 there were four streetcar-related deaths. The biggest cause of injuries was the result of a practice called the "flip"—people jumping on and off moving streetcars. Tragically, children playing on the tracks were regularly maimed or run down by streetcars.

COURTESY MISSOURI HISTORICAL SOCIETY, ST. LOUIS

population at that time. In 1915, the population of St. Louis was estimated at 730,000.

The many different trolley lines allowed the population to expand toward the city limits, and streetcars were a big factor in helping create the suburbs. Despite the "Great Divorce," it would no longer be possible to view St. Louis removed from the greater St. Louis County region. St. Louis County had many small communities. Florissant had been established in the 18th century, Kirkwood in the 1850s, and Clayton was created as the new St. Louis County seat in 1876. Before the streetcars, a horse or carriage was the only way to travel between these communities or into the City of St. Louis. The county roads were notoriously bad. The anticipated cost of building hundreds of miles of new county roads was in fact a cause of the Great Divorce.

The consolidated service of United Railways made for cheap and fast transportation across the City and County and opened rural areas to development. By the time Webster Groves was formally incorporated in 1896, it was touted as the "Queen of the Suburbs." The age of the commuter had begun.

The noticeable creases on this map indicate it was not made for display, but rather as a folded pocket map to be used by tourists and locals as an aid to using the trolley system.

MERAMEC HIGHLANDS

The streetcar system was not only a means to commute, but also a means to escape summer heat in an increasingly crowded and soot-filled city. One of the more popular escapes was the Meramec Highlands, established in the southwestern corner of Kirkwood in 1891. Built along the bluffs at a bend in the Meramec River, the resort featured a large hotel, a general store, and 15 quaint cottages all served by the steam railroad. By the summer of 1898, the electric streetcar tracks were extended to the Highlands, allowing for cheaper and more regular trips from the City. This 1905 flier proclaimed, "the temperature averages about 5 to 8 degrees below that of St. Louis during the day, and 10 to 12 degrees during the night. . . . [I]t is one of the healthiest resorts in the United States. No malaria, no mosquitos, no dust, no noise or bustle." A mineral bath and massage cost $.50.

COURTESY MISSOURI HISTORICAL SOCIETY, ST. LOUIS

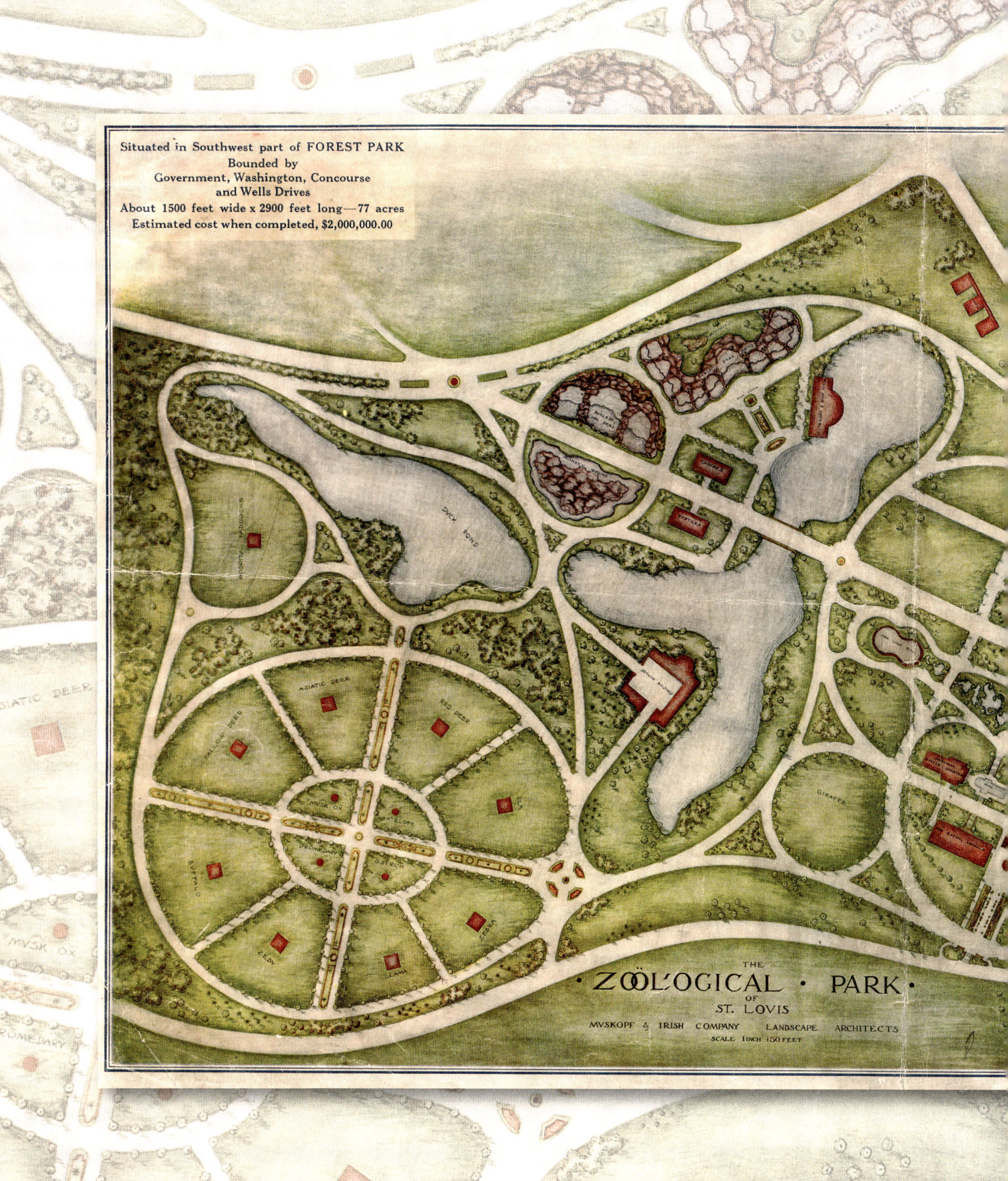
Situated in Southwest part of FOREST PARK
Bounded by
Government, Washington, Concourse
and Wells Drives
About 1500 feet wide x 2900 feet long—77 acres
Estimated cost when completed, $2,000,000.00
DUCK POND
ASIATIC DEER
RED DEER
FALLOW DEER
BUFFALO
ZEBRA
LLAMA
GIRAFFE
ASIATIC DEER
MUSK OX
DROMEDARY
THE
ZOÖL'OGICAL · PARK
OF
ST. LOUIS
MUSKOPF & IRISH COMPANY LANDSCAPE ARCHITECTS
SCALE 1 INCH 150 FEET

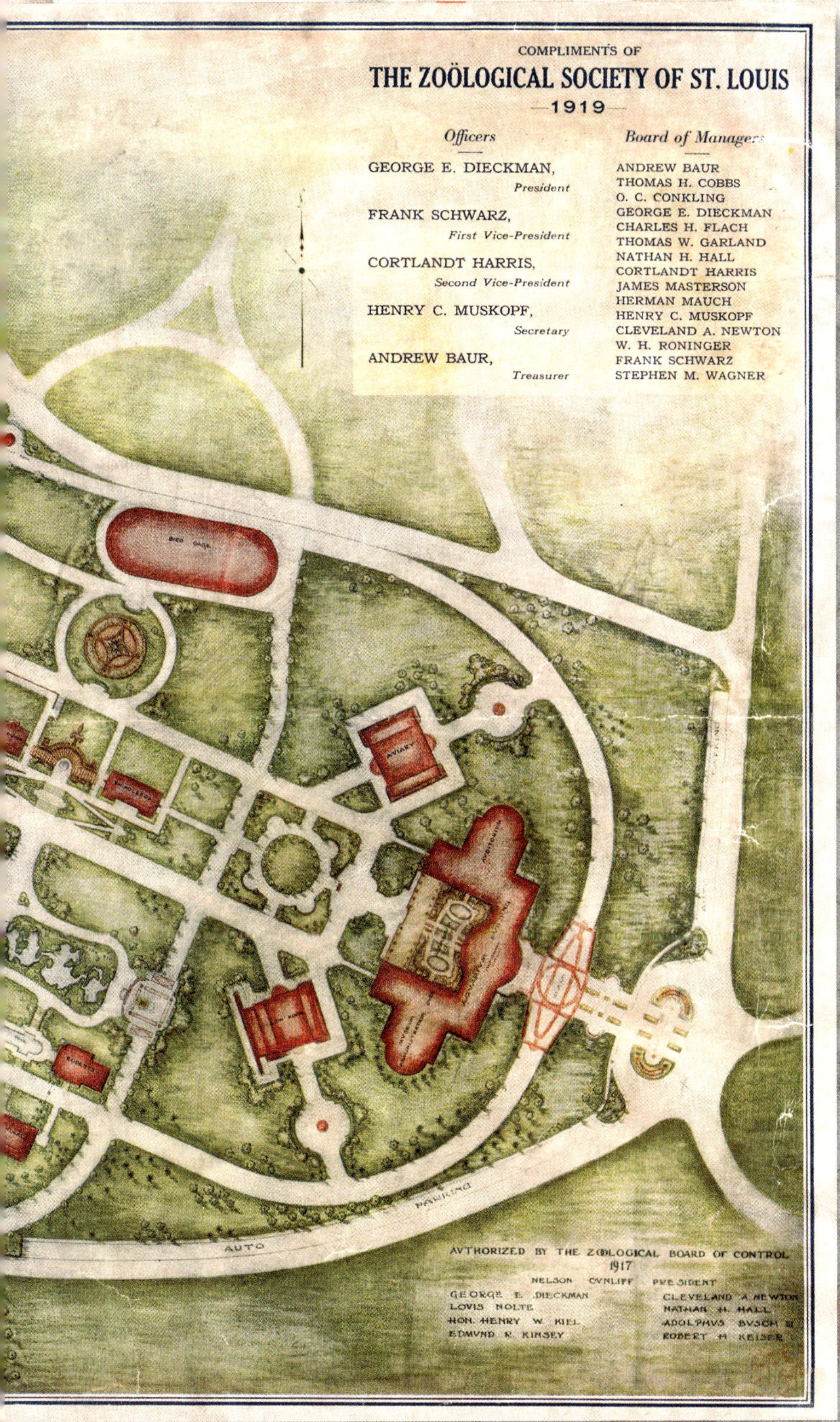

COMPLIMENTS OF

THE ZOÖLOGICAL SOCIETY OF ST. LOUIS

—1919—

Officers

GEORGE E. DIECKMAN, *President*

FRANK SCHWARZ, *First Vice-President*

CORTLANDT HARRIS, *Second Vice-President*

HENRY C. MUSKOPF, *Secretary*

ANDREW BAUR, *Treasurer*

Board of Managers

ANDREW BAUR
THOMAS H. COBBS
O. C. CONKLING
GEORGE E. DIECKMAN
CHARLES H. FLACH
THOMAS W. GARLAND
NATHAN H. HALL
CORTLANDT HARRIS
JAMES MASTERSON
HERMAN MAUCH
HENRY C. MUSKOPF
CLEVELAND A. NEWTON
W. H. RONINGER
FRANK SCHWARZ
STEPHEN M. WAGNER

AVIARY
PARKING
AUTO

AVTHORIZED BY THE ZOOLOGICAL BOARD OF CONTROL
1917
NELSON CVNLIFF PRESIDENT

GEORGE E. DIECKMAN
LOVIS NOLTE
HON. HENRY W. KIEL
EDMVND R. KINSEY

CLEVELAND A. NEWTON
NATHAN H. HALL
ADOLPHVS BVSCH III
ROBERT H. KEISER

1919

The Saint Louis Zoo

The Zoological Park of St. Louis

Zoological Board of Control *(publisher)*

Color lithograph

14 × 22 inches

St. Louis Public Library

PARK •

1919

IN 1913, 77 acres of Forest Park were formally set aside to house a permanent zoo. While the zoo is universally loved today, establishing it inside Forest Park was widely criticized as a waste of greenspace, most notably by St. Louis Park Commissioner Dwight Davis (the founder of the famous Davis Cup tennis tournament, he also created the first municipal tennis courts in the US, today called Dwight Davis Tennis Center).

As early as 1875, when Forest Park was being planned, a zoo was suggested. Planners emphasized that the zoo "should be open to all, free of any admission charge so it could best serve as an institution of public instruction and amusement." Soon after the park opened in 1876, St. Louisans donated American animals like prairie dogs to the park, which were cared for by the Parks Department.

The first major expansion of the park's zoo collection came in 1890 when five American bison, then "in danger of being exterminated by the progress of civilization and the cultivation of the soil" were brought to Forest Park. A large enclosed area was set aside so the bison could live "as nearly to a wild state as possible." Even before the Saint Louis Zoo was officially established, the policies were set that have guided it since—to be open for free; to both entertain and educate; to serve as a survival center for endangered species; and to display animals in natural settings.

By 1900, there were about 150 animals on exhibit in the Forest Park Zoo. For the 1904 World's Fair, the Smithsonian Institution erected a large walk-through flight cage displaying over 1,000 birds. The cage was 228 feet long, 84 feet wide, and 50 feet high. After the Fair, the City bought the cage for $3,500 (it had reportedly cost more than $17,000 to build), and the remaining zoo animals were all moved to the vicinity of the cage. Just a year later, in 1905, a city official told a *St. Louis Globe-Democrat* reporter, "the astonishing attendance this summer leaves no doubt that the bird cage, with a zoo around it, will become the chief feature of the park." In order for this to happen, an organization would have to be created

The original zoo in Forest Park was located where the Muny parking lot is today. A wide avenue was part of a formal central axis that Moskopf and Irish planned for the east end of the new Saint Louis Zoological Park. The oval flight or bird cage from the 1904 World's Fair can be seen at the top of this detail. Its location was the determining factor for the Zoo being located in the southwest part of the park. The simple sea lion pond shown on the far left was replaced by the much larger Sea Lion Sound exhibit that opened in 2012.

1904 BIRD CAGE

Designed by Frank Baker and constructed by the St. Paul Foundry Co. in St. Paul, Minnesota, the bird cage was restored in 1967 and again in 1996. It remains one of the largest free flight cages in the world today.
COURTESY MISSOURI HISTORICAL SOCIETY, ST. LOUIS

to take over the Zoo's operation from the St. Louis Parks Department.

The Saint Louis Zoological Society was formed and began a campaign to build and operate a large and permanent zoo in Forest Park. In 1913, Mayor Kiel signed an ordinance establishing the Saint Louis Zoological Park. The Zoo's first elephant, Miss Jim, was purchased in 1916 with pennies donated by St. Louis schoolchildren. Inspired by this example, later that same year St. Louis voters approved a special zoo tax—making the Saint Louis Zoo the first municipally supported zoo in the world. Now that funding was secure, planning for a large, permanent zoo could begin.

The plan for the new zoo was created in 1919 by the St. Louis architectural landscape firm of Muskopf and Irish. Henry Muskopf and Henry Irish began their partnership in 1912 after Irish left the Missouri Botanical Garden, where he had served as superintendent and horticulturalist for 18 years. The firm is best remembered today for its design of the grounds of the Mississippi State Hospital, which is renowned as a "City Beautiful" campus.

Implementation of the 1919 zoo plan was estimated to cost $2 million (or about $36 million today). The bear pits shown at the top of the plan became standards for zoos across the country when they were installed in 1922. Most of the buildings on the plan were never built.

SEA LION POND

This image of the sea lion pond was taken in 1918. Photographer O. C. Conkling took a number of important photos documenting the early construction of the new Zoo. His name is also listed on the map as a member of the Zoo's board of managers.
COURTESY MISSOURI HISTORICAL SOCIETY, ST. LOUIS

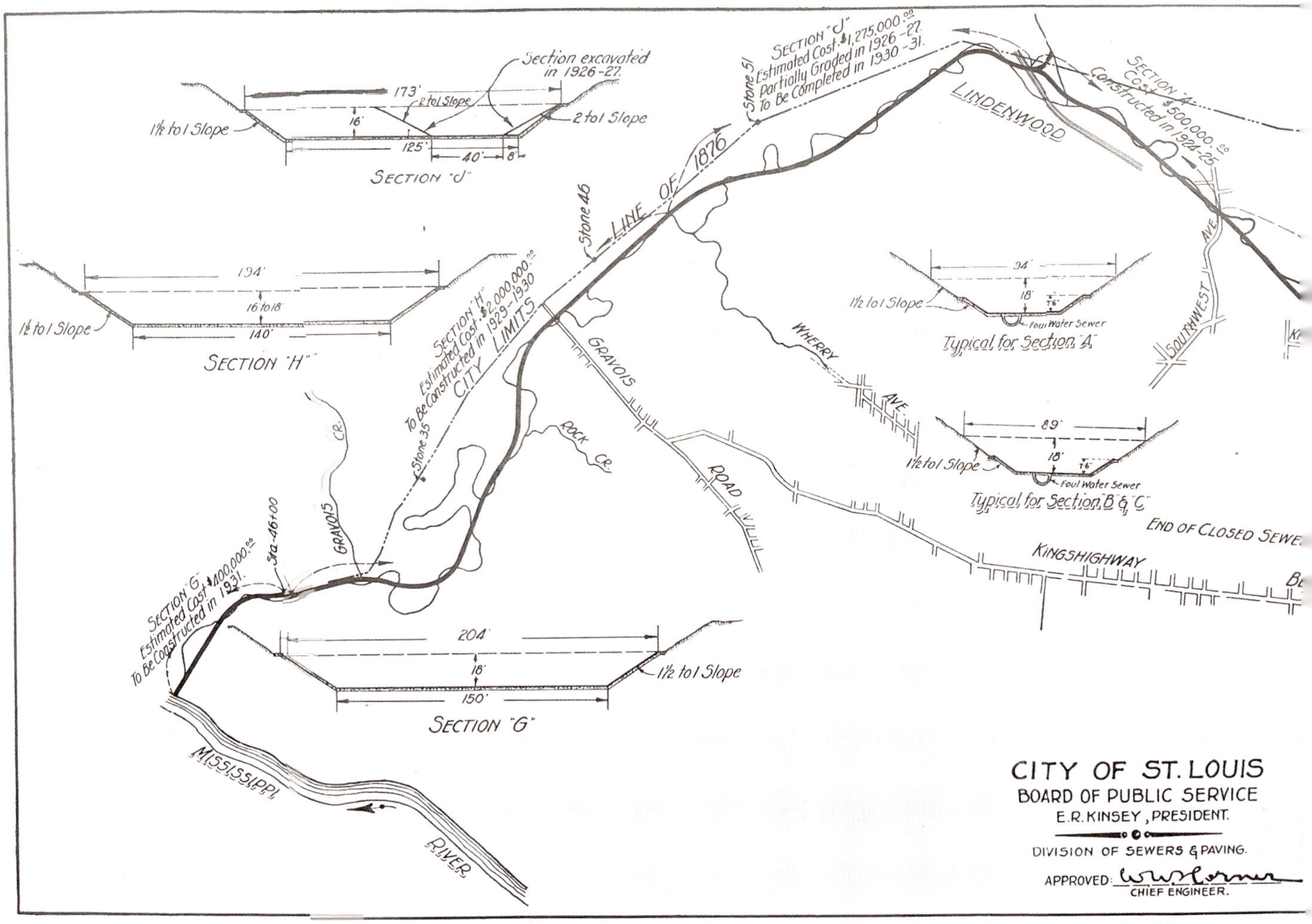

Section excavated in 1926-27.
173'
2 to 1 Slope
1½ to 1 Slope
16'
125'
40'
8'
2 to 1 Slope
SECTION "J"
SECTION "J" Estimated Cost $1,275,000.00 Partially Graded in 1926-27. To Be Completed in 1930-31.
Stone 51
LINDENWOOD
SECTION "A" Cost $500,000.00 Constructed in 1924-25
LINE OF 1876
Stone 46
134'
16 to 18'
140'
1½ to 1 Slope
SECTION "H"
SECTION "H" Estimated Cost $2,000,000.00 To Be Constructed in 1929-1930
CITY LIMITS
Stone 35
GRAVOIS
94'
18'
1½ to 1 Slope
Foul Water Sewer
Typical for Section "A"
SOUTHWEST AVE.
WHERRY AVE.
ROCK CR.
ROAD
89'
18'
1½ to 1 Slope
Foul Water Sewer
Typical for Section "B" & "C"
END OF CLOSED SEWER
KINGSHIGHWAY
Sta. 46+00
GRAVOIS CR.
SECTION "G" Estimated Cost $400,000.00 To Be Constructed in 1931.
204'
18'
150'
1½ to 1 Slope
SECTION "G"
MISSISSIPPI RIVER
CITY OF ST. LOUIS
BOARD OF PUBLIC SERVICE
E.R. KINSEY, PRESIDENT.
DIVISION OF SEWERS & PAVING.
APPROVED: W.W. Horner
CHIEF ENGINEER.

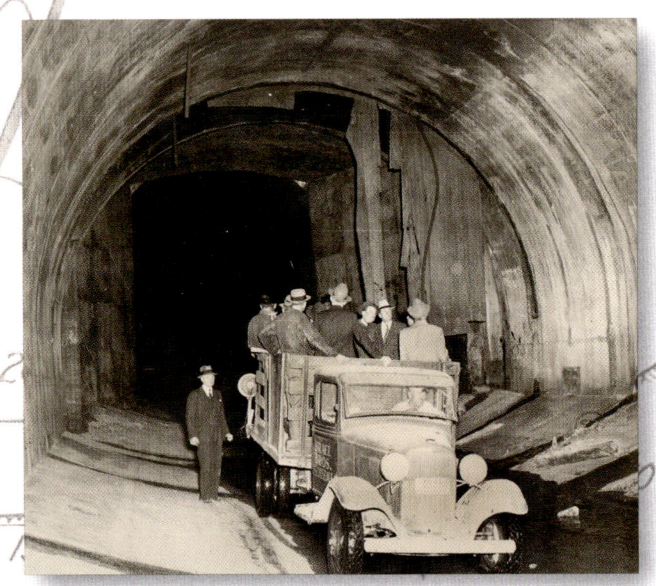

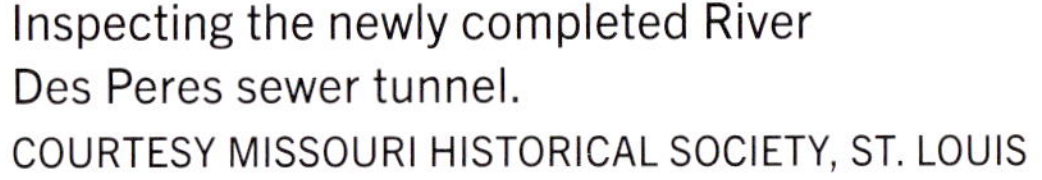

Inspecting the newly completed River Des Peres sewer tunnel.
COURTESY MISSOURI HISTORICAL SOCIETY, ST. LOUIS

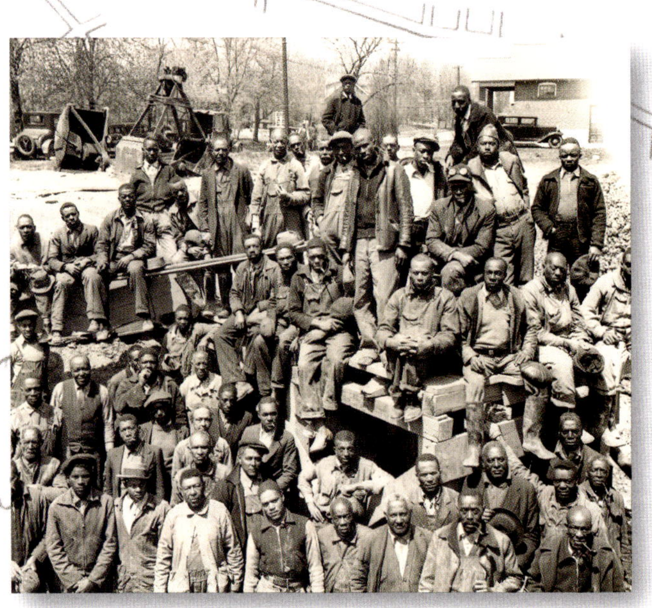

African-American workers on the River Des Peres sewer project.
COURTESY MISSOURI HISTORICAL SOCIETY, ST. LOUIS

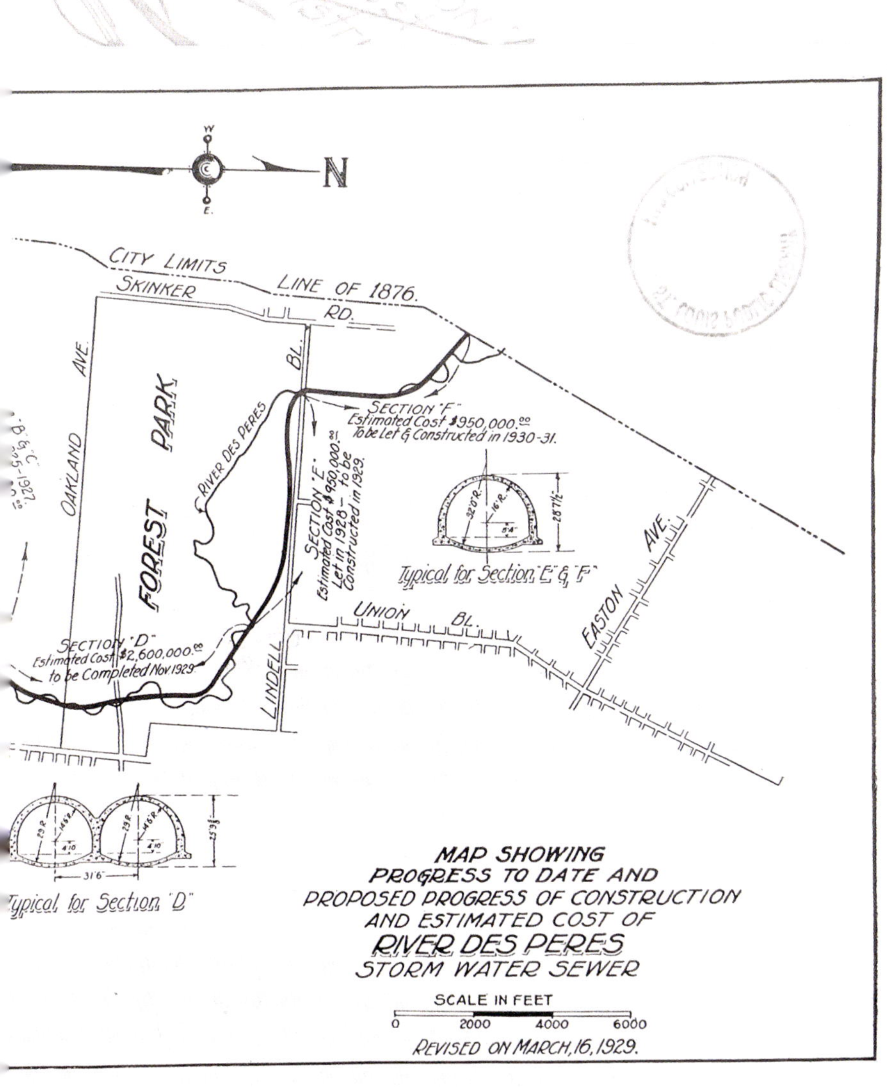

Excavating trench for section D, south of Union Blvd in Forest Park.
COURTESY MISSOURI HISTORICAL SOCIETY, ST. LOUIS

1929

River des Peres

Map Showing Progress to Date and Proposed Progress of Construction and Estimated Cost of River des Peres Storm Water Sewer

City of St. Louis, Board of Public Service, Division of Sewers and Paving *(publisher/printer)*

Lithograph

17 × 8 inches

St. Louis Public Library

1929

THE MISSISSIPPI RIVER fostered the economy and growth of St. Louis. The great river itself was sustained through numerous tributaries, both large and small. One of the smaller of these tributaries is the River des Peres, which originally meandered from what is now Overland in St. Louis County through the northern and eastern sections of Forest Park before heading south and emptying into the Mississippi River at the southern edge of Carondelet. The name River des Peres, or River of the Fathers, comes from a short-lived Jesuit mission built in 1700 at its confluence with the Mississippi.

Describing the river as "a romantic little stream," Forest Park's designer and superintendent Maximillian Kern transformed its floodplains and lagoons into a series of interconnected lakes. All the lakes in Forest Park are artificial, created with water from the River des Peres. At the time, the river's waters were described as crystal-clear where sport fish jumped.

Unfortunately, these transformations were impacted by the flow of the sewer system into the river—resulting in a fetid swamp rather than clear lakes. The *St. Louis Post-Dispatch* reported in 1894 that it was "practically nothing less than a monster open sewer, poisoning the air with the most dangerous corruption and menace to health known, the corruption of sewage." The problem became worse after extensive flooding in 1892 and 1897.

When Forest Park was chosen as the site of the 1904 World's Fair, the river was considered so unhealthy and unattractive that major action was necessary. The meandering course of River des Peres can clearly be seen on the *1904 maps*, which illustrate that the river was buried at great expense under the fairgrounds in the western half of the park. This was a temporary fix.

In 1915, a tropical storm dropped nearly 11 inches of rain on St. Louis in just 17 hours, causing devastating flooding. Claiming 11 lives and the homes of 1,000 families, the flood focused public and government attention onto the problems of the river.

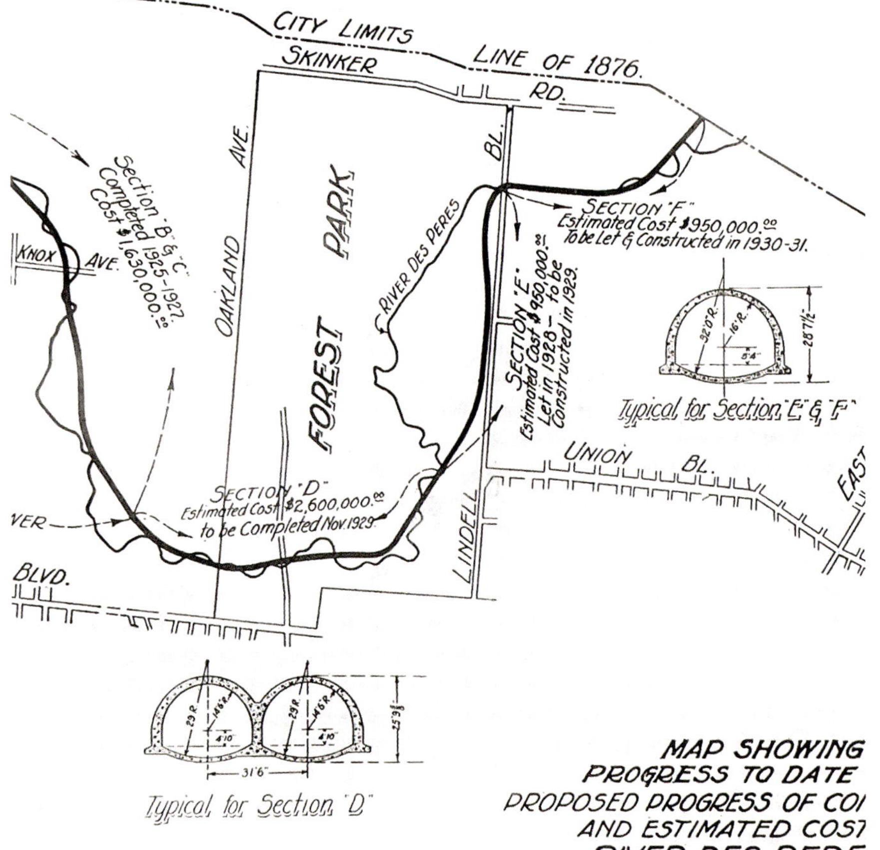

The heavy black line indicates the path of the new River des Peres sewer as it travels from its source northwest of the City through Forest Park. The work required constraining the winding path of the river into the straighter line of a new concrete sewer. The concrete sewer tunnels are enormous, measuring nearly 30 feet high. The construction of sewer sections "D" and "E" through the park cost $3.5 million, and the project was completed in 1931.

RIVER DES PERES, 1890

In his landmark two-volume history of St. Louis, Thomas Scharf described the River des Peres as "a romantic little stream," and this atmospheric photo from 1890 certainly paints that picture. However, as more residents moved to this area of the City, their sewage followed, turning the stream into a sewer.

COURTESY MISSOURI HISTORICAL SOCIETY, ST. LOUIS

A 1923 bond issue was introduced to fix those problems. In advance of the vote to approve the bonds, a billboard in the park was erected with the message, "Think this over. What other big city would have an open sewer running through a fine big park?" It worked, and the bond issue passed 3-1.

This map from 1929 illustrates the progress and scope of work on the River des Peres since the passing of the bond issue. The plan placed the River des Peres sewer underground from the northern boundary of the City to just south of Forest Park. From that point, an open, concrete-lined drainage continues south and east to the Mississippi River. This open section is what is most commonly referred to as River des Peres today. The green space around this open section is a city park and has been designated as River des Peres Greenway, part of the larger Great Rivers Greenway system.

RIVER DES PERES SEWER PROJECT, 1929

The photo shows part of section "E" looking east toward the Jefferson Memorial Building (the Missouri History Museum) after completion of the concrete tunnel, but before backfilling. The American Society of Civil Engineers has designated the 13-mile River des Peres sewage and drainage project as a National Historic Civil Engineering Landmark for "the calculations involved, the large-scale trench dewatering methods, and the soil stabilization procedures."

COURTESY MISSOURI HISTORICAL SOCIETY, ST. LOUIS

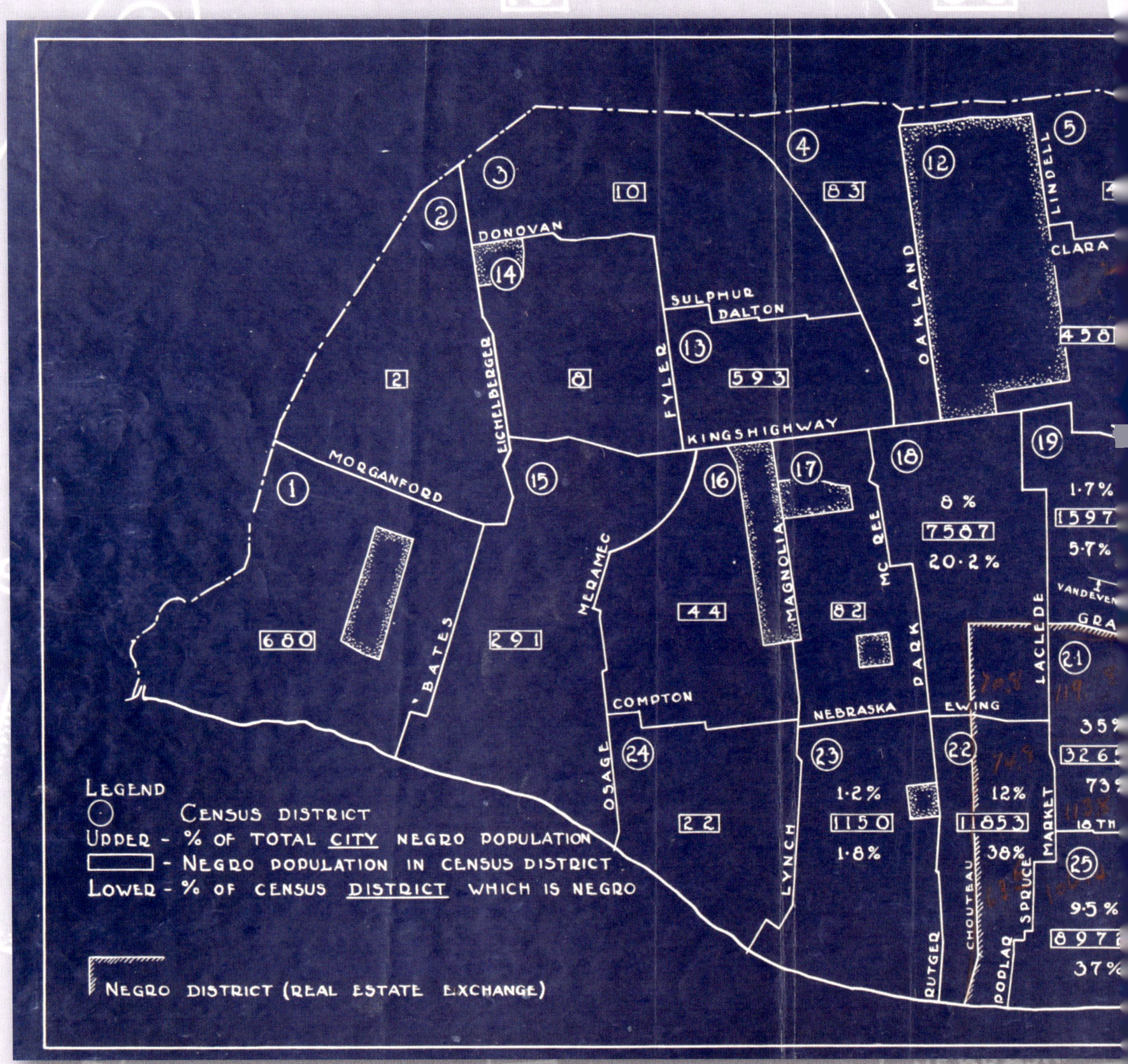

LEGEND
◯ CENSUS DISTRICT
UPPER - % OF TOTAL CITY NEGRO POPULATION
▭ - NEGRO POPULATION IN CENSUS DISTRICT
LOWER - % OF CENSUS DISTRICT WHICH IS NEGRO

NEGRO DISTRICT (REAL ESTATE EXCHANGE)

Census workers tabulating data.
COURTESY LIBRARY OF CONGRESS

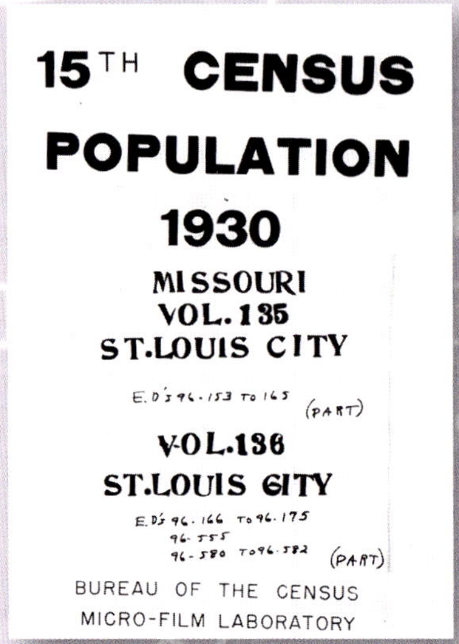

15TH CENSUS
POPULATION
1930
MISSOURI
VOL. 135
ST.LOUIS CITY
E.D's 96-153 TO 163 (PART)
VOL. 136
ST.LOUIS CITY
E.D's 96-166 TO 96-175
96-555
96-580 TO 96-582 (PART)
BUREAU OF THE CENSUS
MICRO-FILM LABORATORY

Blank to Be Filled Out to Help Complete Census

Chamber of Commerce, 511 Locust St., St. Louis, Mo.:

The following persons have not been enumerated in the census:

No.	NAME	No. Persons in Family	Street Address	St. Louis City or County	Ward
1.					
2.					
3.					
4.					
5.					
6.					

THE Chamber of Commerce, in order to obtain an accurate census and insure St. Louis its just rank among the cities, is asking all persons in St. Louis and St. Louis County who were missed by the census enumerators to fill out the above blank and mail it to the chamber. The chamber's supplementary enumeration is in no sense a reflection on the accuracy of the Census Bureau's count, but there are doubtless persons who were not at home when the enumerator called, or who were missed for other reasons. With sixth place in the standing of cities for population at stake for St. Louis, the chamber desires that everyone shall be counted.

St. Louis Globe-Democrat, May 24, 1930.
COURTESY LIBRARY OF CONGRESS.

1930

U.S. Census in St. Louis

Map of the City of St. Louis, Distribution of Negro Population

City of St. Louis Plan Commission *(publisher/printer)*

Cyanotype

10.75 × 19.75 inches

Missouri Historical Society, St. Louis

1930

IN MANY WAYS the dreams and plans for St. Louis that were promoted by the 1904 World's Fair went unfulfilled. At the start of the First World War in 1914, there were increasing suspicions about, and prejudice against, the large German population in St. Louis. In addition, the effects of the Great Migration changed St. Louis's population dynamics forever. Beginning in 1910, millions of Black Americans left the Jim Crow South for cities like St. Louis. The 1930 census would be one of the first documents to map a changing St. Louis during the Great Depression.

According to the US Constitution, a census of "population, agriculture, irrigation, drainage, distribution, unemployment, and mines to be taken by the director of the census" shall be authorized every 10 years by an act of Congress. In addition to 48 states, the census also counted the population of US territories—Washington, DC, Alaska, Hawaii, and Puerto Rico. The census was scheduled to be completed in just 30 days during the month of April 1930.

Just four months after the 15th Census Act was approved, the US suffered the greatest economic disaster in its history—the stock-market crash of October 1929 and the beginning of the Great Depression. The event greatly increased interest in census data like the rate of unemployment in big cities (in 1930, St. Louis was the seventh-largest city in the US).

On April 1, almost 88,000 enumerators began counting. Enumerators were charged with collecting

DENSITY OF NEGRO POPULATION

A variation of the "negro distribution map," this plan charts the density of the Black population shown in designations of between 1 and 100 Black residents per acre. The largest concentration of 81 to 100 Black residents per acre was in the area called Mill Creek. The Mill Creek neighborhood extended from Union Station (18th Street) on the east, to Grand Avenue on the west, and was bounded on the north by Olive/Lindell Streets, and the south by the railyards. The area was never considered an ideal residential location because the valley accumulated run-off from rain and sewers (see *1855 map*). Nevertheless, the location in the heart of midtown St. Louis was a bustling mix of (low cost and older) residential, commercial, and industrial buildings. Following the Great Migration after World War I, the area thrived as one of the largest African American communities in the US. Mill Creek was bulldozed in a call for urban renewal in the 1950s (see *1969 map*).

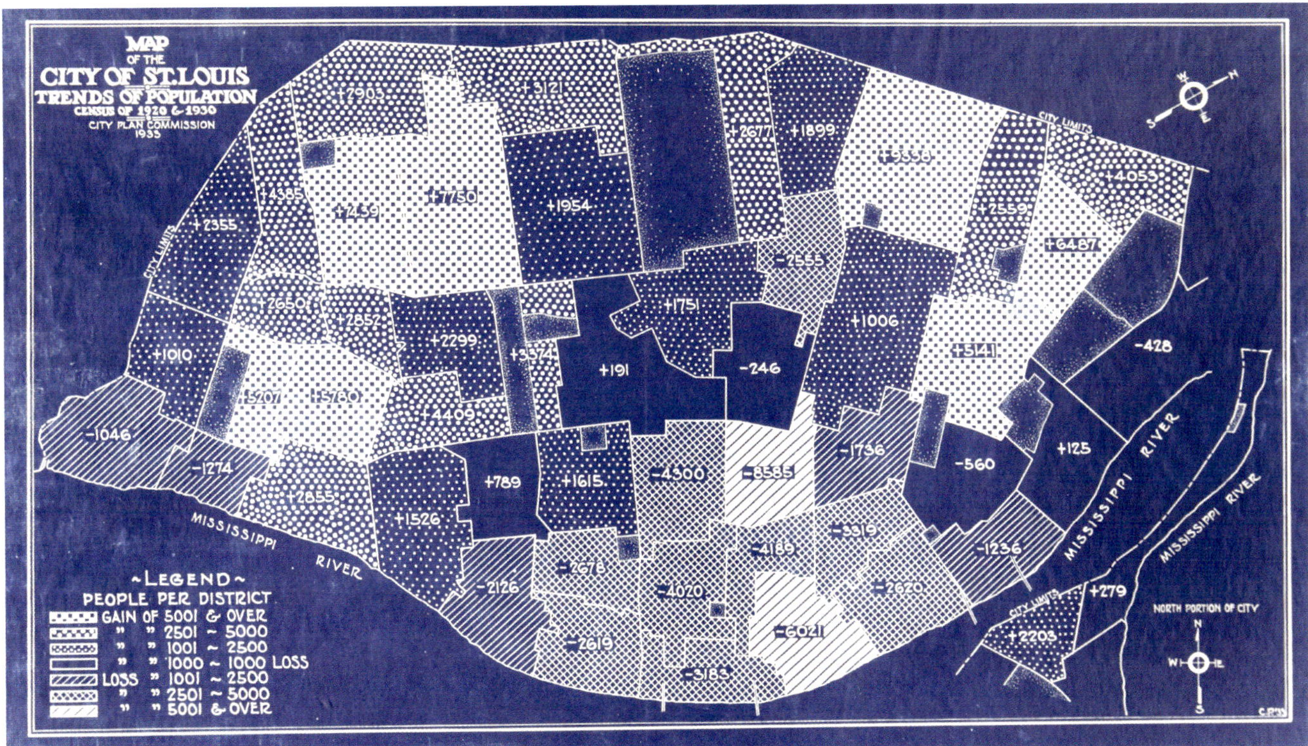

TRENDS OF POPULATION

Areas highlighted with dotted patterns indicate population gains of more than 1,000 people. Areas with lined patterns show population loss of more than 1,000 people. Solid areas show stable populations with very small changes.

The greatest area of loss was in the old central core of the City, and the greatest gains were on the outer edges of St. Louis. The 1930 census counted 821,960 people in St. Louis. According to the 2020 census, the population of the City of St. Louis was 301,578.

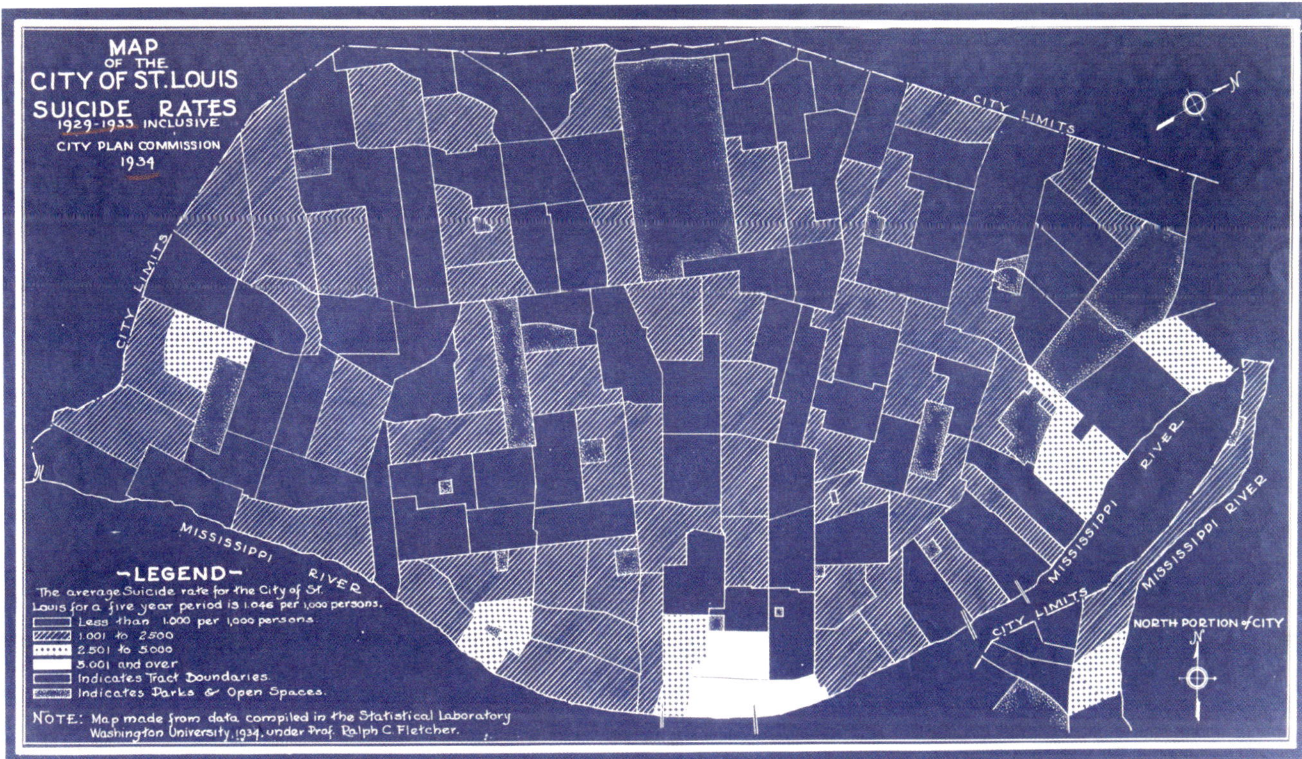

SUICIDE RATES

This map shows the grim statistic of an average of 1.046 suicides in St. Louis per 1,000 people between 1929 and 1933. Downtown had the highest rates of suicide. While death rates were not enumerated as part of the 1930 census, the City Plan Commission created maps in this series from its own dataset.

St. Louis Globe-Democrat.

)RIAL | ST. LOUIS, SUNDAY MORNING, JUNE 22, 1930

What Board in Year

ative Sales Agen- General Aid in Help Them- in Efforts.

sident Hoover signed the he farm relief law is of- r the signing of the law

NEW CENSUS FIGURES WHICH REVEAL SHIFT FROM FARM TO CITY

Striking Social and Economic Problem Seen as Presented by the Unabated Movement from the Country to Urban Centers.

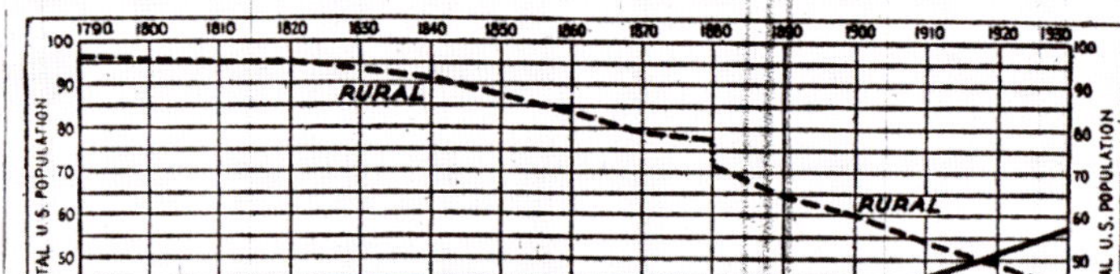

Survey Liquor Exam

Royal Commission Body of Eviden There as Result for America by

By Arrangement with the New Y

ONTO the battlefield been dropped a b Wickersham, chair

St. Louis Globe-Democrat, May 24, 1930.
COURTESY LIBRARY OF CONGRESS

basic information like address along with name, sex, age, and marital status for every individual living in their assigned area. Other questions included whether a home was rented or owned and what was the monthly rent or the home's value. It was the first census to ask if a house contained a radio, a household feature had not existed 10 years earlier.

The 1930 census also asked the place of birth for every person, along with that of their parents.

APPROXIMATE RENTALS

This map used the data coming directly from census questions about home ownership and expenses. The "high rent" neighborhood in 1930 was the Central West End, while the cheapest rents were in the neighborhoods with the oldest buildings closest to the river.

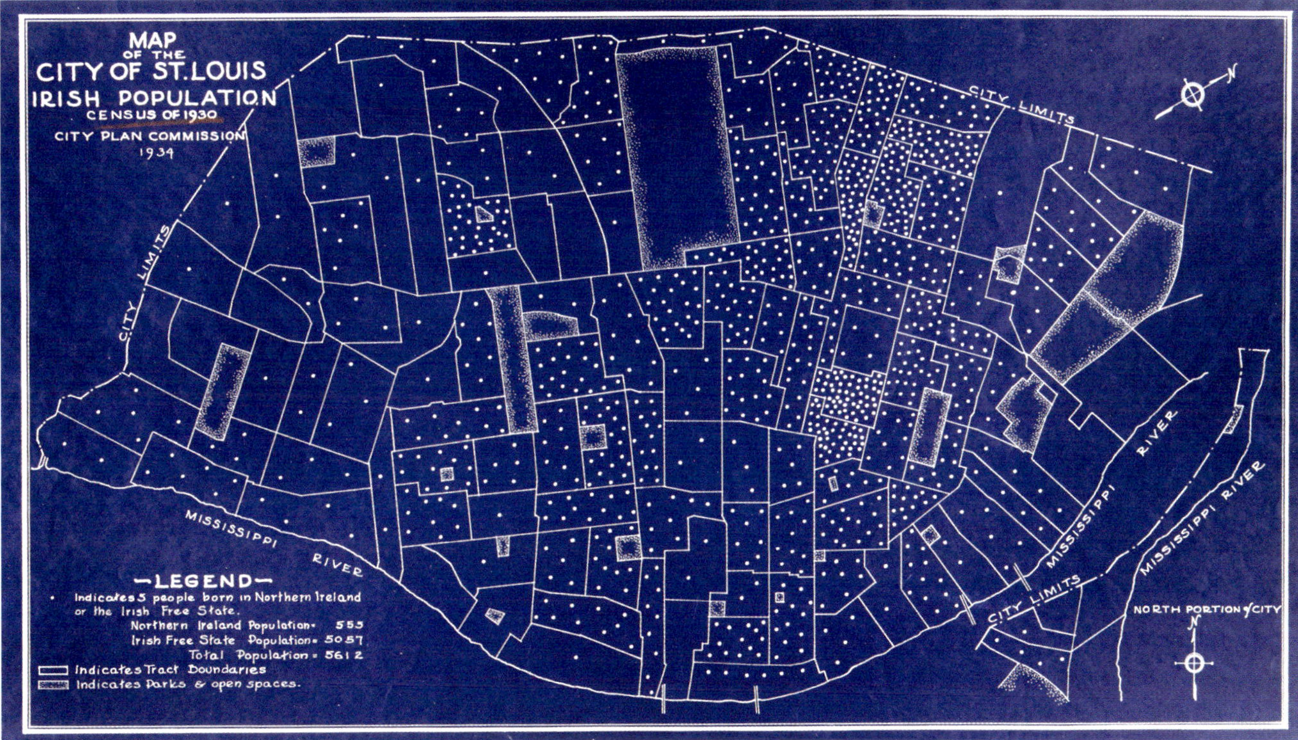

IRISH POPULATION

This map shows 5,612 people born in Ireland and living in St. Louis in 1930. The foreign-born group of maps is the most numerous in this City Plan Commission series. Maps pinpointing the locations of foreign-born people living in St. Louis included the nations of Canada, Poland, Italy, Germany, Greece, Austria, Russia, Lithuania, France, Spain, Switzerland, England, Scotland, Wales, Syria, Czechoslovakia, Hungary, Romania, Yugoslavia, Denmark, Norway, Sweden, and the Netherlands.

If a person was foreign born, they were asked the language spoken at home before coming to the US, the year of immigration, and whether they were a naturalized citizen. This census ultimately cost $40 million ($744 million in 2024) and generated more data than any census up to that date. The census counted 122,775,406 people living in America. There were 821,960 people living in the City of St. Louis and 211,593 in St. Louis County.

After the census numbers were released in 1931, the St. Louis City Plan Commission (see *1907 map*) created a series of maps that plotted different points of census data. The commission also collected its own data, like mortality rates and causes. It used these data to create almost 50 detailed maps. Because St. Louis census data mapping on this scale only occurred once, it is probable that this project was a Depression-era job program for unemployed cartographers, planners, and demographers.

This "Distribution of Negro Population" map records 93,580 Black people living in St. Louis. The map (and most of the others in this series) starkly illustrate the poverty and forced segregation of the City's Black population. Sometimes this map is referred to as a "red line map" because it outlines the "negro district (real estate exchange)."

From the late 19th century until the 1960s, the real estate industry, backed by local laws, created these districts. They were the only areas where Black residents could buy, sell, and inquire about property without "violating City of St. Louis ordinances." These real estate boundaries were outlined on this map with red pencil by an unknown hand.

More than 80 percent of St. Louis's Black population in 1930 lived in the central corridor of the City, split evenly between two designated "negro districts." The first "negro district" is made up of the zones marked 25, 21, and parts of zones 22 and 18. This area was

Map detail showing populations figures for the 1930 census in St. Louis County.
COURTESY MISSOURI HISTORICAL SOCIETY, ST. LOUIS

roughly bounded by the Mississippi River on the east, Chouteau Avenue on the south, Grand Avenue on the west, and Cass Avenue on the north. The second and largest "negro district" comprised only part of zone 11. It was bounded by St. Louis Avenue, Taylor Avenue, Vandeventer Avenue, and Delmar Avenue on the south. This is the genesis of the "Delmar divide"—the area north of Delmar has a population that is 24 percent Black, while the area south of Delmar shows a Black population of just 1.7 percent.

All the maps in this census series are cyanotypes, an economical type of printing that was popular for blueprints. All the maps in this series have large blank areas outlined with dotted patterns, which represent parks and cemeteries, from Calvary and Bellefontaine cemeteries on the north to Carondelet Park on the south.

Yes poster for school tax vote, April 1938.
COURTESY MISSOURI HISTORICAL SOCIETY, ST. LOUIS

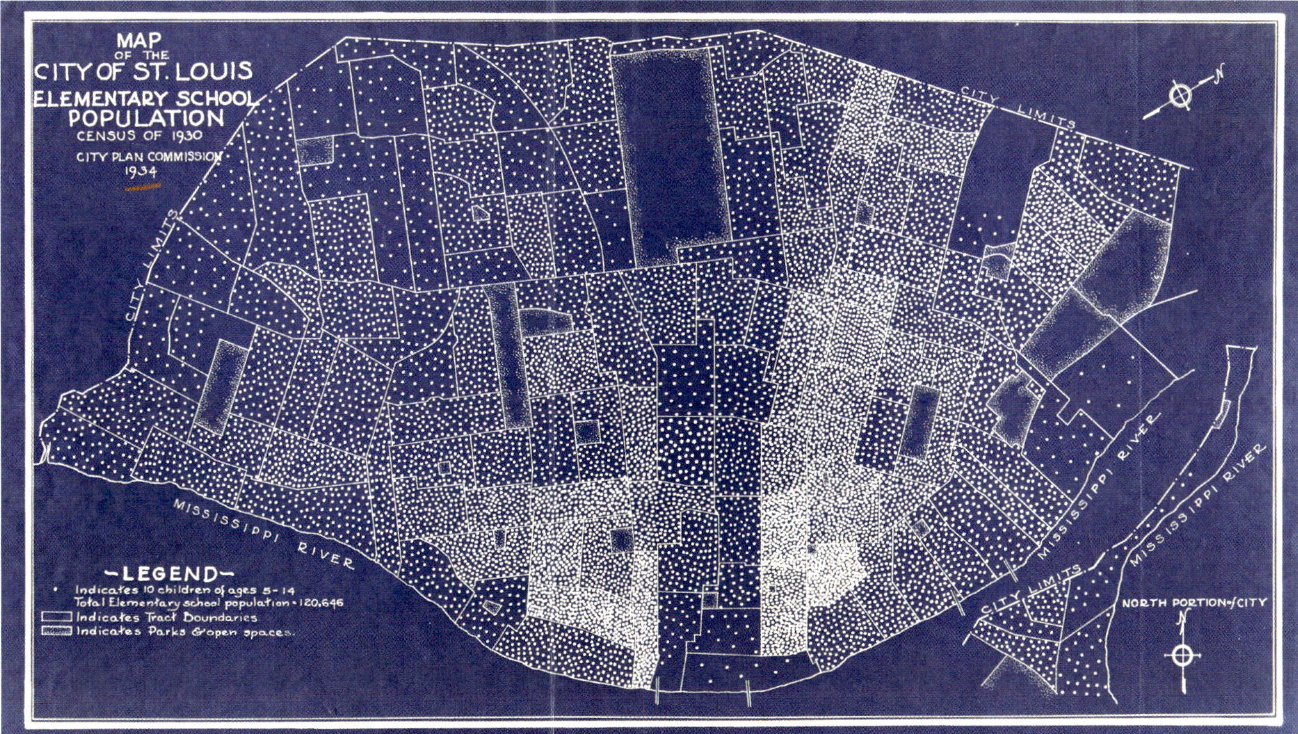

ELEMENTARY SCHOOL POPULATION

The 1930 census recorded 120,646 children between the ages of five and 14 living in St. Louis.

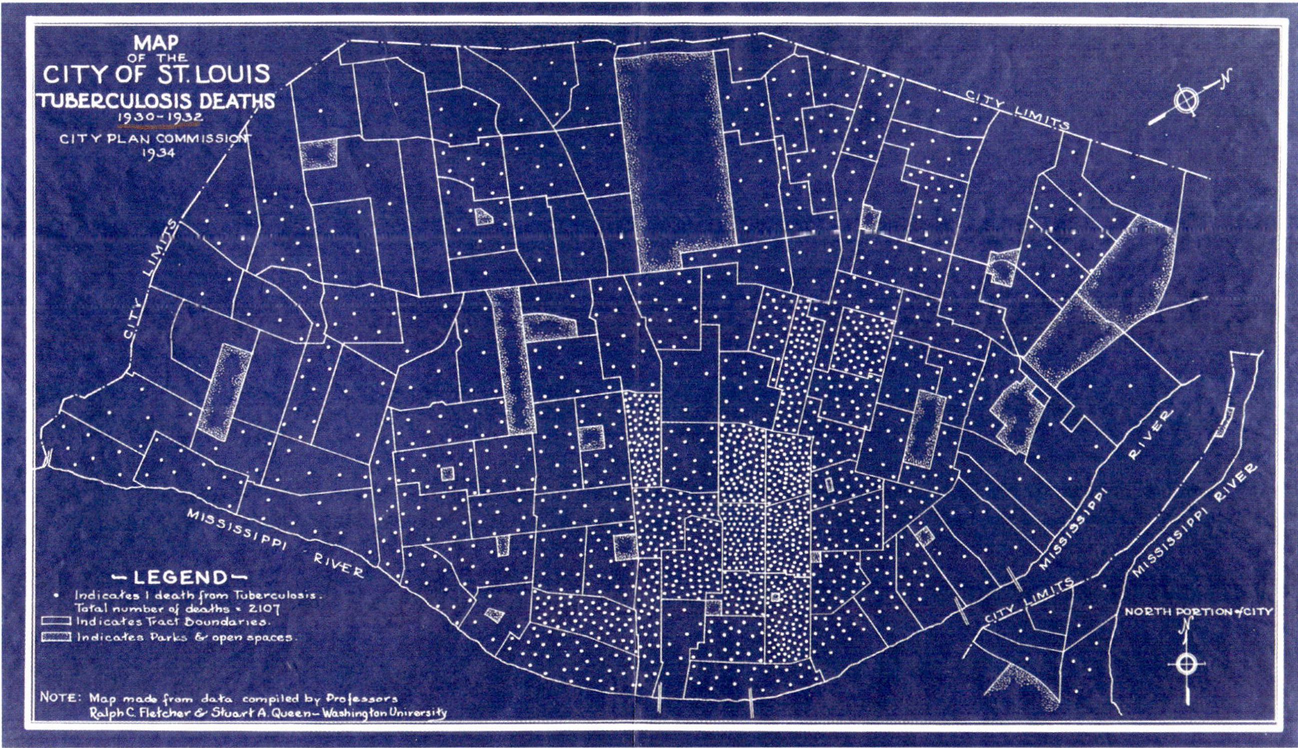

TUBERCULOSIS DEATHS

Rarely diagnosed in the US today, tuberculosis was a major killer in the recent past. This map plots deaths from tuberculosis between 1930 and 1932, when 2,107 tuberculosis deaths occurred. These deaths are clustered in the central corridor and are especially concentrated in the poorest neighborhoods.

THE COMMON SEAL OF THE CITY OF ST. LOUIS
1765
1770
1775
1780
1787
1788 – 1798
1800
1803
1804
St. Ange de Bellerive established St. Louis as the Capital of Upper Louisiana
Mayzo, Piernas assumed authority (Spain)
The building of the Cathedral begun. 1776. War between England and American Colonies
Indian Attack.
The year of the ten boats. Ten barges arrive in company at St. Louis from New Orleans
MANUEL PEREZ Commandant 1788
ZENON TRUDEAU Commandant 1793
CHARLES D. DELASUS Commandant 1798
Louisiana retroceded to France by Spain
Signing of the Treaty.
Lewis and Clark Expedition started from St. Louis up the Missouri.
DESOTO AT THE MISS. RIV.
1541
MARQUETTES VOYAGE
1673
LACLEDE AT ST. LOUIS
1764
1834
1825-26-62
1840
1846
1853
Map of St. Louis showing all major streets, present & to be all parks, cemeteries, hospitals
Fire Dept.
Police Sta.
Public Library
High School
Church
Hospital
Cemetery
Post Office
1932
MAPLEWOOD
RICHMOND HEIGHTS
CLAYTON
FOREST PARK
ART MUSEUM
CARONDELET
MISSISSIPPI RIVER
EAST ST. LOUIS, ILLINOIS.
LACLEDE'S MAP OF SAINT LOUIS 1764
1859
1849
AUGUST CHOUTEAU
1764

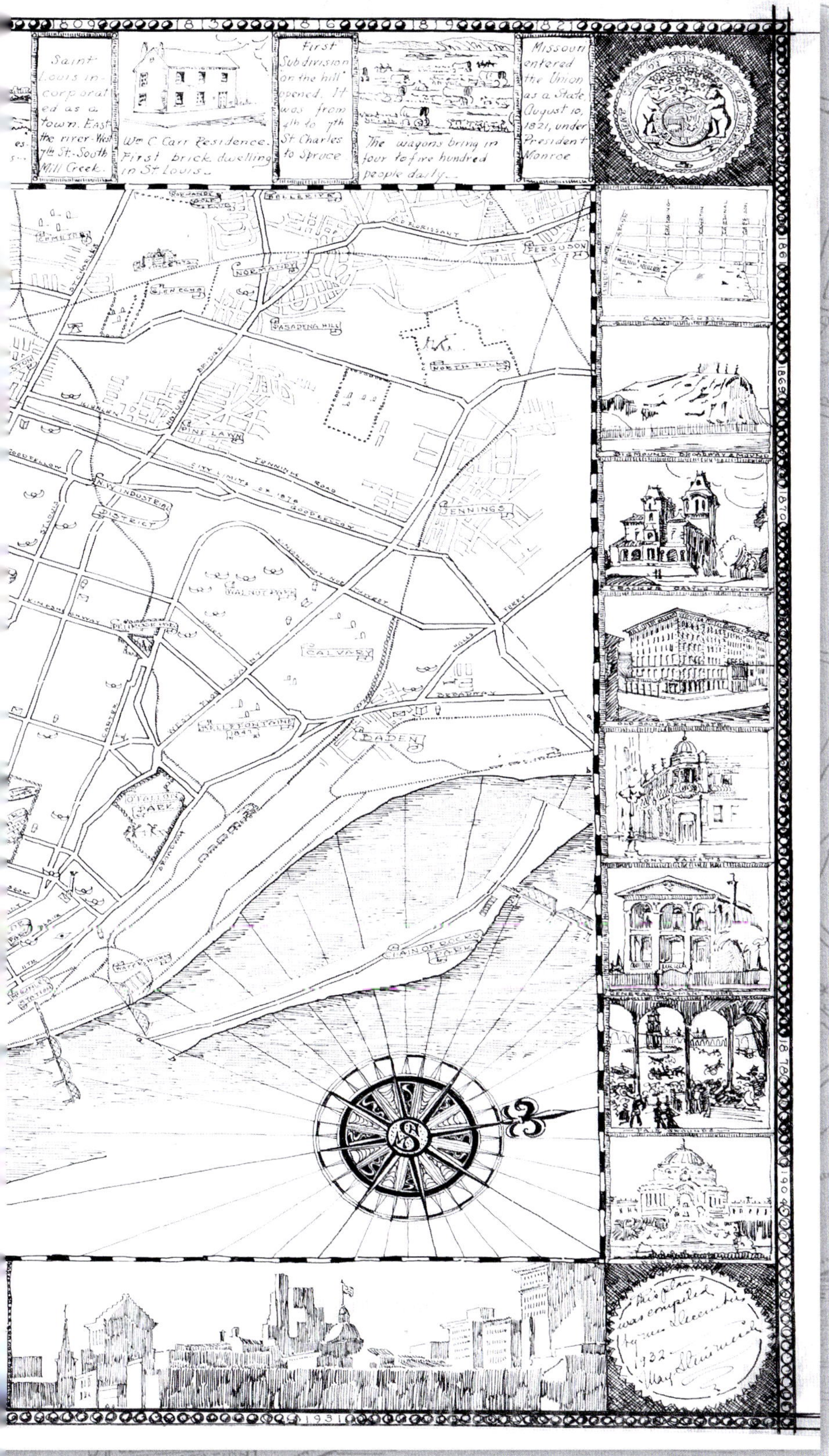

1932

Historical St. Louis

Map of St. Louis, showing all major streets, present & to be, all parks, cemeteries, hospitals

May Steinmesch
(artist/cartographer)

Manuscript, black ink

21.5 × 29.5 inches

Missouri Historical Society, St. Louis

1932

ARCHITECT May Steinmesch drew this pictorial map of St. Louis in 1932, highlighting her hometown's history with an elaborately designed and decorated border.

Henrietta May Steinmesch was born in St. Louis in 1893. In 1915, she earned a bachelor of architecture degree from Washington University as one of the first women to graduate from the program. The architecture program, established in 1902, was a relatively new offering at the university. In her last year of study, she and three classmates founded an organization that would become the Association of Women in Architecture (AWA). The association encouraged contact among women architects at other universities. May Steinmesch also became a

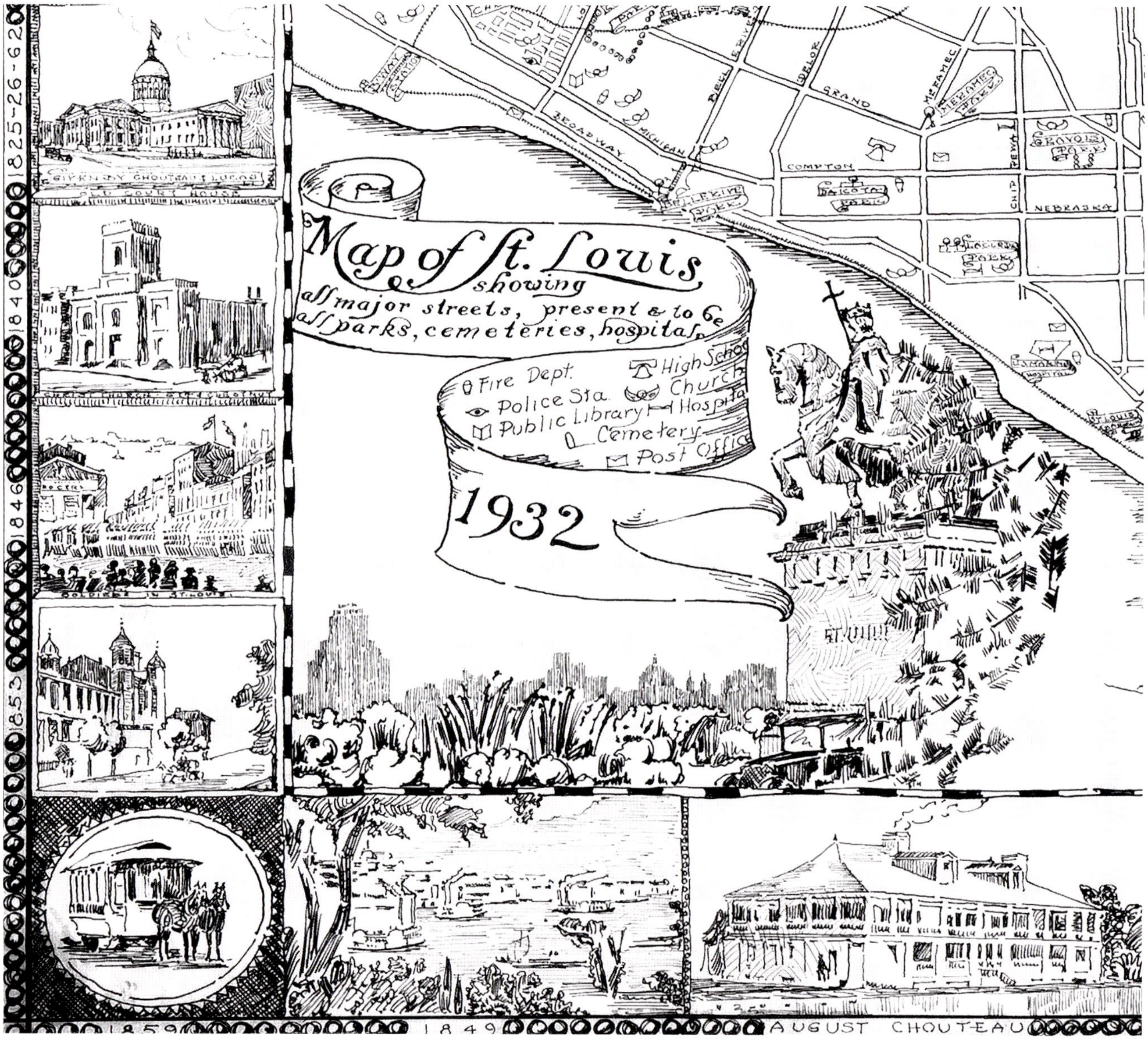

The title block of May Steinmesch's map features a depiction of the statue *Apotheosis of Saint Louis* overlooking the City and Forest Park. The statue was a gift from the Louisiana Purchase Exposition to the City of St. Louis in 1906. For decades it was the principal symbol of St. Louis, later supplanted in part by the Gateway Arch. The lower left corner of the border shows the City's first horse-drawn omnibus. By 1850 there would be 56 omnibuses operated by six companies serving all parts of the City. After a successful 40 years, omnibuses were replaced with trolleys, both electric and cable-driven (see *1915 map*).

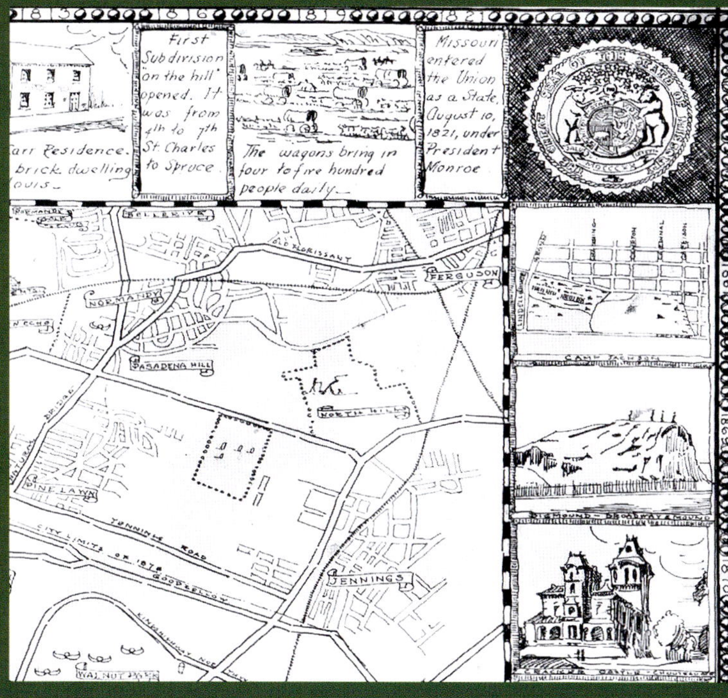

In addition to pictorial scenes, the map's border also features a timeline. The date for each image or event is in very small print that almost disappears into the outer border. These small details speak to Steinmesch's skill at the drafting table. The illustrations shown in this detail are, from top to bottom: the State Seal of Missouri, an 1861 map of Camp Jackson, the 1869 destruction of the Big Indian Mound, a large house called the "Cracker Castle" in 1870, and finally, the Southern Hotel.

respected art teacher at Washington University in the 1930s.

In contrast to most of the maps featured in this book, Steinmesch's pictorial map (also called an illustrated map) depicts St. Louis in an artistic rather than technical style. Pictorial maps are often enhanced with illustrations of buildings, people, and historical events. Steinmesch drew a very accurate representation of the City's layout, even though she added cartoon-like vignettes of parks, bridges, and important buildings.

The map accurately shows the major streets and rail lines, along with all the fire stations, high schools, police stations, churches, public libraries, hospitals, cemeteries, and post offices. They are pinpointed with special symbols as designated by the key in the title block.

MAY STEINMESCH
(1893–1979)

The map's border is filled with 31 precisely drawn buildings or events. All the imagery was copied from well-known prints or photographs. The border also features two historical St. Louis maps. The large map at the bottom center marked as "Laclede's Map of St. Louis—1764" is the same as the *1780 map*, and in the upper right corner is a map of Camp Jackson, as seen on the *1861 map*. The cartouche in the lower right corner of the border bears the inscription, "This plan was compiled by me, December 1932—May Steinmesch"

As a licensed architect, Steinmesch initially worked on projects for the St. Louis City Plan Commission (see the *1930 map*) and the Army Corps of Engineers at Scott Field (today's Scott Air Force Base). During World War II, she moved to San Francisco to work with the United Service Organization designing their West Coast facilities. In 1953, she moved to Pasadena and established her own practice.

H. May Steinmesch was her professional name. Using her first initial may have been an effort to disguise her sex, as women architects were rare and faced widespread discrimination during the years of her career. In 1975, 60 years after she received her degree, Steinmesch noted in an interview, "things haven't changed that much, women are still being discriminated against and the reason has not changed: men don't like knowing that women can do their job."

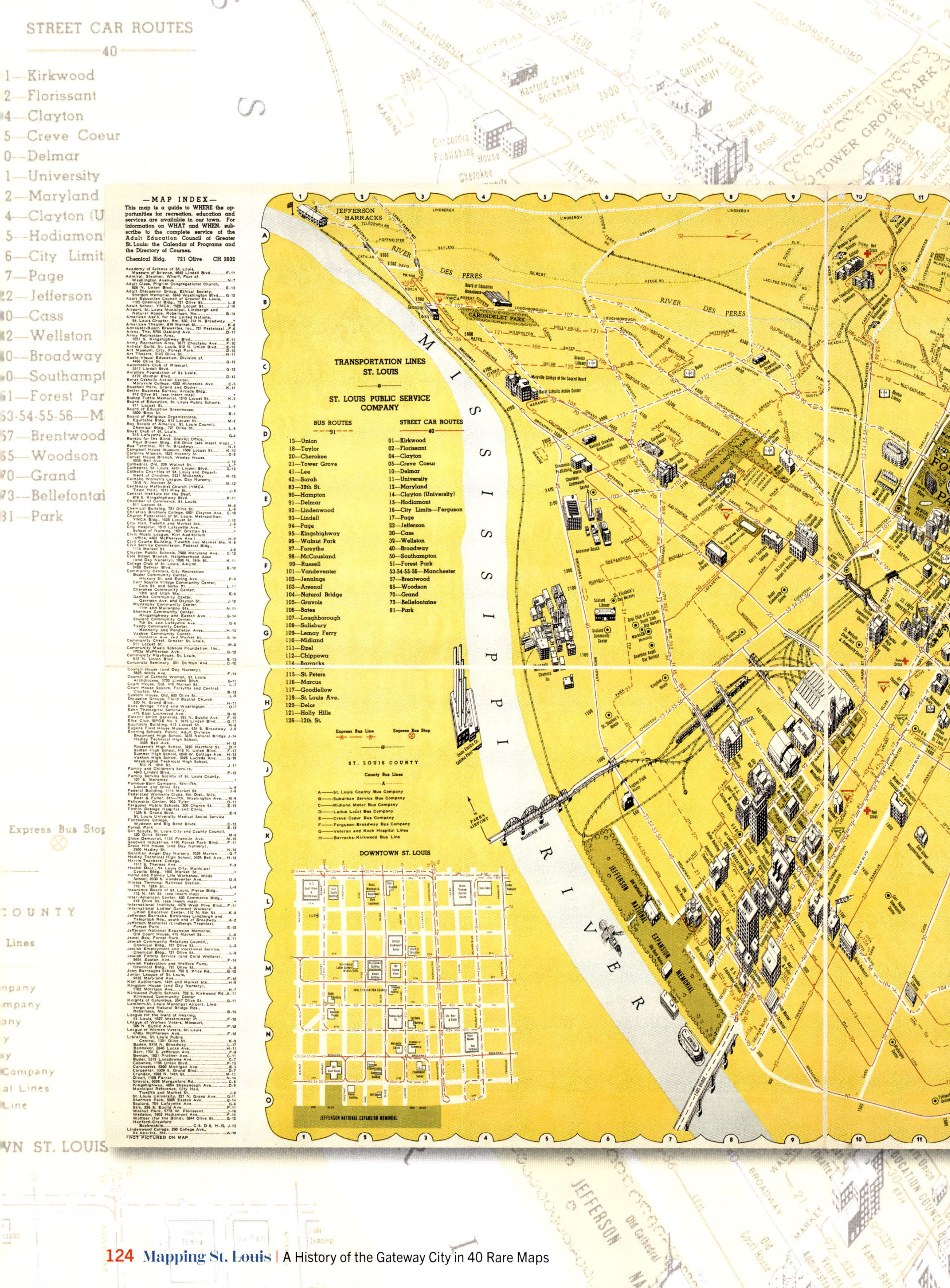

STREET CAR ROUTES
40
1—Kirkwood
2—Florissant
4—Clayton
5—Creve Coeur
0—Delmar
1—University
2—Maryland
4—Clayton (U
5—Hodiamon
6—City Limit
7—Page
2—Jefferson
0—Cass
2—Wellston
0—Broadway
0—Southampt
1—Forest Par
3-54-55-56—M
7—Brentwood
5—Woodson
0—Grand
3—Bellefontai
1—Park
Express Bus Stop
COUNTY
Lines
—MAP INDEX—
This map is a guide to WHERE the opportunities for recreation, education and services are available in our town. For information on WHAT and WHEN, subscribe to the complete service of the Adult Education Council of Greater St. Louis: the Calendar of Programs and the Directory of Courses.
Chemical Bldg. 721 Olive CH 2632
*NOT PICTURED ON MAP
TRANSPORTATION LINES ST. LOUIS
ST. LOUIS PUBLIC SERVICE COMPANY
BUS ROUTES 91
STREET CAR ROUTES 40
13—Union
18—Taylor
20—Cherokee
21—Tower Grove
41—Lee
42—Sarah
83—39th St.
90—Hampton
91—Delmar
92—Lindenwood
93—Lindell
94—Page
95—Kingshighway
96—Walnut Park
97—Forsythe
98—McCausland
99—Russell
101—Vandeventer
102—Jennings
103—Arsenal
104—Natural Bridge
105—Gravois
106—Bates
107—Loughborough
108—Salisbury
109—Lemay Ferry
110—Midland
111—Etzel
112—Chippewa
114—Barracks
115—St. Peters
116—Marcus
117—Goodfellow
119—St. Louis Ave.
120—Delor
121—Holly Hills
126—12th St.
01—Kirkwood
02—Florissant
04—Clayton
05—Creve Coeur
10—Delmar
11—University
12—Maryland
14—Clayton (University)
15—Hodiamont
16—City Limits—Ferguson
17—Page
22—Jefferson
30—Cass
32—Wellston
40—Broadway
50—Southampton
51—Forest Park
53-54-55-56—Manchester
57—Brentwood
65—Woodson
70—Grand
73—Bellefontaine
81—Park
Express Bus Line
Express Bus Stop
ST. LOUIS COUNTY
County Bus Lines
A—St. Louis County Bus Company
B—Suburban Service Bus Company
C—Midland Motor Bus Company
D—Ladue Local Bus Company
E—Creve Coeur Bus Company
F—Ferguson-Broadway Bus Company
G—Veteran and Koch Hospital Lines
H—Barracks-Kirkwood Bus Line
DOWNTOWN ST. LOUIS
JEFFERSON NATIONAL EXPANSION MEMORIAL
JEFFERSON BARRACKS
RIVER DES PERES
CARONDELET PARK
MISSISSIPPI RIVER
TOWER GROVE PARK
JEFFERSON NATIONAL EXPANSION MEMORIAL
MAP INDEX

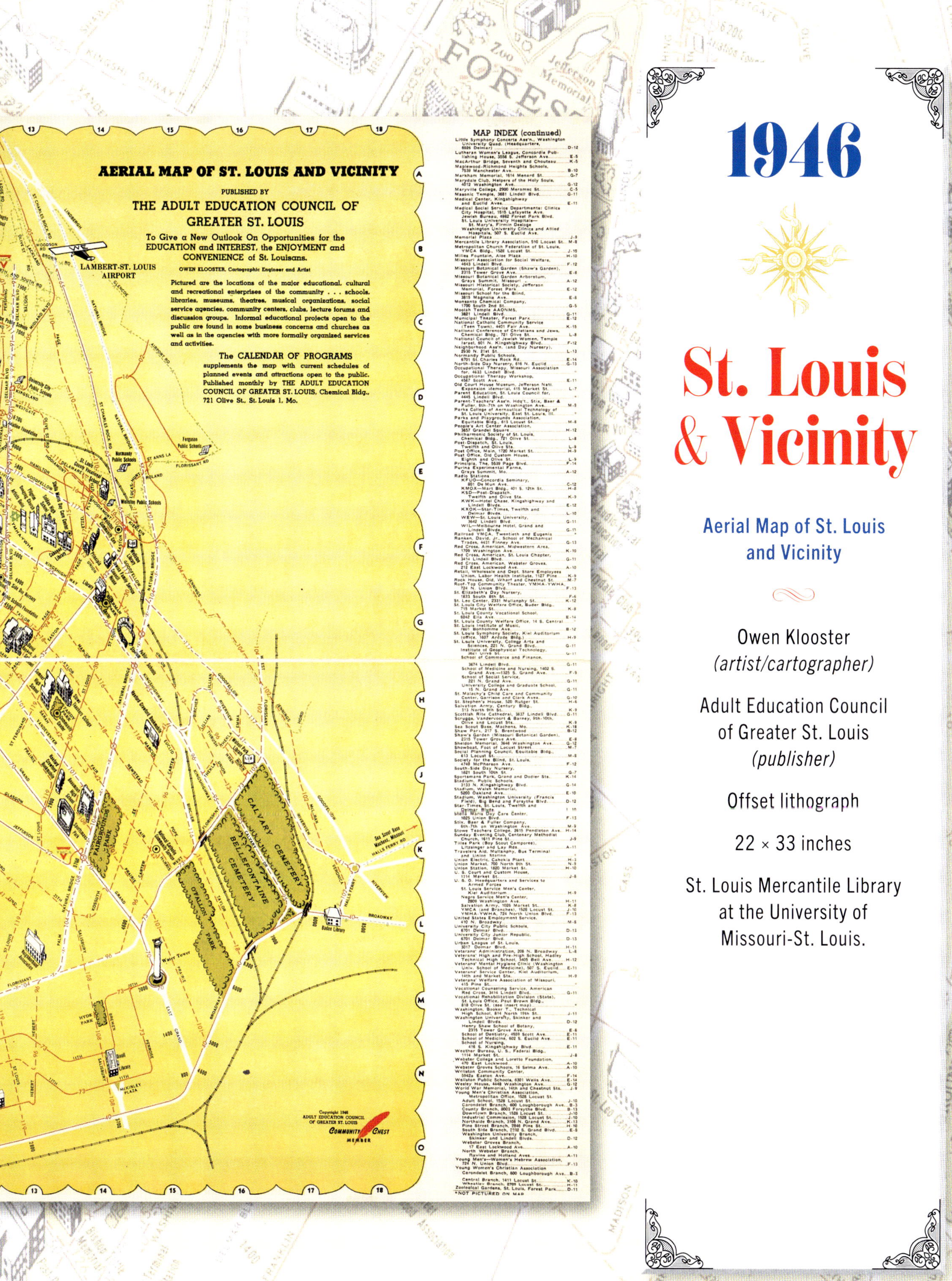

1946

St. Louis & Vicinity

Aerial Map of St. Louis and Vicinity

Owen Klooster
(artist/cartographer)

Adult Education Council of Greater St. Louis
(publisher)

Offset lithograph

22 × 33 inches

St. Louis Mercantile Library at the University of Missouri-St. Louis.

1946

THIS PICTORIAL MAP above shows St. Louis in a rather distorted aerial view. The map was intended as "a guide to where the opportunities for recreation, education and services are available in our town." An emphasis was placed on the breadth of educational institutions in St. Louis, which was the mission of the map's producer, the Adult Education Council. As with the *1915 map* and the *1932 map*, it is not possible to produce a map of St. Louis without adding "the vicinity" to the west.

The Adult Education Council was established in 1937 as a clearinghouse for educational institutions and agencies that offered adult and continuing-education programs in St. Louis. No doubt that following WWII, the Adult Education Council wanted to promote these services to returning servicemen and a postwar generation of St. Louisans.

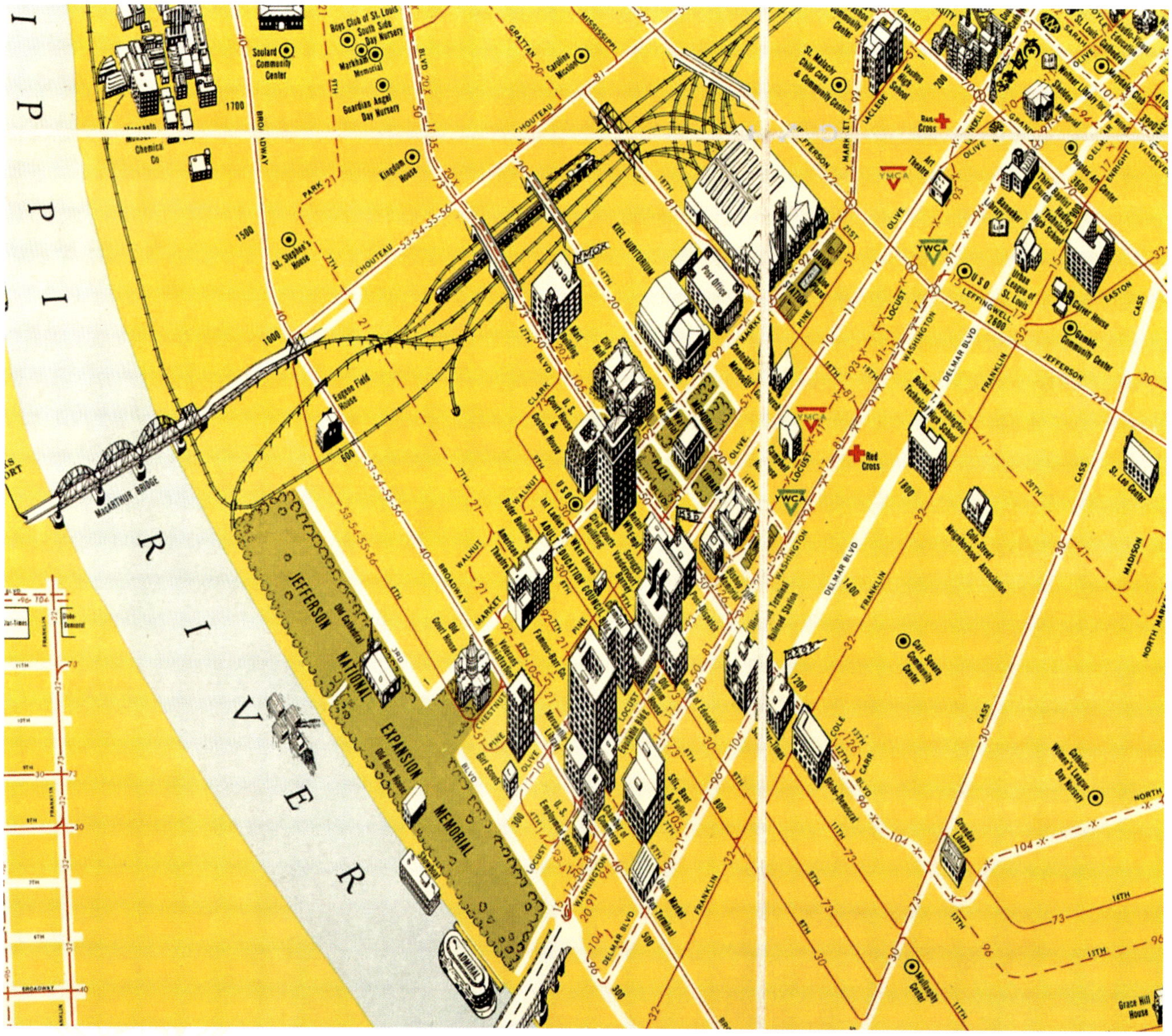

This view of downtown St. Louis highlights in green along the river the new Jefferson National Expansion Memorial. This was the site of the original colonial village as shown in the *1780 map*. It was also the area of destruction in the Great Fire illustrated in the *1849 map*. By the 1930s, this neighborhood was considered to be blighted, and after enlisting the help of the National Park Service, the entire area was cleared of more than 400 buildings. The year after this map was created, the Gateway Arch was selected as the monument for the site. It would not be completed for 20 years.

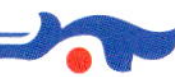

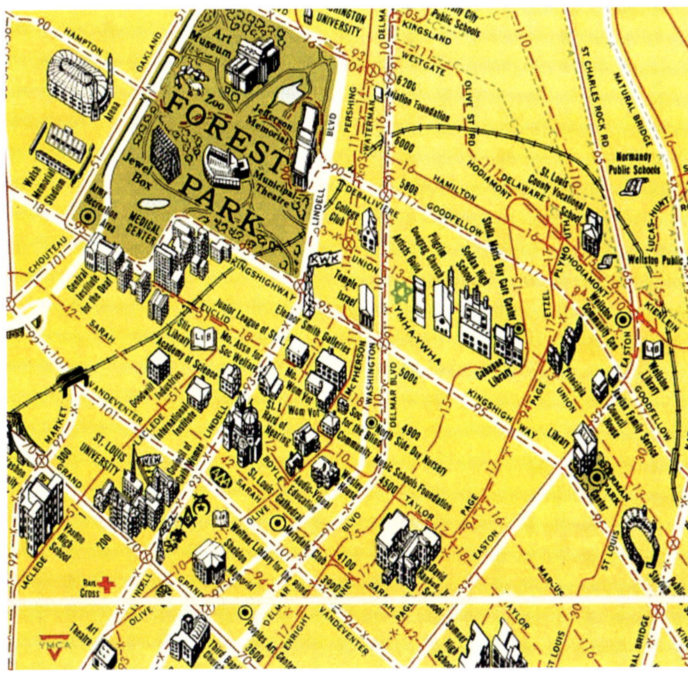

In 1946, the area around Forest Park featured a high concentration and wide variety of schools. Washington and Saint Louis universities have always been at the heart of learning in the City. Four of the City's public high schools—Sumner, Soldan, Vashon, and Hadley Technical—were all within a few miles of each other. Private and specialty schools like Saint Louis University High School, Principia, Central Institute for the Deaf, David Ranken School, the Academy of Science, the International Institute, and Stowe Teachers College, can also be seen in this detail.

Here and There in St. Louis

Stowe Teachers' and Junior College Opened

STOWE TEACHERS COLLEGE

In 1890, Stowe Teachers College was established inside of Sumner High School to provide training for aspiring Black teachers. Just as the public schools were segregated until the 1950s, so were most of the colleges that trained teachers. Stowe later used a vacant elementary school and in 1940 occupied the new purpose-built structure shown here. Located at 2615 Pendleton Avenue in The Ville neighborhood, the building cost $450,000 and its first year enrollment was 354 students. In 1954, Stowe combined with the all-White Harris Teachers College to form what is today known as Harris-Stowe State University. Today Harris-Stowe occupies the old Vashon High School in what was Mill Creek Valley.

COURTESY OF THE AUTHOR

Up until the 1970s, the council published an annual directory of education classes and educational referral services.

Only a small percentage of the City's streets are included on this map. Most St. Louisans in 1946 traveled via public transportation and not by car. There were no interstate highways, so consequently there are more streetcar and bus routes depicted than roads. The St. Louis Public Service Co. operated the 36 bus and 23 streetcar routes in the city. These routes are indicated by the red lines with the numbered routes. The index down each side of the map gives the coordinates for key locations across the City, especially libraries, schools, YMCAs, and YWCAs. And, unique for any St. Louis map, the stops for bookmobiles are indicated.

As an aid in visually identifying locations, dozens of buildings are shown on the map. They are drawn in an architectural format called axonometric projection, which makes them look three-dimensional. The *1875 map* and plates from Compton and Dry's *Pictorial St. Louis* use the same axonometric projection. Among the buildings illustrated is Sportsman's Park. The Cardinals would beat the Boston Red Socks in a seven game series that culminated there on October 15, 1946.

St. Louisan Owen Klooster was the "cartographic engineer and artist" who created this map. His best known work is a series of maps and charts of the "Bible lands."

Just four years after this map was published, the City of St. Louis reached its greatest population at 856,796.

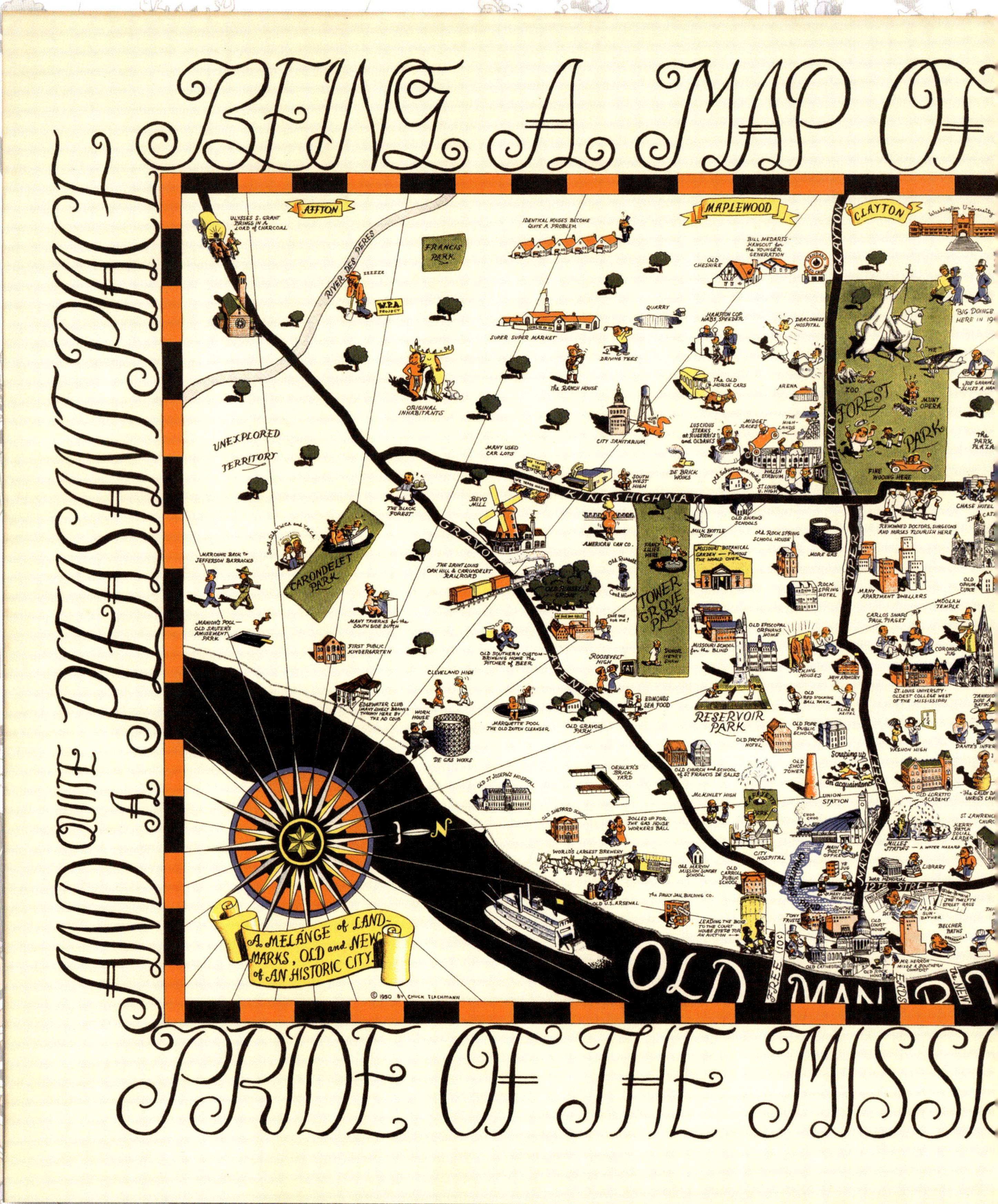

BEING A MAP OF
AND QUITE A PLEASANT PLACE
PRIDE OF THE MISSI
AFFTON
MAPLEWOOD
CLAYTON
FRANCIS PARK
RIVER DES PERES
W.P.A. PROJECT
ULYSSES S. GRANT BRINGS IN A LOAD of CHARCOAL
IDENTICAL HOUSES BECOME QUITE A PROBLEM
SUPER SUPER MARKET
QUARRY
OLD CHESHIRE
HAMPTON COP NABS SPEEDER
DEACONESS HOSPITAL
ORIGINAL INHABITANTS
THE RANCH HOUSE
DRIVING TEES
THE OLD HORSE CARS
ARENA
CITY SANITARIUM
MIDGET RACES
UNEXPLORED TERRITORY
MANY USED CAR LOTS
FOREST PARK
ZOO
MUNY OPERA
FIRE WOOING HERE
KINGSHIGHWAY
GRAVOIS
BEVO MILL
THE BLACK FOREST
CARONDELET PARK
MARCHING BACK TO JEFFERSON BARRACKS
AMERICAN CAN CO.
TOWER GROVE PARK
MISSOURI BOTANICAL GARDEN
MORE GAS
CHASE HOTEL
REKNOWNED DOCTORS, SURGEONS AND NURSES FLOURISH HERE
MANY APARTMENT DWELLERS
MANY TAVERNS for the SOUTH SIDE DUTCH
FIRST PUBLIC KINDERGARTEN
CLEVELAND HIGH
ROOSEVELT HIGH
RESERVOIR PARK
OLD EPISCOPAL ORPHANS HOME
MISSOURI SCHOOL for the BLIND
EDMONDS SEA FOOD
PACKING HOUSES
NEW ARMORY
VASHON HIGH
MARQUETTE POOL
OLD GRAVOIS PARK
DE GAS WORKS
WORK HOUSE
OLD ST. JOSEPH'S HOSPITAL
McKINLEY HIGH
UNION STATION
CITY HOSPITAL
OLD SHEPARD SCHOOL
WORLD'S LARGEST BREWERY
OLD U.S. ARSENAL
LIBRARY
MARKET STREET
12th STREET
N
A MELANGE of LAND-MARKS, OLD and NEW of AN HISTORIC CITY
© 1950 BY CHUCK TLACHMANN
OLD MAN RIV

1950

A Melange of St. Louis Old and New

A Melange of Landmarks, Old and New of an Historic City

Chuck Flachmann
(artist)

Off-set lithograph

11 × 18 inches

Missouri Historical Society, St. Louis

1950

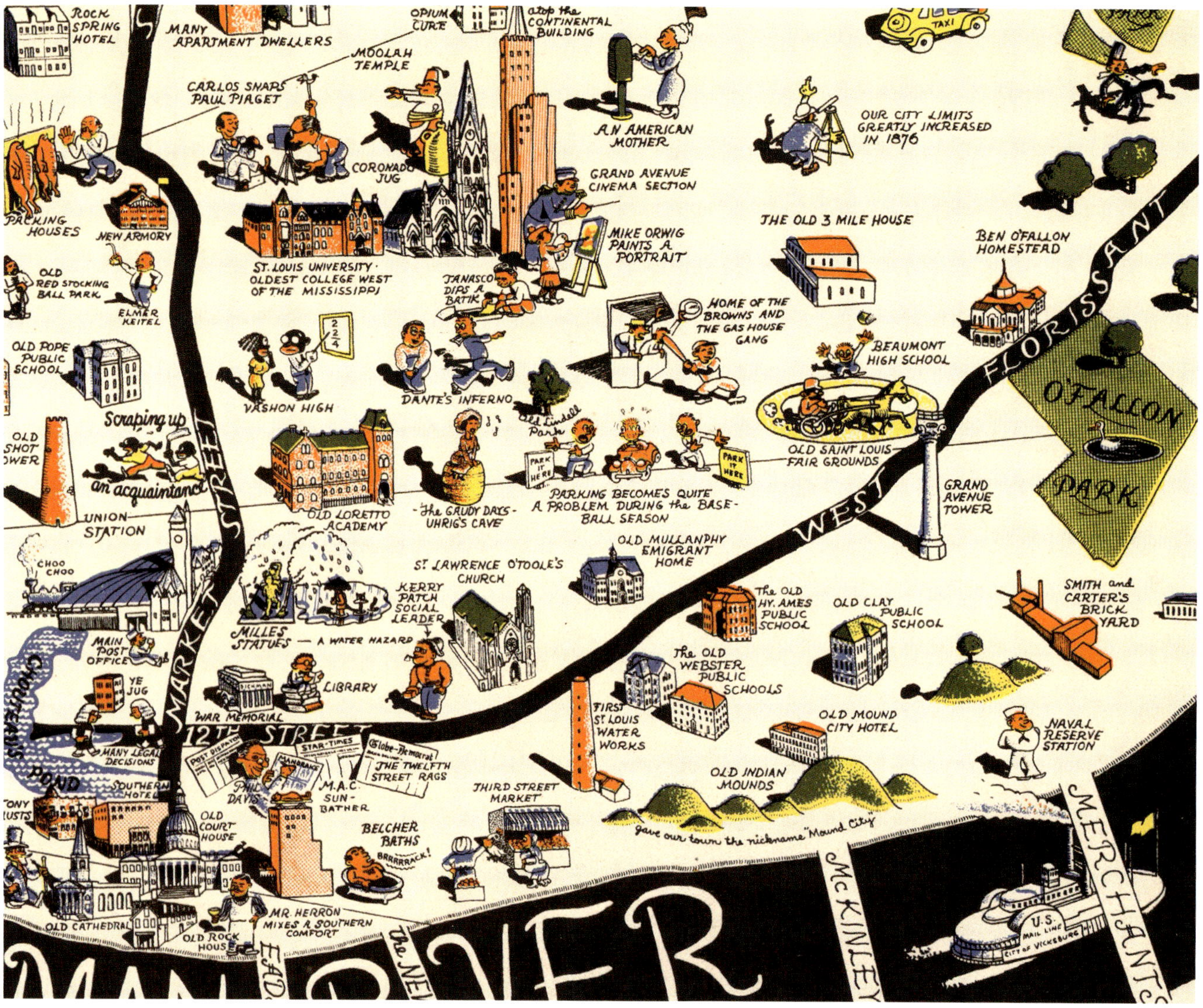

THE INFORMAL and artistic nature of a pictorial map can skillfully impart the local flavor of a place. This map displays many of the colloquialisms of St. Louis in 1950—from its historic charm to a deep-seated racism.

This map boldly announces in elaborate hand-lettered script around the border, "BEING A MAP OF SAINT LOUIS, KNOWN AS THE MOUND CITY, PRIDE OF THE MISSISSIPPI VALLEY AND QUITE A PLEASANT PLACE." However, St. Louis was more pleasant for some than others.

In the summer of 1949, city officials desegregated all city pools and playgrounds. On the opening day of the pool season, the *Post-Dispatch* and *Globe-Democrat* published the desegregation story on the front page.

The only roads shown on this map were the main thoroughfares in 1950—Kingshighway, Gravois, West Florissant, and Market Street, all drawn as heavy black lines. While this is not a map for navigation, the artist has illustrated many St. Louis stories, both historical and contemporary. The Old Indian Mounds had been gone almost a century but are recognized as having "[given] our town the nickname 'Mound City.'" Dante's Inferno in Midtown was one of the first gay bars in St. Louis, and was known for drag shows. It is represented on the map with a homophobic depiction of a man in drag. The map also includes many sexist views of women.

Later that day, about 30 Black children joined the hundreds of White youths swimming at Fairgrounds Park Pool. A group of White citizens (primarily adolescents, but also some adults) surrounded the pool, shouting threats at the Black children. Police

arrived to escort the children safely out of the pool area, but later that evening, the violence escalated. Thousands more Whites arrived, many holding bats and clubs. They chased down Black people they found throughout the Fairgrounds Park neighborhood. Ultimately, it took 12 hours and hundreds of police to quell the violence. At least a dozen people were hospitalized with injuries (10 were Black) and eight people (three White and five Black) were arrested for inciting violence. In an effort to prevent more violence, the mayor immediately reinstituted segregation at all municipal pools. In 1950, all City pools and playgrounds would be permanently desegregated.

This map bears the same racist attitudes that sparked the Fairgrounds Pool race riot. Near the Old Courthouse, a man in a top hat can be seen "leading the boys to the courthouse steps for an auction." The auction is a slave auction. The "boys" are enslaved and depicted chained together with the worst type of racist physical features. There are numerous other sexist and racist scenes on the map, including some of Indigenous peoples.

It is unknown what motivated the artist to create this map, but it could have been born out of a commission. It is also important to note that on June 10, 1950, President Harry S. Truman was in St. Louis to dedicate the ground for the Jefferson National Expansion Memorial, which contemporary advertisements proclaimed was "planned to make our city, more than ever, the pride of the Mississippi Valley." The Gateway Arch had yet to be constructed and does not appear on the map.

An alternate version of this map, also dated 1950, was created for the Anheuser-Busch Brewery. It features the company logo in place of the compass rose, along with the brewery buildings and Clydesdales.

To commemorate St. Louis's bicentennial in 1964, a second, less-colorful edition of this map was released. In this second edition, all the racist depictions of Black St. Louisans were removed and the Gateway Arch, completed on October 28, 1965, was added. A depiction of W. C. Handy was also added and bears the moniker "creates our blues." This was an inequitable representation for a city where 30 percent of the population was Black at the time.

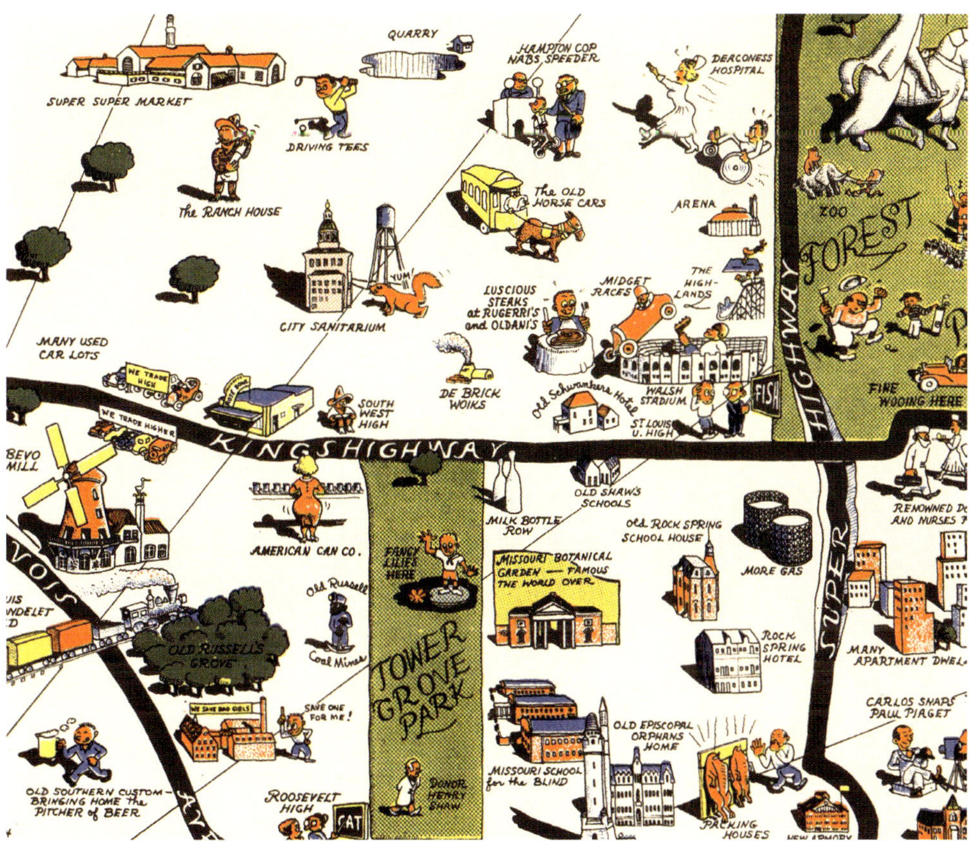

This map is mostly about St. Louis people: a man enjoys "luscious steaks at Rugerri's and Oldani's" on the Hill. South of Gravois, a man practices the "old southern custom of bringing home the pitcher of beer." And nearby, a "Hampton cop nabs a speeder," which is just a young boy on a scooter.

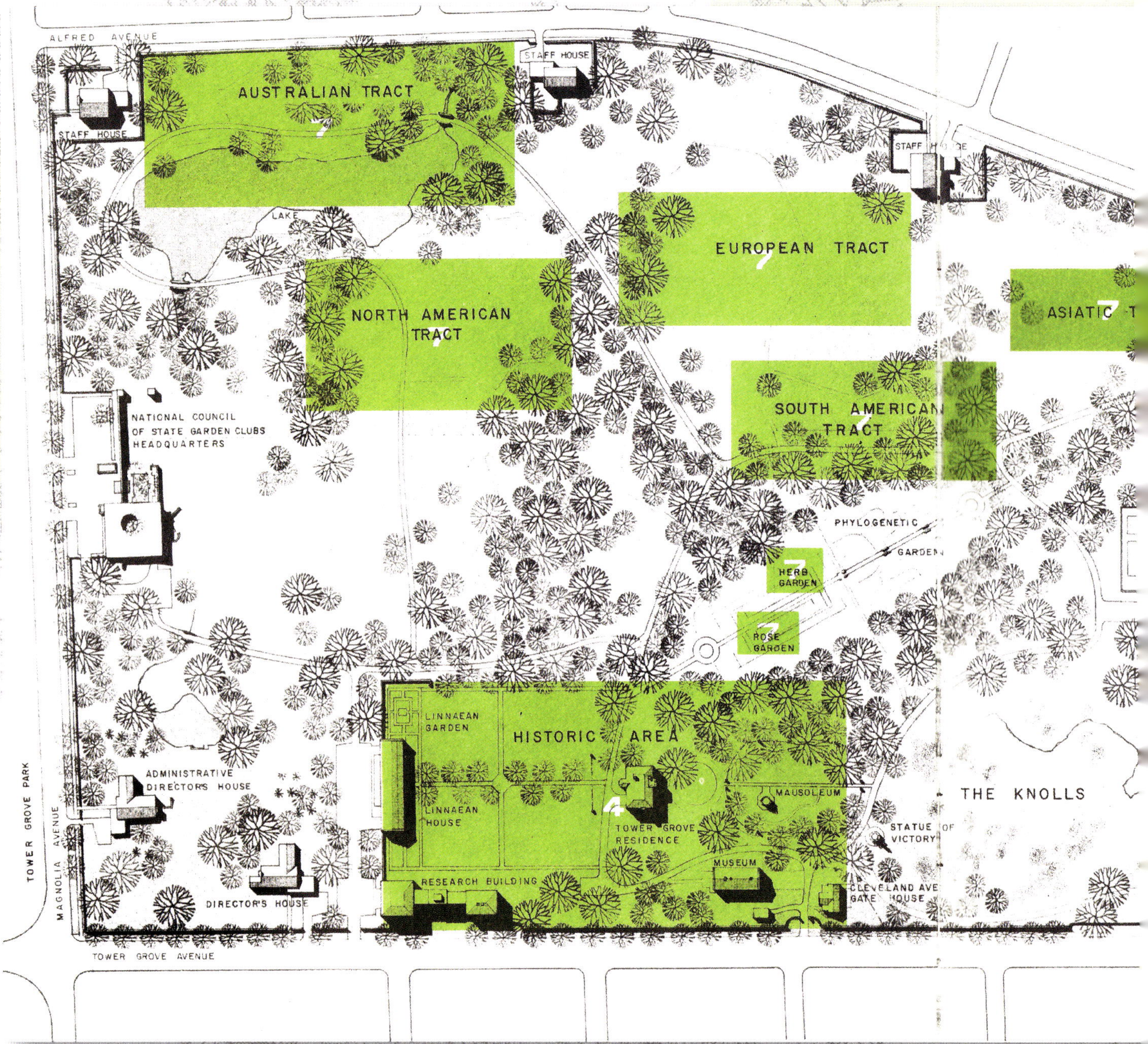

ALFRED AVENUE
STAFF HOUSE
AUSTRALIAN TRACT
STAFF HOUSE
STAFF HOUSE
LAKE
EUROPEAN TRACT
NORTH AMERICAN TRACT
ASIATIC T
SOUTH AMERICAN TRACT
NATIONAL COUNCIL OF STATE GARDEN CLUBS HEADQUARTERS
PHYLOGENETIC GARDEN
HERB GARDEN
ROSE GARDEN
LINNAEAN GARDEN
HISTORIC AREA
THE KNOLLS
ADMINISTRATIVE DIRECTOR'S HOUSE
LINNAEAN HOUSE
MAUSOLEUM
TOWER GROVE RESIDENCE
STATUE OF VICTORY
TOWER GROVE PARK
MAGNOLIA AVENUE
MUSEUM
RESEARCH BUILDING
CLEVELAND AVE GATE HOUSE
DIRECTOR'S HOUSE
TOWER GROVE AVENUE

Shaw's original entrance gate on Tower Grove Avenue.
COURTESY LIBRARY OF CONGRESS

Missouri Botanical Garden Centennial Souvenir, 1959.
COLLECTION OF THE AUTHOR

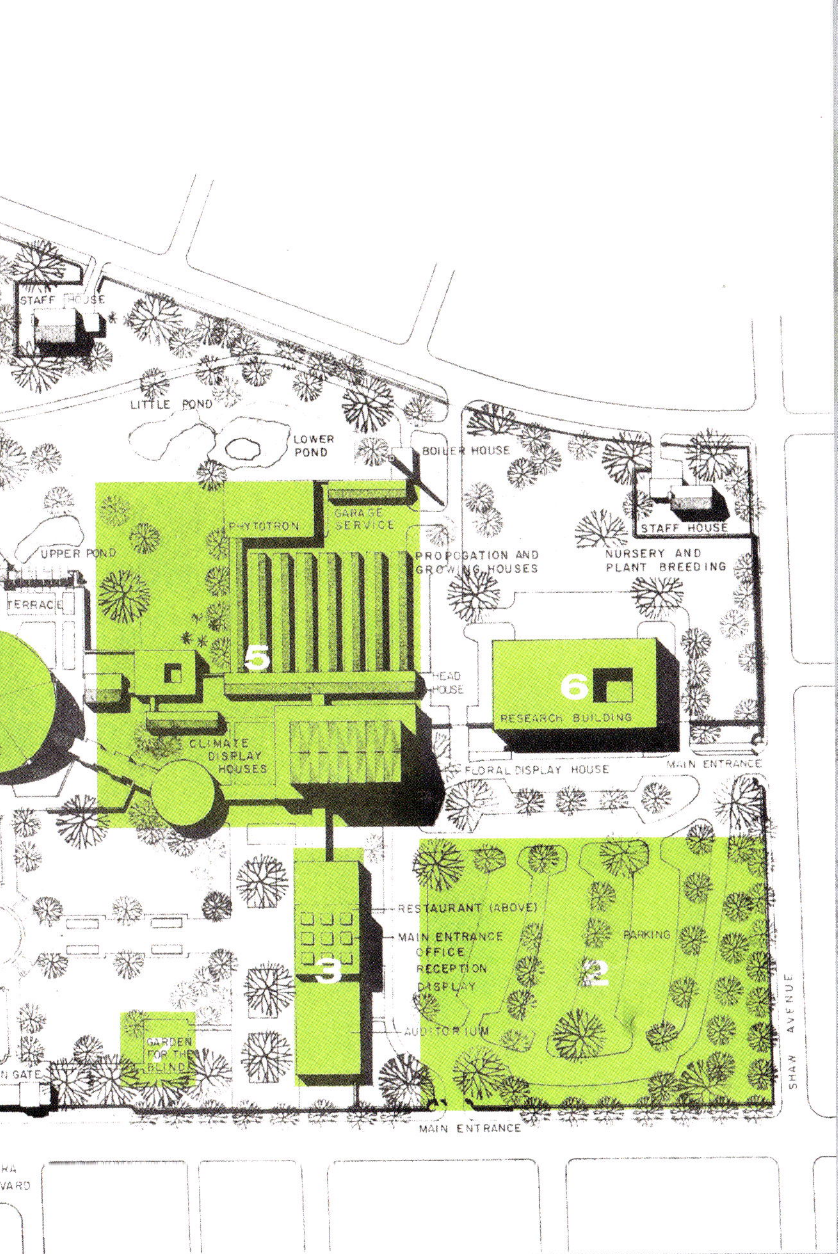

Shaw's Old Conservatory.
COURTESY MISSOURI HISTORICAL SOCIETY, ST. LOUIS

1959

Shaw's Garden Centennial Plan

Missouri Botanical Garden Master Plan for the Future

Murphy & Mackey Architects
(artist/cartographer)

Missouri Botanical Garden
(publisher)

Off-set lithograph

8 × 13 inches

Collection of the Author

THE CLIMATRON

Construction on the Climatron began in 1959. It was built on the site of the 1913 Palm House, which had become structurally deficient and was considered old-fashioned. Covering over half an acre, the Climatron was the first major construction project at the garden in over 50 years. Its radical, futuristic design was based on the geodesic dome concept of architect Buckminster Fuller. The dome was designed by the St. Louis firm Murphy and Mackey, who were responsible for many mid-century designs in St. Louis. The Climatron was an overnight success, receiving press coverage worldwide as the "only geodesic dome greenhouse" and one of the first computer-designed structures in the world. This concept drawing of the Climatron was published in the garden's *Centennial Souvenir* publication in 1959. COLLECTION OF THE AUTHOR

NO OTHER AREA in St. Louis combined the beauty of a park with the refinements of a museum as did Henry Shaw's Missouri Botanical Garden. Though commonly referred to as "Shaw's Garden," Henry Shaw himself had officially named it the Missouri Botanical Garden, which first opened to the public in 1859. For the rest of his life, the creation and care of the garden would be Shaw's passion and principal occupation.

Shaw immigrated to St. Louis from England in 1819. After achieving great success in the St. Louis hardware business, he retired with large land holdings southwest of the city limits. In 1849, he built a country house on this land and named it Tower Grove. Two years later, Shaw traveled to his native England, visiting the Royal Botanic Gardens at Kew and the sprawling gardens at Chatsworth. During his walk through Chatsworth, Shaw conceived the idea of creating a garden on his own land at Tower Grove.

From the beginning, Shaw not only wanted the garden for himself, but also for the people of St. Louis. To welcome visitors, he built an impressive entrance gate on Tower Grove Avenue, which was part of the tall stone wall built along the northern and eastern sides of the garden.

After Shaw's death in 1889, the garden began to set a course for its future without its founder. Frederick Law Olmsted was hired in the late 1890s to develop a master plan for the future of the garden. Olmsted was probably the most important park and garden designer of the 19th century. He designed plans for

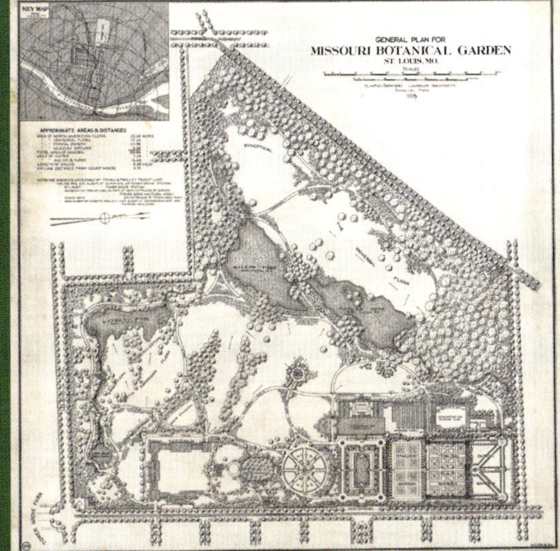

THE OLMSTEAD PLAN, 1905
The westernmost section of the garden (the triangular piece shown at the top of this plan) was sold by the garden in 1923 and developed into the residential streets familiar today. COURTESY LIBRARY OF CONGRESS

New York's Central Park and dozens of other public parks and university campuses across the country.

The Olmsted firm suggested demolishing the conservatory and building a larger building in line with the entrance gate at Tower Grove and Flora avenues. This larger building, called the Palm House, was built in 1913. The conservatory was demolished in 1916.

Olmsted's most ambitious proposal was to use the undeveloped areas on the west side of the garden to highlight a collection of plants from North America called the "North American Tract." Included in this tract was to be a large pond created by damming a small stream. This pond still exists today as half of the lake in the Japanese Garden. Most of the rest of the recommendations from the Olmsted Plan were never implemented.

In 1959, celebrations and renewed Plans for the future were held to mark the 100th anniversary of the public opening of Shaw's Garden. This map was produced as part of the 1959 *Master Plan for the Future*, which sought to "revolutionize the age-old concept of the botanical garden." The futuristic Climatron was the plan's focal point and is marked 1 on the map. The plan also called for a new parking area (marked 2 and still in use today) along with a new entrance (marked 3). A newly designated historical area included Tower Grove House, the 1859 museum building, Shaw's former town house (which was moved brick by brick from its original location at Seventh and Locust Streets), and the Linnean House, which was to be moved about 1,700 feet south from its original location within the garden. The multiple areas marked 7 were undeveloped open spaces to be covered with representative plants from across the globe. Except for the Climatron and new parking area, funding for the rest of this plan never materialized.

OLD CONSERVATORY & NEW PALM HOUSE, 1915
This rare photo shows both Shaw's old conservatory (at right) and the new Palm House (at left) during the few brief years they stood together. The Palm House was completed in 1913 and the old conservatory was demolished in 1916. COURTESY MISSOURI HISTORICAL SOCIETY, ST. LOUIS

Map of the Municipal County of St. Louis Proposed by the Missouri C

The boroughs shown on this map preserve the character and identity of the major existing communities of city and county. The borough lines have been drawn to give every citizen in city and county an equal voice as a voter in the affairs of the new "Municipal County of St. Louis."

ST. LOUIS PUBLIC LIBRARY MAP COLLECTION

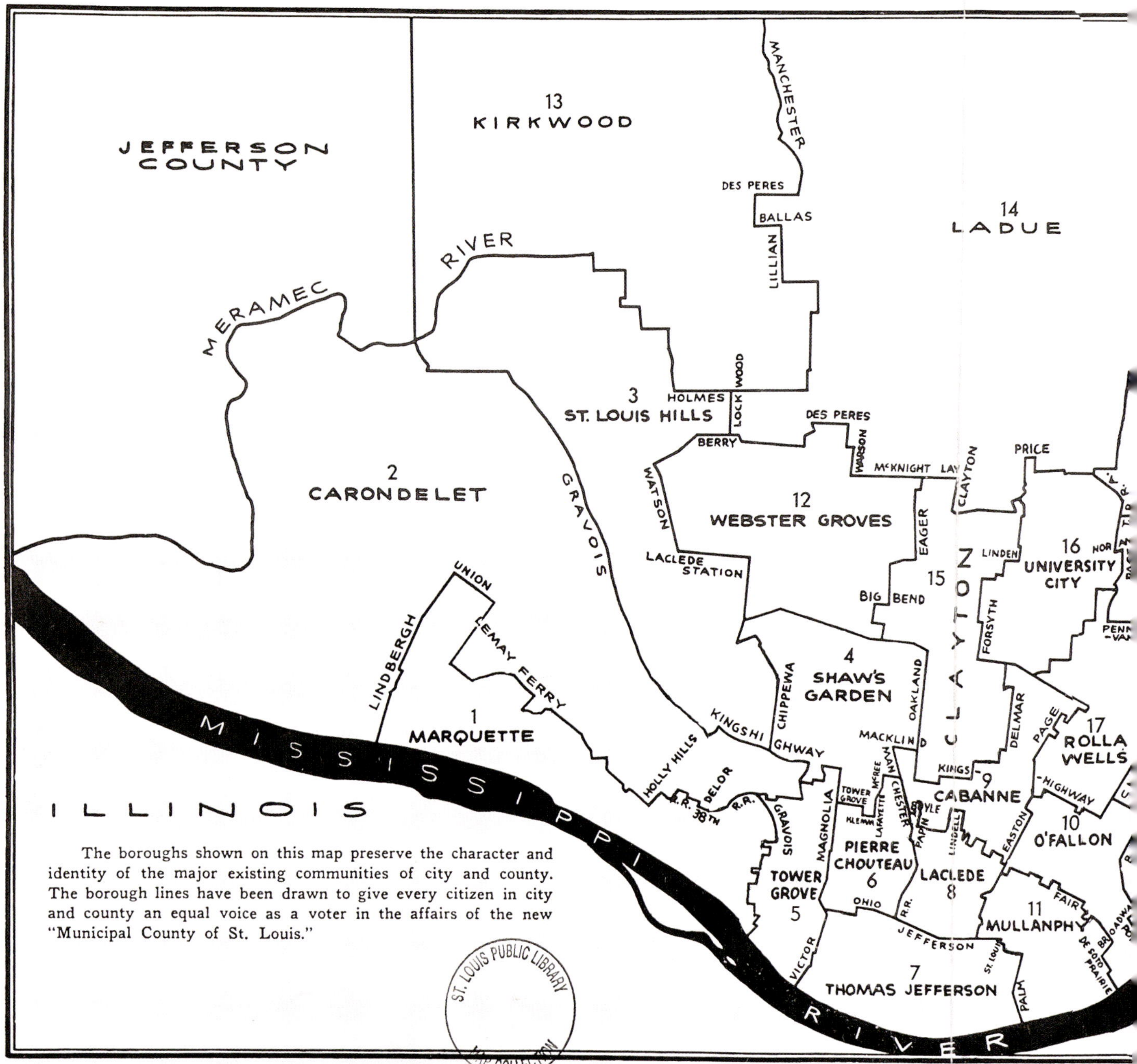

ree for the Borough Plan to Reunite St. Louis

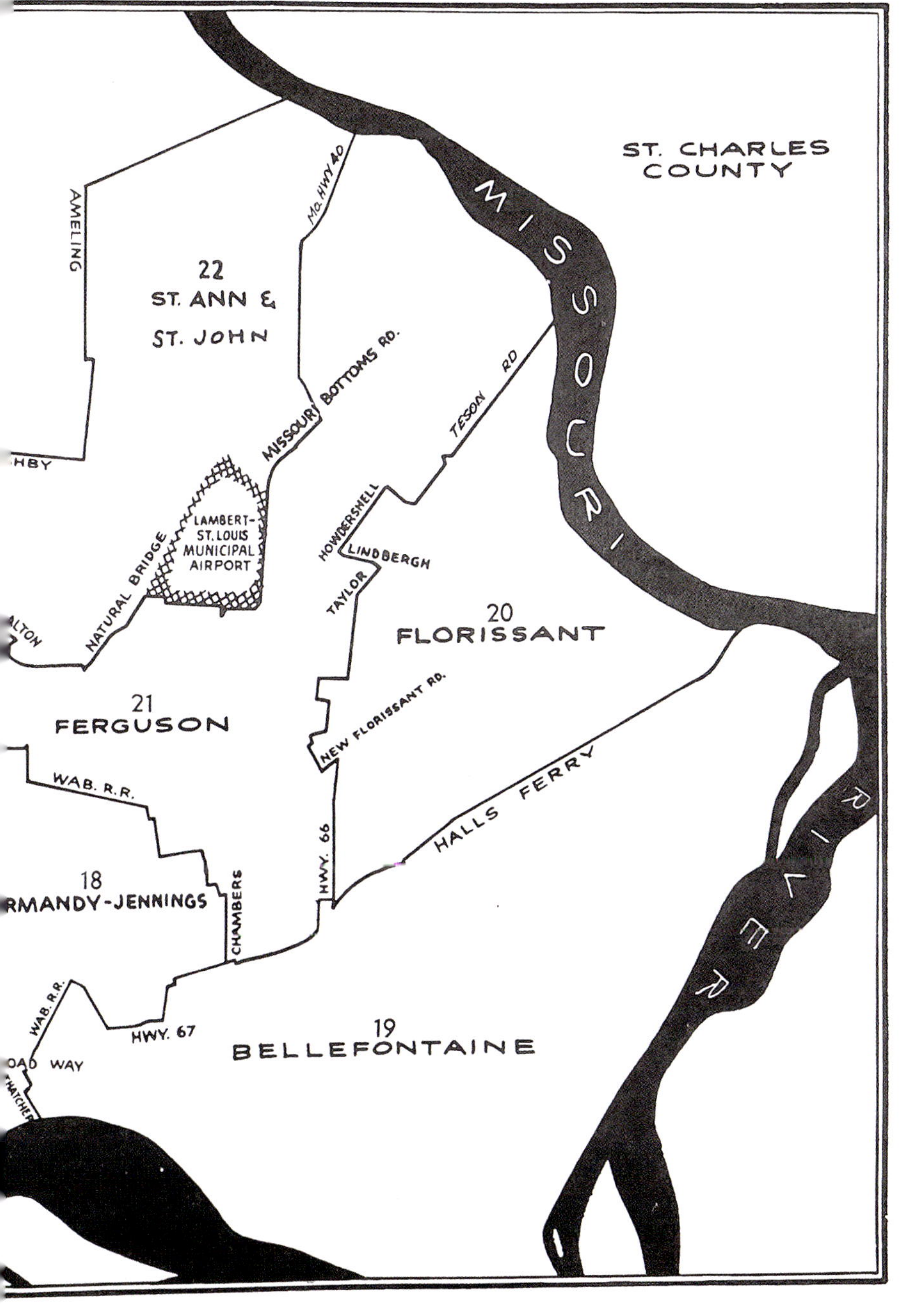

1962

St. Louis Borough Plan

Map of the Municipal County of St. Louis Proposed by the Missouri Committee for the Borough Plan to Reunite St. Louis

Missouri Committee for the Borough Plan to Reunite St. Louis *(publisher)*

Offset lithograph

11 × 16.5 inches

St. Louis Public Library

1962

NEARLY 90 YEARS before this map was produced, the "Great Divorce" separated the City of St. Louis from St. Louis County. The *1882 map* tells the full back story.

Ever since, efforts to repair the divorce have become akin to putting Humpty Dumpty back together again. In 1926, a plan was proposed where the City would annex the entire county and divide it into six wards, enlarging the St. Louis Board of Aldermen from 28 to 34 seats. Not all County residents were opposed to the measure. On the eve of the vote, County resident Joseph Forshaw Jr. told the *Post-Dispatch*, "some people say they like their little governments, [but]

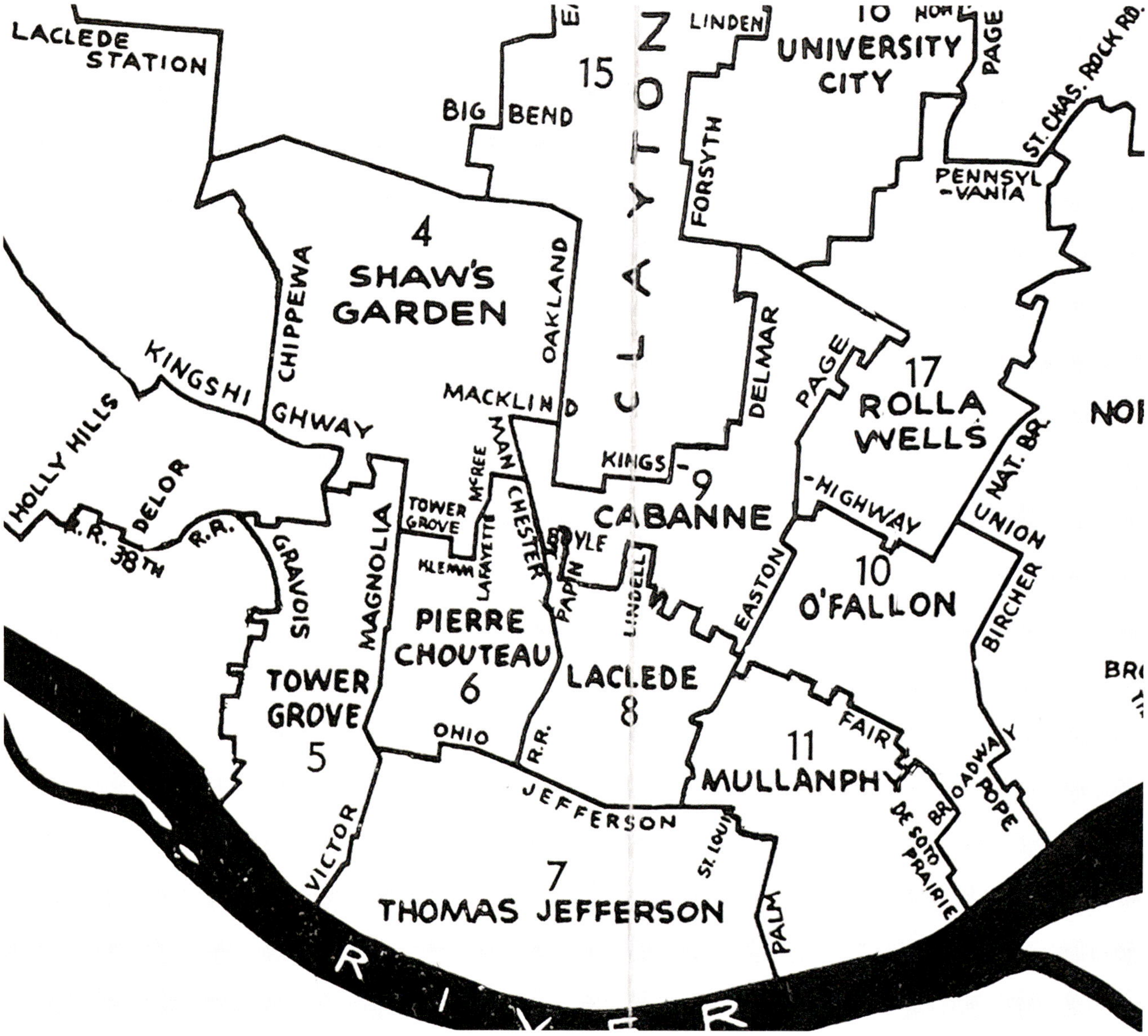

In 1962, the largest segment of Missouri's population was living in the City of St. Louis and the municipalities that ringed the city limits. Consequently, more than half of the newly proposed 22 boroughs were concentrated in this area. There were eight in the City (Thomas Jefferson, Mullanphy, Laclede, Pierre Chouteau, Tower Grove, Cabanne, O'Fallon, and Shaw's Garden), seven in the county (Webster Groves, Kirkwood, Ladue, St. Ann & St. John, Ferguson, Florissant, and Bellefontaine), and seven straddling the City–County line (Marquette, Carondelet, St. Louis Hills, Clayton, Rolla Wells, Normandy, and University City). The borough designations were selected from the names of historical St. Louis figures (Rolla Wells, Laclede, Cabanne, etc.) or to reflect an existing municipal designation (Florissant, Kirkwood, etc.).

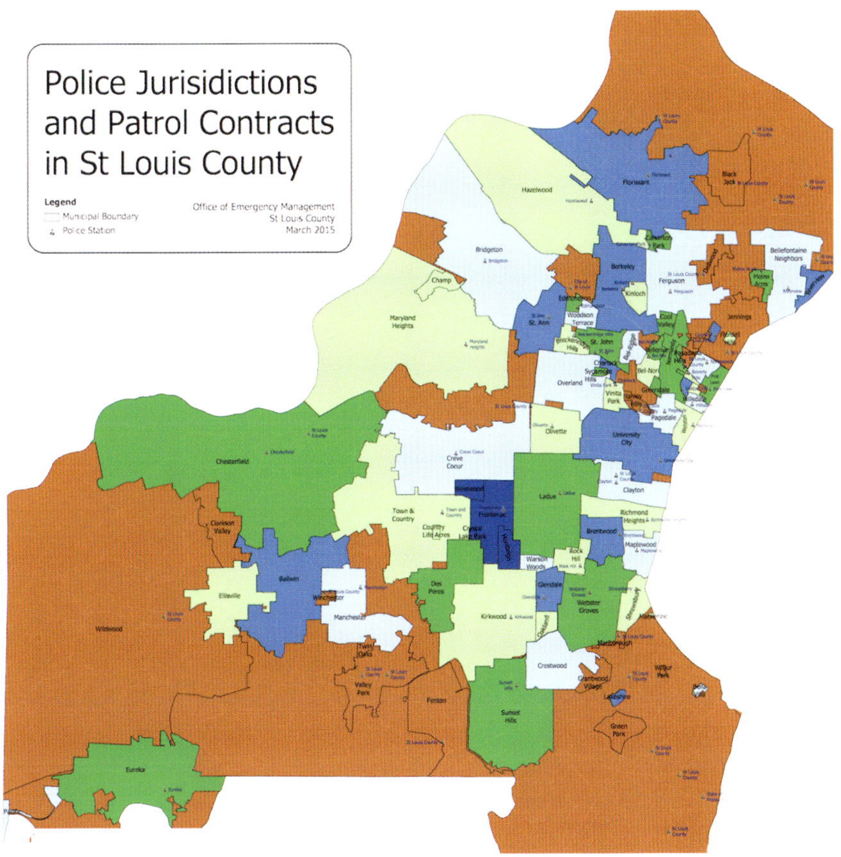

POLICE IN ST. LOUIS COUNTY, 2015

Dramatically illustrating the fragmented law-enforcement network in St. Louis County, this map was created by the St. Louis County Office of Emergency Management in 2015. Across the City of St. Louis and St. Louis County, 60 police departments provide service to 1.3 million people spread over 589 square miles. These departments differ as widely in size, demographics, and resources as do the 92 municipalities they serve. In total, the region spends more than $468 million each year on policing. The St. Louis County Police Department is the largest in the County. Its coverage area is shown in brown on the map. Issued by Better Together, this map accompanied the report *Overcoming the Challenges and Creating a Regional Approach to Policing in St. Louis City and County.*

they are behind the times." Nevertheless, the 1926 plan failed in the County by 67 percent, even though it passed in the City by 87 percent.

Over the next 35 years, there would be three very successful areas of City–County cooperation that hinted at the possibility of a future reunification. In 1949, the Missouri and Illinois legislatures created the Bi-State Development Agency, which combined more than a dozen local bus companies to create a unified metro transit system. Today, it is called Metro and includes MetroLink. In 1954, large voter majorities in the City and parts of the County created the Metropolitan St. Louis Sewer District, combining the City Sewer Department with 40 municipal and district systems. And in 1962, the City and County overwhelmingly passed the creation of a shared Junior College District, which built three campuses: Forest Park, Meramec, and Florissant Valley. That same year, another effort took shape to consolidate the City and County.

This 1962 map proposed 22 boroughs in a politically unified City and County. Similar to the system in New York, each borough would elect two members to a legislative council that, along with a mayor and a few other officials elected at large, would govern the new (unified) Municipal County of St. Louis. The result would have been a metropolitan area of nearly 1.5 million people, making St. Louis the sixth-largest city in the nation. St. Louis had been 10th in the 1960 census, the last time it was in the top 10 list. Voters in both the City and County decisively rejected the plan, and reunification was pronounced unpopular and impossible.

But the issue would not go away. Better Together was formed in 2013 to again look at reunification. Their stated mission was to act as a "catalyst for the removal of governmental, economic, and racial barriers to the region's growth and prosperity for all of our citizens by promoting unity, trust, efficiency, and accountability." The group studied and ultimately proposed a City–County merger initiative. However, in May of 2019, after months of widespread criticism, Better Together pulled their consolidation proposal from ballot consideration.

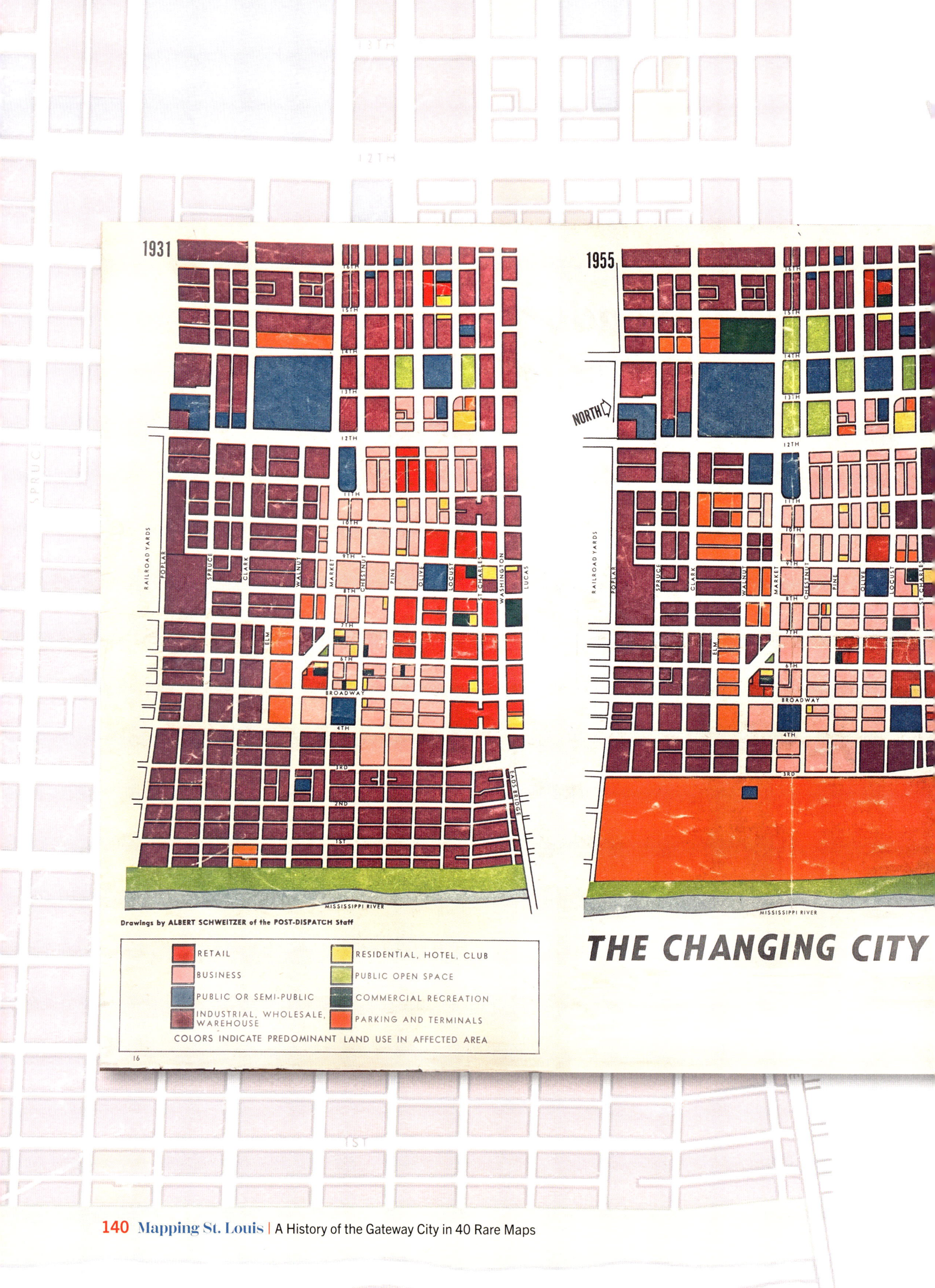
1931
1955
NORTH
16TH
15TH
14TH
13TH
12TH
11TH
10TH
9TH
8TH
7TH
6TH
BROADWAY
4TH
3RD
2ND
1ST
RAILROAD YARDS
POPLAR
SPRUCE
CLARK
WALNUT
MARKET
CHESTNUT
PINE
OLIVE
LOCUST
ST CHARLES
WASHINGTON
LUCAS
ELM
EADS BRIDGE
MISSISSIPPI RIVER
Drawings by ALBERT SCHWEITZER of the POST-DISPATCH Staff
RETAIL
BUSINESS
PUBLIC OR SEMI-PUBLIC
INDUSTRIAL, WHOLESALE, WAREHOUSE
RESIDENTIAL, HOTEL, CLUB
PUBLIC OPEN SPACE
COMMERCIAL RECREATION
PARKING AND TERMINALS
COLORS INDICATE PREDOMINANT LAND USE IN AFFECTED AREA
16
THE CHANGING CITY

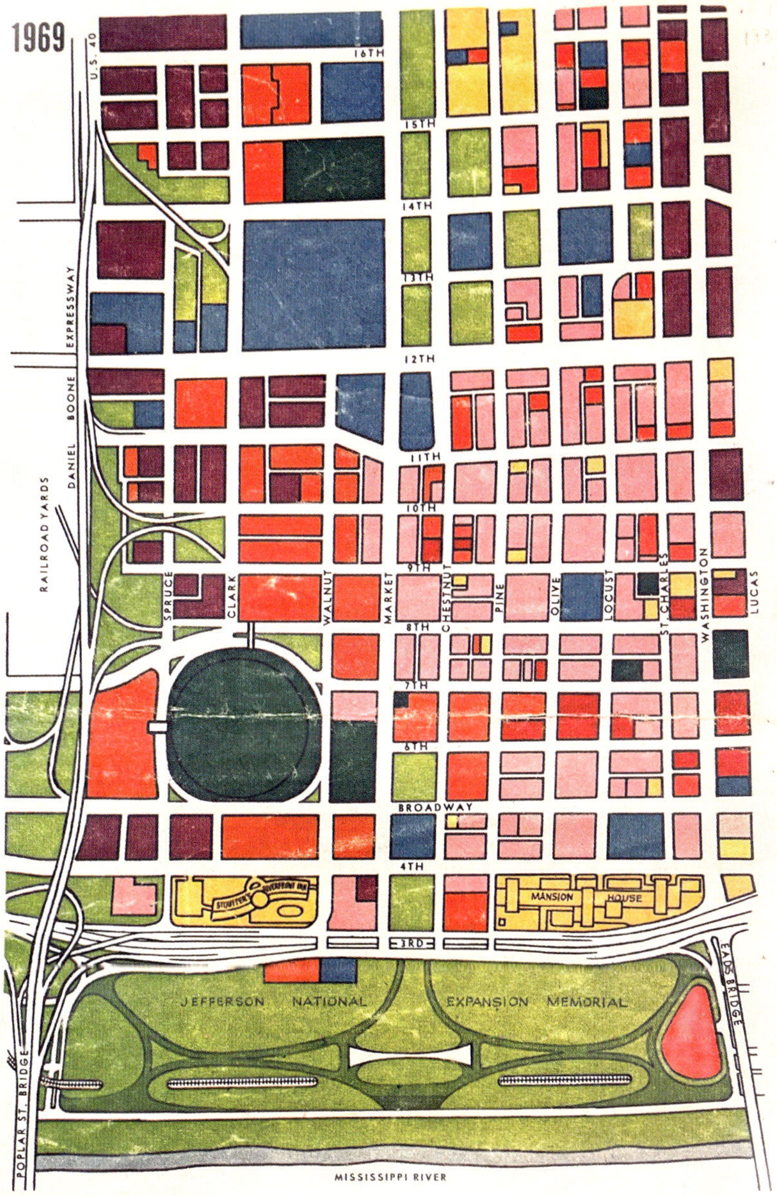

1969

Downtown St. Louis Evolves

The Changing City

Albert Schweitzer
(artist/cartographer)

St. Louis Post-Dispatch
(publisher)

Offset lithograph

21.5 × 12.5 inches

St. Louis Public Library

BETWEEN THE 1930s and 1960s the layout and landscape of downtown St. Louis changed dramatically. This colorful map, printed in the "Pictures" section of the *St. Louis Post-Dispatch* on June 15, 1969, reflects these changes. The map shows the city center for three specific years: 1931, 1955, and 1969.

In 1931, the downtown area was composed primarily of industrial and warehouse space along with commercial offices and some retail. The riverfront and near south side were almost exclusively the domain of "product trading" warehouses, manufacturing firms, wholesale companies, transportation companies, and light industry. The street grid in this area still followed the colonial-village layout as created in the 1760s. The two blue squares closest to the river (classified on the map as "public or semi-public" space) are the Old Cathedral and the Old Courthouse. There was very little parking space (shown in orange) in this era, the car still being a relatively new commodity.

By 1955, the exodus of much of the retail heart of St. Louis to suburban shopping centers had left its mark on downtown. Three of the remaining retail establishments were the landmark department stores: Famous-Barr; Stix, Baer and Fuller; and Scruggs, Vandervoort and Barney—each one accounting for an entire red square on the map. The greater dependence on the automobile is evident by the areas now designated as parking lots. The large parking area on the riverfront is the site of the future Gateway Arch. The land having been cleared and the street grid erased, it was used for parking until funding for the Arch monument could be secured.

RIVERFRONT, CIRCA 1930

When this aerial photo was taken, the riverfront and levee had changed very little since the Great Fire of 1849, 90 years earlier (see *1849 map*). As indicated on the map, the area was mostly industrial and warehouse space. The Old Courthouse is visible on the far left.
COURTESY MISSOURI HISTORICAL SOCIETY, ST. LOUIS

The 1969 map of downtown St. Louis shows a complete transformation. The riverfront has now been built up with the new Gateway Arch and its acres of greenspace. Significant new space has been classified as "commercial recreation" and shown in dark green, most notably the new Busch Stadium, which can be recognized by its large, round shape. Other older institutions like the Kiel Opera House, the Ambassador Theater, and the Campbell House Museum also fit the recreation designation. As St. Louis continued its expansion from the central core; the move of Busch Stadium *east* from Grand Avenue to the riverfront area illustrates the emphasis placed on urban renewal in this era. Sizable new residential areas (colored yellow), including the Mansion House and Plaza Square developments, contained more than 2,000 apartments between them.

RIVERFRONT, CIRCA 1955

After the demolition and clearing of the buildings along the riverfront was completed in the early 1940s, the large open space was used for parking. This lasted nearly two decades. Thousands of cars are parked in the area that had been the entire site of colonial St. Louis and would soon become the Jefferson National Expansion Memorial (today the Gateway Arch National Park).

COURTESY MISSOURI HISTORICAL SOCIETY, ST. LOUIS

RIVERFRONT, CIRCA 1967

The newly completed Gateway Arch and Busch Stadium are the two largest features in a downtown that now boasts acres of public greenspace and recreation options. In the distance, the large, cleared area west of downtown was the Mill Creek Valley neighborhood.

COURTESY MISSOURI HISTORICAL SOCIETY, ST. LOUIS

A major justification of the 1960s urban renewal efforts included the construction of a highway system through downtown. By 1969, Interstate 70 had been constructed between the Arch and the rest of downtown, and the Daniel Boone Expressway (today called Interstate 64) was built in place of Poplar Street. West of downtown, this new expressway destroyed the Mill Creek Valley neighborhood and 20,000 Black residents were displaced in the name of "urban renewal." Unlike the White residents of neighborhoods like Lucas Place and Vandeventer Place, who chose to move to the western suburbs, these Black residents had no choice in their relocation.

All three maps were drawn by Albert Schweitzer, a longtime artist for the *St. Louis Post-Dispatch*, where he was the fifth cartoonist to draw the front-page Weatherbird, the oldest continually drawn daily cartoon feature in the country. The architectural firm of Peckham Guyton Associates of St. Louis produced the graphics on which this map is based, following a regional land survey of the area commissioned by the Linclay Corp., a commercial real estate firm.

CITY SCHOOL SYSTEM
Primary Schools
Primary Branch Schools
Primary School Districts
Overcrowed Schools
Under-Capacity Schools
FOREST
PARK
SOLDAN
SAINT LOUIS
DEVELOPMENT
PROGRAM

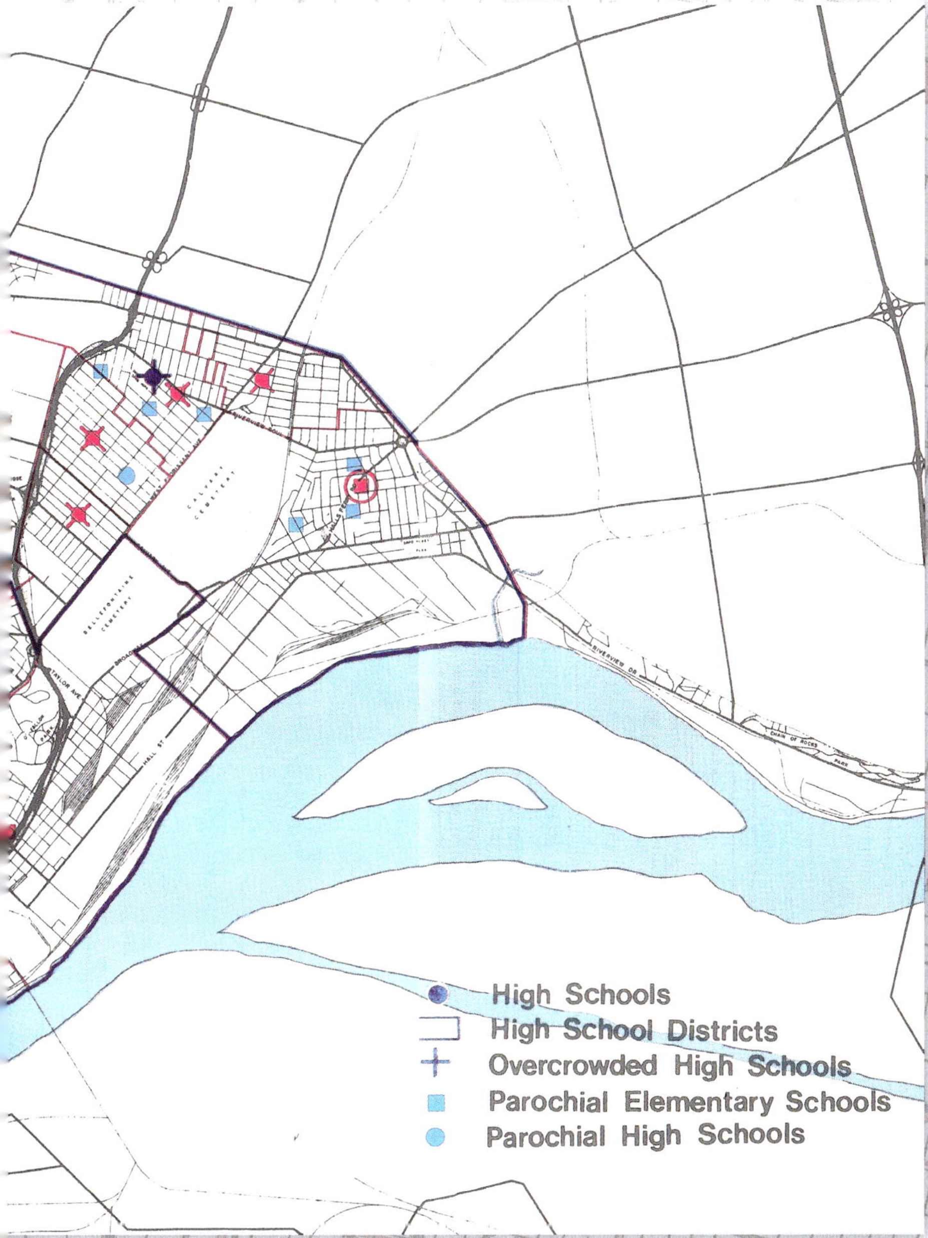

1973

St. Louis Schools

City School System
from the *Saint Louis*
Development Plan of 1973

City Plan Commission
(artist/cartographer)

City of St. Louis
(publisher)

Off-set lithograph

6 × 12.5 inches

Collection of the Author

High Schools
High School Districts
Overcrowded High Schools
Parochial Elementary Schools
Parochial High Schools

First grade at Fanning School, circa 1910.
COURTESY MISSOURI HISTORICAL SOCIETY, ST. LOUIS

1973

THIS MAP emphasizes the challenges faced by the City of St. Louis since World War II. It was prepared by the City Plan Commission as one of dozens of maps published for the landmark 1973 *Saint Louis Development Program*. The introduction to this comprehensive program noted: "The City of St. Louis is one of the great cities of the nation, but at the same time, it is caught up in all the problems of the urban crisis created by nation-wide forces of socio-economic change. . . . We must set our City in order, decide what the City can be, what it can no longer be, and rebuild our concepts and our City in the light of new and realistic goals and policies."

One of the greatest challenges facing the City in 1973 was the education system. In 1970, there were 150,416 children enrolled in schools inside the City limits—110,425 in public schools and 39,991 in parochial schools. This was a drop of 10,000 students in just three years from more than 160,000 total students in 1967.

The first two public elementary schools in St. Louis opened in 1838, and the City opened a high school in 1856—the first west of the Mississippi. The High School (its official name, as it was the only one for almost 40 years) was one of the first coeducational high schools in the country. When it was completed at 15th and Olive Streets in the shadow of the new and fashionable Lucas Place neighborhood, it was described as the "most lavish schoolhouse west of New York."

From 1868 to 1880 the public schools were led by Superintendent William Torrey Harris, who built St. Louis schools into a national model, combining "systematic teaching methods, strong discipline, and basic proficiencies." Susan Blow proposed to Harris that St. Louis try the new "kindergarten" concept, an experiment in teaching young children needed skills before they started elementary school. He authorized Blow to create the nation's first public kindergarten at Des Peres School in 1873. So effective was the system Harris built

THE HIGH SCHOOL
This impressive school cost some $50,000 to build, and within five years more than 300 girls and boys were enrolled. It was designed by architect William Rumbold, who is best remembered as the architect of the Old Courthouse dome and as a consulting architect for the construction of the dome of the US Capitol in Washington, DC, both built in the 1860s. After being in use for only 38 years, the High School was demolished in 1895.
COURTESY MISSOURI HISTORICAL SOCIETY, ST. LOUIS

that St. Louis won five grand prizes at the 1900 Paris Exposition for the work of local elementary and high school students. As noted on the *1946 map*, a local teacher's college was named for him.

At the start of the 20th century, architect William B. Ittner was St. Louis School Board commissioner. He quickly became a national leader in the design of school buildings. Ittner used ideas from urban planning to build schools with better traffic flow and classrooms created for specific uses. Many of Ittner's schools remain in use and are considered some of the finest examples of early 20th-century architecture in St. Louis.

SCHOOL ARCHITECT
Architect William B. Ittner (1864–1936) designed more than 425 school buildings in Missouri and has been described as the most influential man in school architecture in the US. He was appointed St. Louis School Board commissioner in 1897 and was responsible for designs that featured natural lighting and beautiful exteriors.
COURTESY MISSOURI HISTORICAL SOCIETY, ST. LOUIS

COTE BRILLIANTE SCHOOL
Built in 1904 at 2616 Cora Avenue in The Ville neighborhood, the Cote Brilliante School was one William B. Ittner's best designs. Like most of Ittner's schools, it looks like a "palace" of education. Cote Brilliante School closed in 2017, and as of 2024 it was listed for sale as one of the St. Louis Public School's "surplus properties."
COURTESY MISSOURI HISTORICAL SOCIETY, ST. LOUIS

When this map was published in 1973, the school population was in decline. The City still offered a wealth of educational options for children: 140 public primary schools, 12 public high schools, 57 parochial primary schools, and 14 parochial high schools. A wide array of new programs were also offered, including Head Start and Project Metro, now called Metro High School. But the map also showed severe school overcrowding in 16 schools, mostly located on the near southside and in the far northside.

In 2024, there were 70 public elementary, middle, and high schools in St. Louis, with a total student population of 18,747.

See!
MUSEUMS OF
Museum of Transportation
Saint Louis Art Museum
The Magic House, St. Louis Children's Museum
Frank Lloyd Wright House in Ebsworth Park
Laumeier Sculpture Park
Thomas Sappington House Museum
Saint Louis Zoo
Ulysses S. Grant National Historic Site
Missouri Botanical Garden
Saint Louis Science Center
Jefferson Barracks
Miniature Museum of Greater St. Louis
Tower Grove Park
Saint Louis University Museum of Art
Samuel Cupples House
Carondelet Historical Society
Missouri
Chatillon-DeMenil Mansion
International Photography Hall of Fame and Museum
Scott Joplin House
Missouri Civil War Museum
Jefferson Barracks Historic Site
River
Field House Museum
Soldiers Memorial Military Museum
Cahokia Courthouse
Illinois
Old Courthouse
W
S
N
E
Greater St. Louis Air & Space Museum
23
Cardinals Hall of Fame & Museum
The Judicial Learning Center
Closed for renovations
Westward Expansion
Inside the Economy Museum
National Blue

2017

Museums of St. Louis

See Museums of St. Louis

Dan Zettwoch
(artist/cartographer)

American Alliance
of Museums
(publisher)

Offset lithograph

20 × 28 inches

Courtesy of Dan Zettwoch
(zettwoch.com)

ST. LOUIS HAS always been a favored stopping point and tourist destination because of its central location, rich history, and civic pride. There were many historic sites to entice visitors. The oldest and largest of these were the Indian Mounds.

The first museum in St. Louis was William Clark's collection of artifacts from the 1804 Lewis & Clark Expedition, which he displayed in an annex to his house at Main and Vine Streets starting in 1816. The annual St. Louis Exposition that predated the 1904 World's Fair always had temporary museum attractions, first at the Fairgrounds Park and after 1883 at the St. Louis Exposition and Music Hall at 14th and Olive Streets, which built permanent exhibits of machinery and fine arts.

25 SELECTED CRITTERZENS OF CITY MUSEUM

To celebrate its 25th anniversary in 2022, the City Museum commissioned Zettwoch to create a special-edition print that highlights its "ever-evolving, always-thrilling, artist-built playground full of weirdly wonderful spaces to explore." Zettwoch added a warning on the print "NOT A MAP/NOT FOR USE AS NAVIGATION." City Museum doesn't offer maps to visitors—visitors are expected to explore (and get lost) all on their own.
COURTESY DAN ZETTWOCH

ST. LOUIS EXPOSITION, 1893

Since the 1870s, the annual St. Louis Exposition attracted thousands of visitors to the City each autumn. In addition to displays of machinery, the "magnificent art galleries" were a big draw. This poster advertises the 1893 Exposition, which featured daily concerts by America's favorite bandmaster, John Philip Sousa.
COURTESY MISSOURI HISTORICAL SOCIETY, ST. LOUIS

The Missouri Historical Society was created in 1866 but had no permanent home for its collection until it purchased the Thomas Larkin mansion on Lucas Place in 1886. Up until the time, the society met at various locations around the City, but its collection was stored in the basement of the Old Courthouse. Plans to build a grand new museum to replace the Larkin Mansion never materialized until the society moved to its current building in Forest Park in 1912.

This pictorial map was produced for the American Alliance of Museums Annual Meeting and Museum Expo, which was held in St. Louis in 2017. St. Louis

STL BEER
Zettwoch has produced other maps of St. Louis, including STL Beer. Before prohibition started in 1920, there were over 100 breweries operating in the City. The St. Louis Brewers Heritage Foundation (STLBeer.org) honors this history and promotes beer brewing in St. Louis today. This is the third edition of the foundation's STL Beer map, and it is designed "to make it easier to map out your quest for the perfect pour." On the map, Zettwoch pinpointed the location of 40 local breweries—from Anheuser-Busch (the biggest and oldest) to the newest (Blue Jay Brewing Co., opened December 2023). Twenty of the breweries featured here are in the City of St. Louis.
COURTESY STLBEER.COM AND DAN ZETTWOCH

artist Dan Zettwoch was commissioned to create the design to highlight the breadth and depth of museums in the St. Louis region. The map features more than 50 museums both large and small, old and new.

The signature Gateway Arch dominates the center of the map, along with the St. Louis Science Center T-rex and the Saint Louis Zoo hippo. Ulysses Grant (Ulysses S. Grant National Historic Site), the Climatron (Missouri Botanical Garden), and the *Spirit of St. Louis* (Missouri History Museum) also figure large in the design. Today, all these attractions contribute to bringing more than 25 million visitors to St. Louis every year.

According to the American Alliance of Museums, house museums are the most plentiful type of museum in America, and St. Louis has dozens of them. Grand houses like the Campbell House and Cupples House, simpler houses like Sappington House and Field House, and architectural marvels like the Frank Lloyd Wright House at Ebsworth Park can all be found within just 12 miles of the Arch.

Cartoonist and printmaker Dan Zettwoch also creates other colorful, jam-packed informational designs inspired by St. Louis history and culture. He has long been a fan of history, and his signature style is by his own admission, "cartoony, very colorful, sort of silly. . . . [B]right colors and a fun style can go a long way in telling history. It's sort of a way of putting a book on one illustration."

In 2015, Zettwoch created dozens of giant wall-sized illustrations for the landmark Missouri History Museum exhibit "A Walk in 1875 St. Louis." His wall-sized illustrations featured scenes of life in St. Louis in 1875—"what it would be like to go to the market and what a baseball game was like." He has since created a map of the breweries of greater St. Louis. Since its creation, this map has been offered for sale at museum gift shops throughout the City.

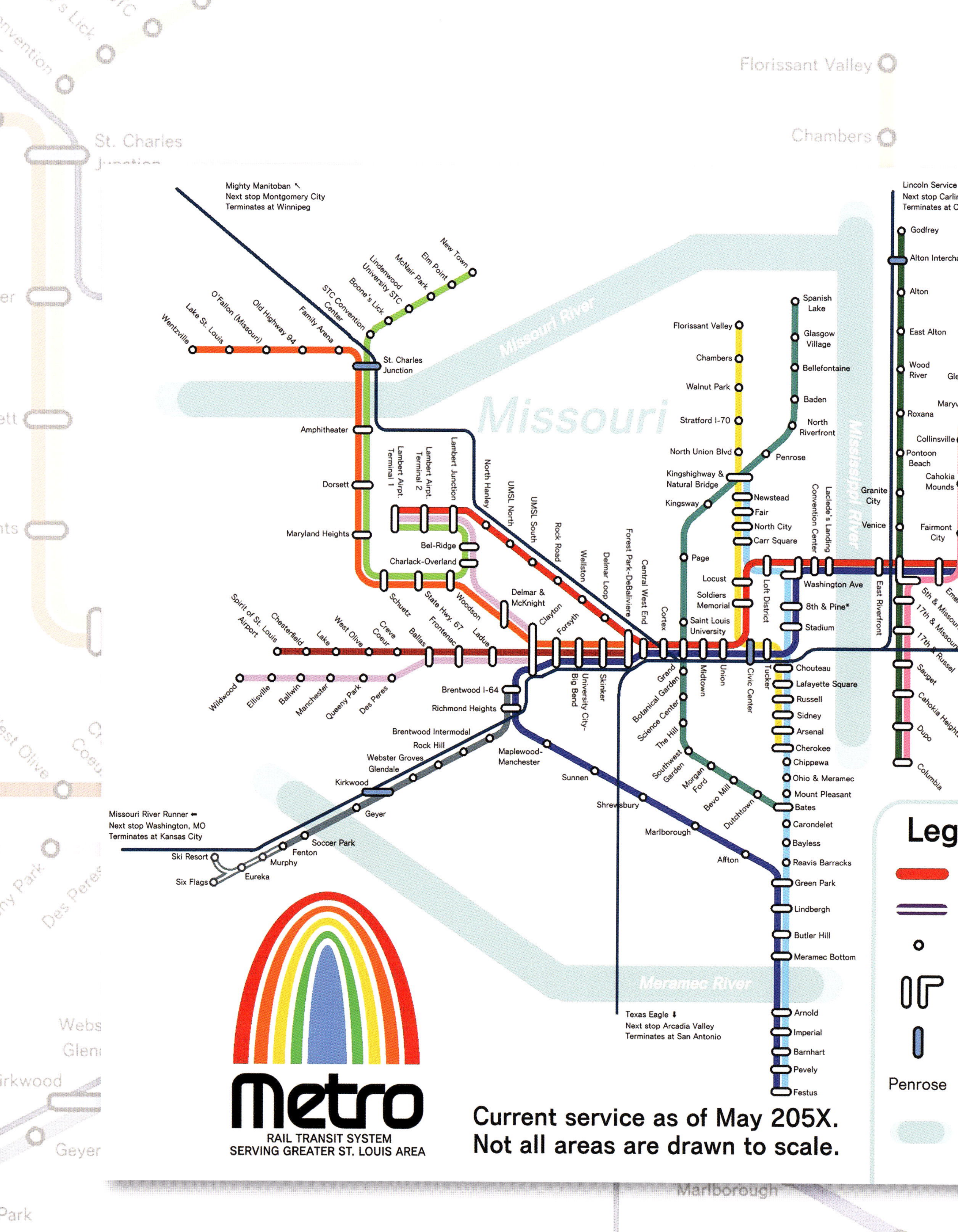

Mighty Manitoban
Next stop Montgomery City
Terminates at Winnipeg
Lincoln Service
Wentzville
Lake St. Louis
O'Fallon (Missouri)
Old Highway 94
Family Arena
STC Convention Center
Boone's Lick
Lindenwood University STC
McNair Park
Elm Point
New Town
St. Charles Junction
Amphitheater
Dorsett
Maryland Heights
Lambert Airpt. Terminal 1
Lambert Airpt. Terminal 2
Lambert Junction
North Hanley
UMSL North
UMSL South
Rock Road
Wellston
Delmar Loop
Forest Park-DeBaliviere
Central West End
Cortex
Bel-Ridge
Charlack-Overland
Delmar & McKnight
Clayton
Forsyth
Schuetz
State Hwy. 67
Woodson
Frontenac
Ladue
Ballas
Creve Coeur
West Olive
Lake
Chesterfield
Spirit of St. Louis Airport
Widwood
Ellisville
Ballwin
Manchester
Queeny Park
Des Peres
Brentwood I-64
Richmond Heights
Brentwood Intermodal
Rock Hill
Webster Groves
Glendale
Kirkwood
Geyer
Maplewood-Manchester
Sunnen
Shrewsbury
Marlborough
Affton
Big Bend
University City-
Skinker
Grand
Botanical Garden
Science Center
The Hill
Southwest Garden
Morgan Ford
Bevo Mill
Dutchtown
Midtown
Union
Civic Center
Tucker
Missouri River Runner
Next stop Washington, MO
Terminates at Kansas City
Ski Resort
Six Flags
Eureka
Murphy
Fenton
Soccer Park
Missouri River
Missouri
Mississippi River
Meramec River
Florissant Valley
Chambers
Walnut Park
Stratford I-70
North Union Blvd
Kingshighway & Natural Bridge
Kingsway
Page
Locust
Soldiers Memorial
Saint Louis University
Newstead
Fair
North City
Carr Square
Loft District
Spanish Lake
Glasgow Village
Bellefontaine
Baden
North Riverfront
Penrose
Convention Center
Laclede's Landing
Washington Ave
8th & Pine*
Stadium
Chouteau
Lafayette Square
Russell
Sidney
Arsenal
Cherokee
Chippewa
Ohio & Meramec
Mount Pleasant
Bates
Carondelet
Bayless
Reavis Barracks
Green Park
Lindbergh
Butler Hill
Meramec Bottom
Arnold
Imperial
Barnhart
Pevely
Festus
Texas Eagle
Next stop Arcadia Valley
Terminates at San Antonio
Godfrey
Alton
East Alton
Wood River
Roxana
Collinsville
Pontoon Beach
Cahokia Mounds
Granite City
Venice
Fairmont City
East Riverfront
5th & Missouri
17th & Missouri
17th & Russell
Sauget
Cahokia Heights
Dupo
Columbia
Penrose
Metro
RAIL TRANSIT SYSTEM
SERVING GREATER ST. LOUIS AREA
Current service as of May 205X.
Not all areas are drawn to scale.

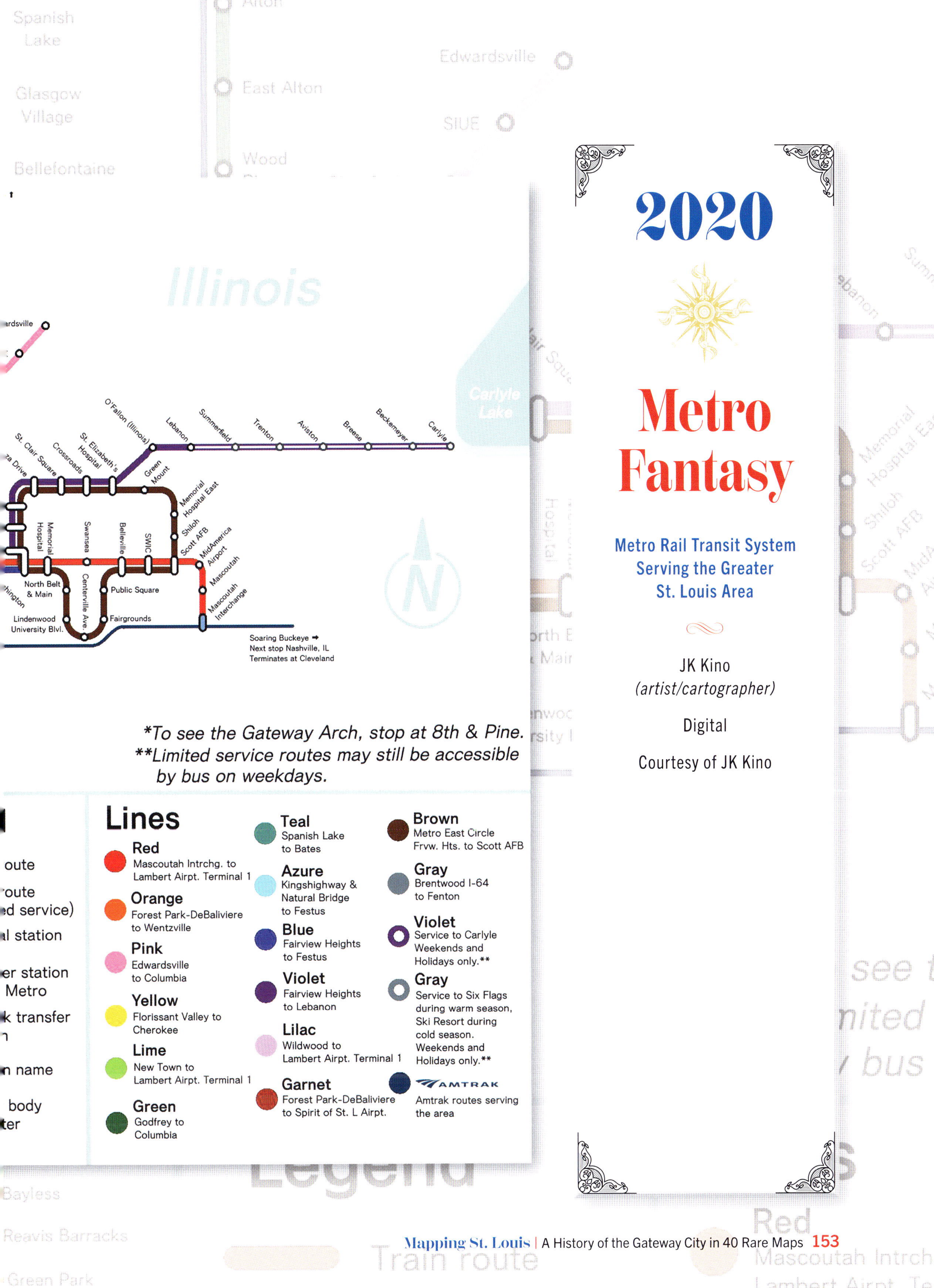
Illinois
Carlyle Lake
O'Fallon (Illinois)
Lebanon
Summerfield
Trenton
Aviston
Breese
Beckemeyer
Carlyle
St. Clair Square
Crossroads
St. Elizabeth's Hospital
Green Mount
Memorial Hospital East
Shiloh
Scott AFB
MidAmerica Airport
Mascoutah
Mascoutah Interchange
Memorial Hospital
Swansea
Belleville
SWIC
North Belt & Main
Centerville Ave.
Public Square
Fairgrounds
Lindenwood University Blvl.
Soaring Buckeye
Next stop Nashville, IL
Terminates at Cleveland
*To see the Gateway Arch, stop at 8th & Pine.
**Limited service routes may still be accessible by bus on weekdays.
Lines
Red
Mascoutah Intrchg. to Lambert Airpt. Terminal 1
Orange
Forest Park-DeBaliviere to Wentzville
Pink
Edwardsville to Columbia
Yellow
Florissant Valley to Cherokee
Lime
New Town to Lambert Airpt. Terminal 1
Green
Godfrey to Columbia
Teal
Spanish Lake to Bates
Azure
Kingshighway & Natural Bridge to Festus
Blue
Fairview Heights to Festus
Violet
Fairview Heights to Lebanon
Lilac
Wildwood to Lambert Airpt. Terminal 1
Garnet
Forest Park-DeBaliviere to Spirit of St. L Airpt.
Brown
Metro East Circle Frvw. Hts. to Scott AFB
Gray
Brentwood I-64 to Fenton
Violet
Service to Carlyle Weekends and Holidays only.**
Gray
Service to Six Flags during warm season, Ski Resort during cold season. Weekends and Holidays only.**
AMTRAK
Amtrak routes serving the area
2020
Metro Fantasy
Metro Rail Transit System Serving the Greater St. Louis Area
JK Kino (artist/cartographer)
Digital
Courtesy of JK Kino

2020

THIS MAP of the St. Louis Metro system is an example of a fantasy map. Fantasy map-making, also called fictional map-making or geofiction, is a type of map design that visually presents an imaginary world or concept, or represents a real-world geography in a fantastic style. A fantasy map could be made for fun or as a planning tool to visualize an as yet undeveloped (and unplanned) future. The artist who created this map did so as an exercise of what a greatly expanded rail transit system in St. Louis might look like.

Mass transit is a critical part of any urban environment. In the 19th century, St. Louis boasted horse-drawn omnibuses, followed by cable cars, and finally electric streetcars. The *1915 map* detailed the extensive network of streetcars in the City, while the *1946 map* noted bus routes that would supplant all the streetcars by the late 1960s. MetroLink, St. Louis's light-rail system debuted in 1993 and today consists of 38 stations along a 46-mile route.

METROLINK SYSTEM, 2024

When it debuted in 1993, MetroLink connected 16 stations along 13.9 miles of track from the University of Missouri–St. Louis to 5th and Missouri in East St. Louis. This red line was expanded the next year when service began to Lambert St. Louis International Airport. It was extended again in 2001 and 2003 in Illinois, extending to the Shiloh-Scott station in Illinois. In 2006 the new cross-county MetroLink extension was completed in St. Louis County. This new blue line runs through University City, Clayton, Richmond Heights, Brentwood, and Maplewood, terminating in Shrewsbury. Service on the red line is slated to expand again when an extension is completed in 2026, connecting the Shiloh-Scott station along a 5.6-mile route to Mid-America Airport in Mascoutah, Illinois. In 2023, there were 6.8 million riders on MetroLink. COURTESY OF METRO

This Metro map imagines more than 200 stations across the City of St. Louis, three Missouri counties, and four counties in Illinois. In scale, this proposed system is more appropriate for a city the size of London, with a population of 9 million and its Underground system of 272 stations. The longest distance represented on

this map is Wentzville, Missouri, to Carlyle, Illinois, a distance of some 85 miles. It would, however, require two transfers to take that fictional journey. To cover such a large geographic area, this map illustrates 14 color-coded routes. A plan of this size would certainly cost many hundreds of billions of dollars and take decades to complete. This timescale is reflected in the note at the bottom of the map: "current service as of May 205X."

There are, however, two aspects to this map that are not fantasy. Three of the Amtrak lines serving the Civic Center, Alton, and Kirkwood stations are real. In addition, the red and blue lines are an accurate representation of the two MetroLink routes currently in service. However, the blue line depicted here continues a fictional 11 stations past Shrewsbury.

Like most modern transit maps, this Metro fantasy map is not geographically accurate. Instead it uses straight lines, fixed angles, and fixed distances between stations—compressing those in the outer area of the system and expanding those close to the center.

In creating this fantasy map, the artist also designed a logo concept as bold as his vision of a greatly expanded transit rail system for St. Louis.

NORTHSIDE-SOUTHSIDE LRT

In 2016 work began to study the five possible routes to expand MetroLink. Two years later, the East-West Gateway Council of Governments (a regional planning authority) recommended a Northside–Southside connector as the first phase of a MetroLink expansion. In 2023, this updated map was issued, detailing the proposed connector route. Called the Jefferson Alignment, the 5.6-mile route travels completely along Jefferson Avenue from Fairground Park on the north to Chippewa on the south. It includes 14 stations and would connect to the existing red/blue MetroLink lines at a new transfer station near Jefferson Avenue. This plan has been criticized as too expensive for what it provides. The estimated cost is $1 billion.
COURTESY OF METRO

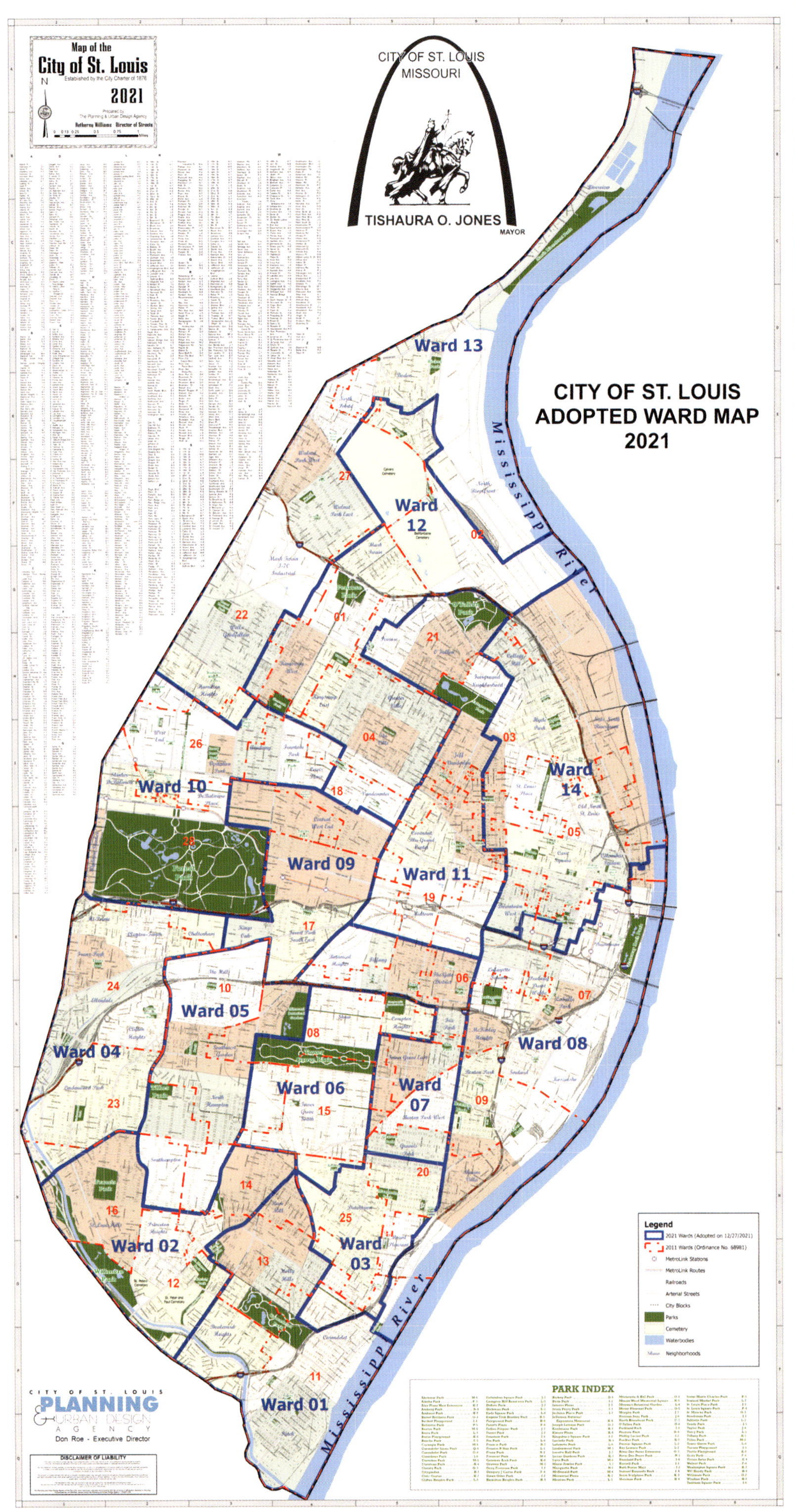
Map of the City of St. Louis
Established by the City Charter of 1876
2021
CITY OF ST. LOUIS
MISSOURI
TISHAURA O. JONES
MAYOR
CITY OF ST. LOUIS
ADOPTED WARD MAP
2021
Ward 13
Ward 12
Ward 14
Ward 10
Ward 09
Ward 11
Ward 05
Ward 04
Ward 06
Ward 07
Ward 08
Ward 02
Ward 03
Ward 01
Mississippi River
Legend
PARK INDEX
CITY OF ST. LOUIS
PLANNING & URBAN DESIGN AGENCY
Don Roe - Executive Director
DISCLAIMER OF LIABILITY

Board of Aldermen's Chambers, City Hall.
COURTESY MISSOURI HISTORICAL SOCIETY, ST. LOUIS

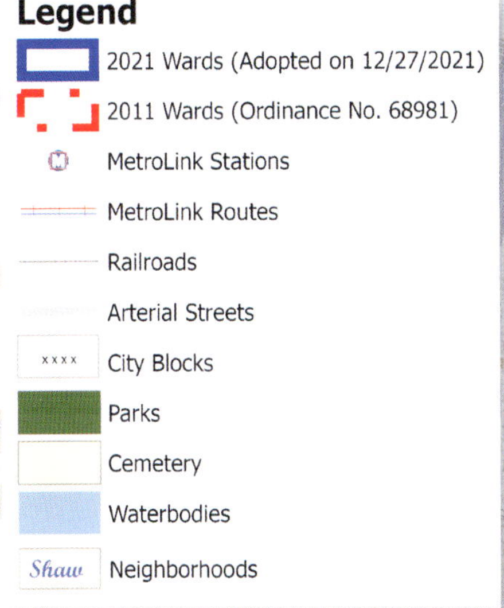

2021

New St. Louis Wards

City of St. Louis Adopted Ward Map

The Planning and Urban Design Agency, City of St. Louis
(artist/cartographer)

City of St. Louis
(publisher)

Digital

City of St. Louis

2021

WARD BOUNDARIES were a common feature on 19th-century maps of St. Louis. The *1844*, *1855*, and *1882 maps* all include these political boundaries. On December 14, 2021, the St. Louis Board of Aldermen passed a bill that established new ward boundaries and reduced the board by half—from 28 wards to 14. It was the largest change in city government in more than 100 years.

The ward is the basic administrative unit of the City of St. Louis and has been since the charter of 1835 was approved by the Missouri Legislature. Since that time, each ward has elected its own representative to the Board of Aldermen. The Board of Aldermen is the legislative body of St. Louis; it creates, passes, and amends local laws, and approves the City's annual budget. Initially, St. Louis had four wards. By the 1880s, the number had increased to 28. In 2021, that number was reduced for the first time.

The new Sixth Ward encompasses the entire neighborhoods of Compton Heights, Shaw, and Tower Grove South, as well as part of Dutchtown. It also includes all of Tower Grove Park. The red dashed lines represent the old ward boundaries where these same neighborhoods were all divided between multiple wards. The numbered city blocks are indicated in light gray. This system of block numbering began to appear on St. Louis maps in 1835.

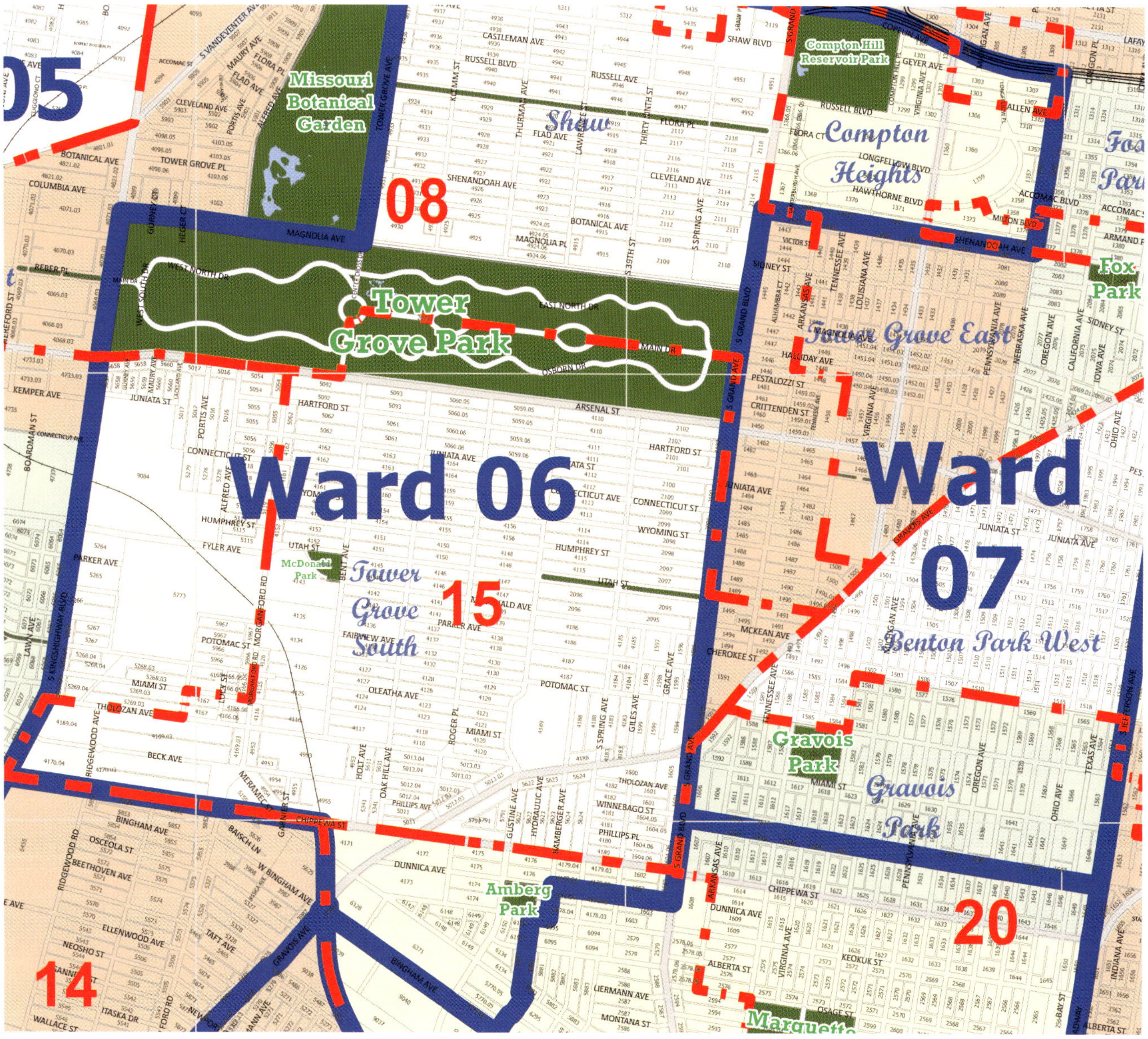

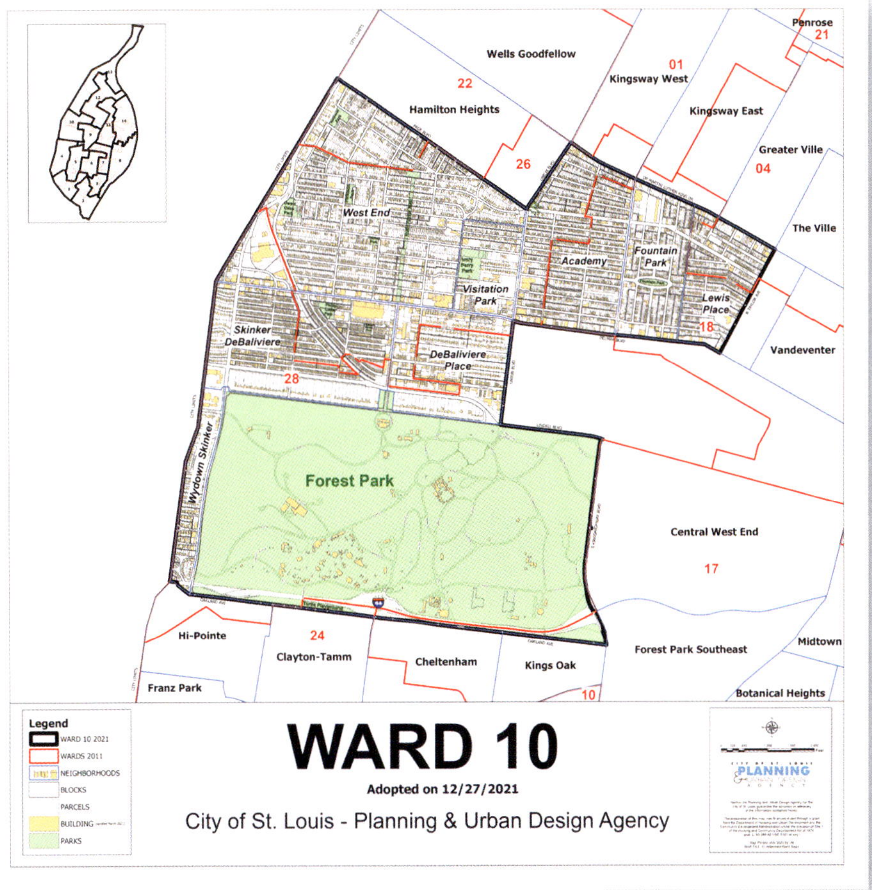

ST. LOUIS 10TH WARD OFFICIAL MAP

The new 10th ward of St. Louis created in 2021 includes all of Forest Park along with the seven neighborhoods to the north.

There were earlier attempts to change the size of the board. In 1957, voters rejected a charter change that would have cut the board to 15. Aldermen killed a similar proposal by two Republican board members in 1981. A petition initiative that got on the ballot in 1983 failed. Most recently, in 2004, voters decidedly rejected a citywide overhaul pushed by some of St. Louis's most influential business and political leaders.

The successful effort began in 2012, when voters passed a city charter amendment that cut the Board of Aldermen to 14 seats. Part of the reason for its passage was the fact that the changes would not go into effect for almost 10 years. An amendment stipulated that the reduction and redrawing of the ward boundaries would begin after the release of the 2020 census numbers in September 2021.

When it came time to redraw the map, controversy was rife. The Legislation Committee of the Board of Aldermen publicly met for months to create a new ward map that was fair, equitable, and legal. The committee made it a priority to put whole neighborhoods and "communities of interest" in a single ward or at most two wards. In the end, only 15 percent of the City's 79 neighborhoods would be split into more than one ward. At the time of its adoption, it was noted that the map had "seven minority preference wards and seven white preference wards." The first election for the newly drawn wards was in 2023.

This new ward map shows 14 wards with heavy blue outlines. There are roughly 21,000 residents in each new ward. However, their land area size varies quite dramatically. Ward 6 covers an area about half the size of ward 14.

Ward boundaries are a common feature on 19th- and 20th-century maps of St. Louis. But the new ward map highlights one important distinction: it is not oriented to the west, as are the majority of the maps in this historical overview of St. Louis (with the exceptions of the *1829*, *1855*, and *1907 maps*). Though most St. Louisans would consider the new wards a positive change, in fact the map outlines what some would consider evidence of decline in St. Louis. The new wards were created not only because of shifting population patterns, but also in response to the dramatic reduction in population from the 1950s—by more than 500,000 people.

Epilogue

DURING THE SUMMER of 2019, St. Louisans were invited to participate in a project called "Public Iconographies," which resulted in the creation of an atlas of "both traditional and unofficial sites of memory" in St. Louis. The project was a joint effort between the Pulitzer Arts Foundation based in Midtown St. Louis and Monument Lab, a Philadelphia-based organization that studies how communities remember their histories through public art and monuments. The stated goal of the project was to explore the relationship between the people of St. Louis and the City's inherited symbols.

Participants made hand-drawn maps that marked monuments and significant places: "current, potential, historical, and/or erased." Ultimately, 750 illustrated maps featuring over 1,000 places across the region were submitted. These maps reflect pre-colonial Indigenous histories, legacies of migration and segregation, and hundreds of sites of civic pride. The Gateway Arch was the site most frequently included on the maps. Most mapmakers acknowledged it with pride as an iconic symbol of St. Louis. Others used the Arch as a window to look at enduring inequalities. The maps were amalgamated into a collective map of the City titled, "How would you map the monuments of St. Louis?"

One cannot look at St. Louis without looking west. Both good and bad, that view has created and shaped St. Louis's place in history. But as we turn our sights both inward and outward, and in all directions, new and more complete maps will be formed. Maps show us where we've been and where we want to go, but they do not predict the future. Only time and the people of St. Louis will draw new maps to record our success or failure.

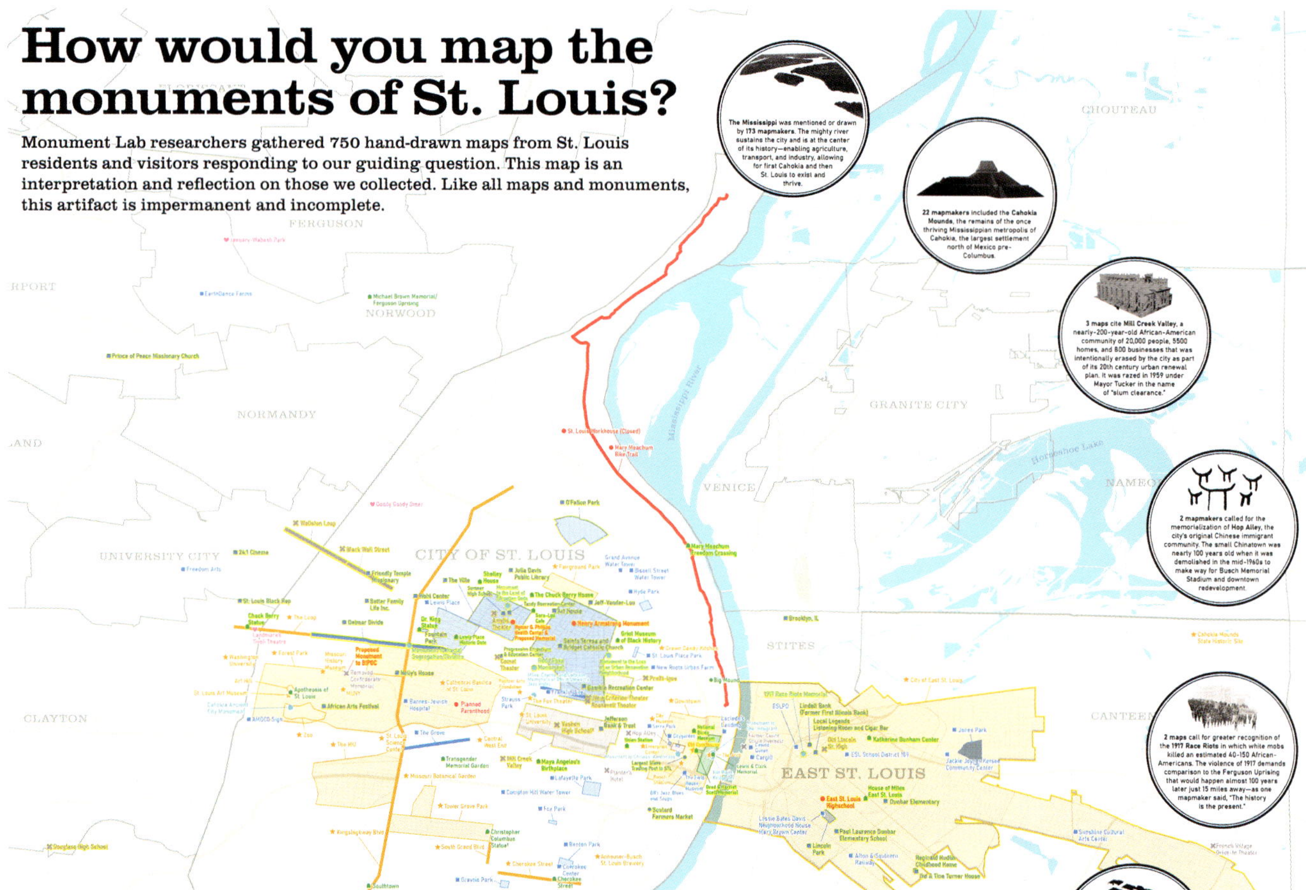

How would you map the monuments of St. Louis? (2020).
COURTESY MONUMENTS LAB

Bibliography 

Hundreds of books, articles, and journals were consulted in the preparation of this book. This selected bibliography notes the key general sources along with those specific to a dated map section.

General

Gordon, Colin (2008). *Mapping Decline, St. Louis and the Fate of the American City*. University of Pennsylvania Press.

Hoover, John Neal (2014). *Mapping St. Louis History: An Exhibition of Historic Maps, Rare Books and Images Commemorating the 250th Anniversary of the Founding of St. Louis*. St. Louis Mercantile Library at the University of Missouri–St. Louis.

Hurley, Andrew, editor (1997). *Common Fields: An Environmental History of St. Louis*. Missouri Historical Society Press.

Primm, James Neal (1998, 4th edition). *Lion of the Valley: St. Louis, Missouri, 1764–1980*. Missouri Historical Society Press.

Reps, John W. (1989). *St. Louis Illustrated*. University of Missouri Press.

Ristow, Walter (1985). *American Maps and Mapmakers: Commercial Cartography in the Nineteenth Century*. Wayne State University Press.

1767

Ekberg, Carl J. and Sharon K. Person (2015). *St. Louis Rising: The French Regime of Louis St. Ange De Bellerive*. University of Illinois Press.

Peterson, Charles E. (2001 reprint). *Colonial St. Louis, Building a Creole Capital*. The Patrice Press.

1780

Kling, Stephen, Jr., Kristine L. Sjostrom, and Marysia T. Lopez (2017). *The Battle of St. Louis, the Attack on Cahokia, and the American Revolution in the West*. THGC Publishing.

1804

Hoover, John Neal (1999). "Frederic Billon" from the *Dictionary of Missouri Biography*. University of Missouri Press.

1822

Beck, Lewis C. (1823). *A Gazetteer of the States of Missouri and Illinois*. Charles and George Webster, Albany.

1829

Davis, Lindsay (2022). "Splitting the Village Share" from *Gateway* (Vol. 42, No. 2). Missouri Historical Society.

1844

Jaycox, Emily Troxell (2002). "Gateway to the West: St. Louis Becomes a City" from *Mapping the West, America's Westward Movement 1524–1890*. Rizzoli International.

1848

Lowic, Lawrence (1982). *The Architectural heritage of St. Louis, 1803–1891*. Washington University Gallery of Art.

1849

Gordon, Christopher Alan (2018). *Fire, Pestilence, and Death: St. Louis, 1849*. Missouri Historical Society Press.

1852

Shepley, Carol Ferring (2008). *Movers and Shakers, Scalawags and Suffragettes: Tales from Bellefontaine Cemetery*. Missouri Historical Society Press.

1865

Gerteis, Louis (2001). *Civil War St. Louis*. University of Kansas Press.

1884

Schworm, William (1968). *A History of the St. Louis Waterworks*. City of St. Louis Water Division.

1893

Toft, Carolyn Hewes and Jane Molloy Porter (1984). *Compton Heights*. Landmarks Association of St. Louis.

1896

Curzon, Julian, editor (1896). *The Great Cyclone at St. Louis and East St. Louis, May 27, 1896*. Cyclone Publishing Co.

1904, 1919 & 1929

Loughlin, Caroline and Catherine Anderson (1986). *Forest Park*. Junior League of St. Louis.

1907 & 1962

Tranel, Mark, editor (2007). *St. Louis Plans: The Ideal and the Real St. Louis*. Missouri Historical Society Press.

1915

Butterworth, Molly (2021). *Trains & Trolleys, Railroad and Streetcars in St. Louis*. Reedy Press.

1950

Silva, Eddie (10/25/2016). "The Longest Day." *The Riverfront Times*.

1959

Faherty, William Barnaby, S. J. (1989). *A Gift to Glory In: The First 100 Years of the Missouri Botanical Garden (1859–1959)*. Harris & Friedrich Publishers

1973

City Plan Commission (1973). *Saint Louis Development Program*. City of St. Louis.

2021

St. Louis City Ordinances 69185 (2012) and 71443 (2021).

Epilogue

monumentlab.com/projects/public-iconographies

Index

Index